Books are to be returned on or before
the last date below.

KT-558-156

WARRIOR WOMEN

WARRIOR WOMEN

3000 Years of Courage and Heroism

ROBIN CROSS & ROSALIND MILES

Quercus

Contents

A portrait dated 1794 of Catherine II of Russia.

Amazon queen Hippolyta as
depicted on an amphora
(Greek jar).

Jacqueline Cochran standing
on the wing of a Canadair F-86
Sabre, with test pilot Chuck
Yeager on the left.

Jewish fighters captured in
1943 by Nazi troops during
the Warsaw Ghetto Uprising.

Introduction

We are the pointing end of the spear. I understand the marching orders, and we will be prepared to deploy ... with an aggressive attitude that we will win. I hope I am a role model to both men and women, because we are a fighting force and should not be concerned with the differences between us.

LIEUTENANT-COLONEL MARTHA MCSALLY TAKING COMMAND OF USAF 354TH FIGHTER SQUADRON, BASED AT DAVIS-MONTHAN AIR FORCE BASE, ARIZONA, 2004

In March 2007, for her bravery in action in Iraq, Private Michelle Norris became the first female soldier to be awarded the Military Cross, one of the British Army's highest honours. The next year, in June 2008, Corporal Sarah Bryant was the first British woman soldier to die on active service in Afghanistan, when her jeep was blown up by a roadside bomb.

Both these events threw into sharp focus a question heavily debated in recent years; in modern warfare, should women fight on the front line? A number of countries, led by the United States, have made significant efforts to integrate women more fully into their armed forces, albeit with certain restrictions. But only guerrilla forces like those of Eritrea or the Tamil Tigers in Sri Lanka have thrust women into front-line infantry positions, risking their lives side by side with men.

Yet today's terms of modern asymmetrical warfare—conflicts between unevenly matched belligerents, notably between conventionally armed First World powers and Third World counter-insurgents—have exploded the conventional notion of front lines in which men fight, and rear areas where women can safely serve in their traditional clerical and medical roles. Michelle Norris was in Iraq as a medical orderly when her commander was severely wounded in an ambush and she saved his life under enemy fire. Sarah Bryant was a Pashtu-speaking officer in the Intelligence Corps, whose main duties were translation and liaison, especially with the women of the region, who under no circumstances would have been accessible to her male colleagues.

Behind this, however, lies a far deeper reality. Throughout history, women have always been active in times of war and conflict. At the battle of the Paris Commune in 1871, women manned the barricades alongside men under relentless cannon fire from government troops; in the words of an independent observer, Georges Clemenceau, 'they fought like devils, far better than the men'.

What makes women like these ready to take up arms and fight? All the same reasons that mobilize men. Although separated by centuries, both the Celtic queen Boudicca and Joan of Arc, 'the Maid of Orléans', fiercely resisted hated invaders of their country, although they paid with their lives. In the Second World War, the women of the secret services of Britain and the United States risked torture and death in Nazi-occupied territory to play their part in the struggle against this ruthless tyranny.

Not all warrior women are so high-minded or driven by patriotic zeal. For many, war and revolution offered a unique avenue of escape from the cramped and stultifying female roles enforced on them, whatever their era or class. Some, like the fiery 'La Saragossa', 18th-century heroine of the Peninsular War, or 'La Pasionaria', the communist icon of the Spanish Civil War, kept their female identity and passed into history as heroines still honoured today.

But many more women, in flight from their female destiny, found their freedom by masquerading as men. No comprehensive list exists of the numbers of women who served in war as men: those who succeeded simply slid into history undetected. But from the early Middle Ages to the 19th century, there are countless known instances of women disguising themselves as men to fight as soldiers and sailors in the Hundred Years War, the War of the Spanish Succession, the Napoleonic War, the American Revolutionary and Civil Wars, and many others. For generations of female mavericks, misfits, malcontents or simply high-spirited girls, taking the chance of adventure alongside men meant living as men, too.

How did they get away with it? On average, women are shorter than men, have half the upper body strength (a key factor in handling weapons and war machinery) and far less overall muscle mass. These factors are also advanced by opponents of women in the military to argue that women simply are not able to do the work of men. But the differences between the sexes were far less marked in historical periods when most of the population were undernourished, thereby reducing visible secondary sexual characteristics like fat on curvaceous breasts and hips.

But the key factor governing the performance of any soldier in combat, as any commander will attest, is mental attitude. Tiny women ran the Ho Chi Min line in the Vietnam War, often carrying almost their own body weight in weaponry, ammunition and supplies, and helped to defeat the most powerful nation on Earth. In the United States, Colonel Martha McSally, the first woman in the United States Air Force to command a combat squadron that fought in Afghanistan, is 1.6 metres (5 ft 3 in) tall, and the rules had had to be changed before this, to enable her to fly on active service in Iraq.

Seventy years ago, any debate about women soldiers would have seemed academic in the Soviet Union, fighting for its life against Nazi Germany. In the Second World War, Russian women fought in the front line. In the First World War, the grimly named all-female 'Battalions of Death' displayed conspicuous bravery fighting for the Russian Imperial Army on the Eastern Front. The nay-sayers would also have received short shrift from women agents of the British Special Operations Executive (SOE), like the brilliant Pearl Witherington, who in the 1940s commanded over 2,000 men of the French Resistance in the field.

All these women and more will be found in this book. The problem was not who to include, but who to leave out: for every woman warrior we chose, there are countless more. Throughout history, women have played vital roles in times of war, a contribution that has yet to be fully recognized. We hope we have begun to do long-overdue justice to the cool and lonely courage so many have displayed so often under fire.

Robin Cross
Rosalind Miles

This book is for Carys Miles, Leila Hanna Miles and Imogen Whitfield, warrior women of the future—may their lives be as full of courage and adventure.

'Golden-shielded, silver-sworded, man-loving, male-child-killing Amazons', wrote the Greek historian Hellanicus in the fifth century BC. Fearless female warriors like these crop up so often in the annals of the ancient world that bands of women fighting together cannot be dismissed as a myth. Modern industrialized warfare, especially in the 20th and 21st centuries, has given women a chance to fight alongside men. But this was a natural right women assumed long before 'civilization' defined them as the weaker sex.

Amazons

Prehistory to the Early Christian Era

Stories of women who organized themselves to fight in bands are found in history, literature and legend from the dawn of time. They are most persistent in the countries around the Mediterranean and the Near East, where written and oral accounts record the existence of a warlike tribe of women warriors who lived and fought together, taking men to sire children, but destroying any boy babies, rearing only the girls.

The original Amazons appear to have lived in Libya, where rock drawings have been discovered dating from around 2000 BC, showing women armed with bows. During the Heroic Age of Greek civilization around 1600 BC, they emerged in mainland Greece, where they appear frequently in stone carvings and other memorials of war. Their heyday came in around 1250 BC in the time of the great Greek heroes, the warrior Heracles and Theseus, the founding father of Athens, just before the Trojan War of around 1200 BC.

Amazons were also famous for their skill in horse-taming, and were among the first people in human history to be recorded fighting on horseback. Their association with horses is evident from the recurrence of the Greek *hippos* (horse) in their names: three Amazons known by name were Hippolyta ('stampeding horse'), Melanippe ('black mare') and Alcippe ('powerful mare').

Most famous of the Amazons was Queen Hippolyta, who became the target of the hero Heracles around 1250 BC, when he demanded her girdle, the symbol of her sacred and sexual power. The whole tribe of Amazons rose against him in anger and Hippolyta met him in pitched battle, where she was thrown from her horse and lay helpless at Heracles' feet.

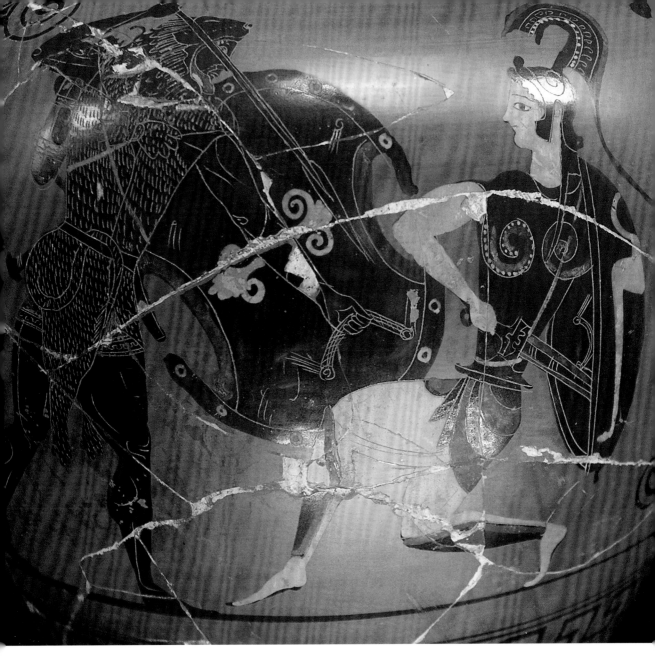

The hero offered to spare Hippolyta's life if she would submit to him. Knowing that this would mean immediate rape and a lifetime of sexual slavery, the warrior queen chose to die rather than yield. Heracles killed her, stripped her of her girdle, seized her battleaxe, and slaughtered all the other Amazon champions, one by one.

Only when the best of the whole tribe had been killed did the Amazon commander, Melanippe, seek a truce. Heracles granted it on condition that she too gave up her girdle, symbolically handing over her power as queen and woman to him. Heracles then raped her and let her go, knowing the humiliation would be worse than death.

Scene painted on an Attic black-figure amphora of around 530–520 BC, showing Heracles (left) joining battle with the Amazon queen Hippolyta.

The Amazons suffered many such assaults at the hands of the Greeks as they imposed their patriarchal rule on tribes who followed the older earth religion of the Great Mother Goddess, a belief system honouring womankind and led by queens. Driven to revenge, the Amazon queen Penthesilea travelled to Troy in around 1250 BC to fight on behalf of the Trojans, who were also at war with the invading Greeks. She fought with great distinction on the Trojan side, and more than once drove the greatest champion of the Greeks, Achilles, from the field.

But in their final encounter, Achilles ran her through. Stripping the dying body of its armour, Achilles realized that his adversary was a woman and falling in love or lust with her as she died, had sex with her body while she was still warm. He then grieved for her death in a way that he never had before, as a warrior hero who had killed many men. Another Greek, the troublemaker Thersites, taunted Achilles for his sexual perversion and his unmanly tears, and boasted that he had gouged out Penthesilea's eyes with his spear while she was still alive.

Achilles promptly killed Thersites for this slight. In revenge, another Greek hero Diomedes, one of Thersites' kinsmen, tied Penthesilea's body to his horse and dragged it round the battlefield by the heels. The battered corpse was finally rescued on Achilles' orders and buried with great honour. Penthesilea was the last true Amazon, and the tribe died with her.

Astonishing stories indeed, but are they truth or myth? Later historians, writing in more restricted times, puzzled over the anomaly of any women who chose to fight. The word 'Amazon' was interpreted as deriving from the Greek *a* ('without') and *mazos* ('breast'). This paved the way for the explanation that these fighting women cut off their right breasts to improve their skill at arms. Faced with this nonsense, traditional historians have dismissed the Amazons as pure myth.

But the written accounts, ranging from travellers' gossip to the work of reputable historians, are too numerous and coherent to ignore. Amazons are described by classical writers as diverse as Homer, Pliny, Strabo, Aeschylus and Plutarch, all of whom treat their existence as fact. In the fifth century BC, the Greek historian Herodotus reported a mutiny on the Black Sea, when a group of Amazon prisoners of war overpowered their Greek captors and escaped to establish a new realm in Scythia and Sarmatia (modern Ukraine and southern Russia). Roman commanders, who never admitted women to their own armies, record encountering women in the ranks of their enemies, especially the Scythians, who regularly included female fighters alongside men.

Like the Romans, the Greece of the classical era from about 500 BC onwards was not interested in women's freedom or equality. When Athenians evolved the world's first 'democracy', women were specifically excluded from voting or any civic involvement, along with slaves, criminals and the insane. The gradual subjugation of women throughout

In the early days of ancient Greece, all young girls led a free, open-air life and were given athletic and gymnastic training to promote both fitness and beauty. Both the Spartans and Athenians trained their girls in the art of war and encouraged their participation in competitive war games.

In Crete, chosen young women trained as *toreras* to take part in the Minoan ritual of bull-leaping, while Ionian women joined in boar-hunts, their weighted nets and spears at the ready. The freedom of the young unmarried women in the military city-state of Sparta was so marked that it scandalized others, as the Athenian playwright Euripides records:

> The daughters of Sparta are
> never at home!
> They mingle with the young men in
> wrestling matches,
> Their clothes cast off, their hips all naked,
> It's shameful!

The hardening of these young women's bodies by sport and the regular practice of nudity had a deliberate aim: it fostered their strength, physical ability and endurance for military service. Plato stated in *The Republic* that women should become soldiers if they wished. Roman theorists followed the Greeks in this. The writer and philosopher Musonius Rufus (AD 30–*c*.101) argued that women and men should receive the same education and training, and any differences should be based on ability and strength, not gender.

Courage and daring were not confined to men. The Roman heroine Cloelia, taken hostage by the Etruscan king, Lars Porsenna, during an attack on Rome in the sixth century BC, escaped, stole a horse and swam the River Tiber to get back to Rome to fight.

WARRIOR WOMEN OF THE ANCIENT WORLD

The Romans promptly handed her back to the Etruscans as an oath-breaker, intent on demonstrating *Romana fides*, the unwavering truth of a Roman pledge. But Lars Porsenna was more impressed by Cloelia's valour than he was by her compatriots' rigid view of honour, and freed her and all her fellow hostages as a mark of respect.

This detail from a fresco found at the palace of Minos at Knossos on Crete depicts a female athlete taking part in the ritual of bull-leaping. It dates from the Middle Minoan period (17th–15th centuries BC).

Greece, and indeed the rest of the civilized world, is mirrored in the story of the Amazons, whose fortunes fell as those of the heroes rose. Powerful, capable, glamorous, gifted and free, they represented the type of woman who had no place in the brave new world of father gods and men of might, and who still had to fight for her right to exist.

Deborah is one of the world's earliest recorded women army commanders, resolute in war and triumphant in peace. A poet, prophet, counsellor and civic ruler whose story is told in the biblical Book of Judges, chapters 4–5, she held both spiritual and temporal power. Seated in her tent under a palm tree on the high ground of Mount Ephraim, she settled disputes of religion, property and law, which over the years gave her the authority to bring about the deliverance of her nation.

Deborah
1209–1169 BC

The fourth and only female judge in Israel before the establishment of the monarchy, she earned the title of 'Mother of Israel' for taking action against her people's long-standing enemy. Under the command of their king Jabin, as the chronicler recorded, the Canaanites had grievously oppressed and enslaved the Children of Israel for 20 years.

The captain of Jabin's army, Sisera, was his most zealous enforcer, and the king had equipped him with the very height of the battle armoury of the time, 900 chariots of iron, which, like modern-day tanks, could repel all the feeble weaponry of those on foot. As judge of all Israel, Deborah held supreme power, and it was to her the Israelites turned and cried out when their oppression became too much to bear.

Deborah is described in English translations as 'the wife of Lapidoth', a man's name not recognized elsewhere in the chronicles. In ancient Hebrew, *eshet Lapidot* could mean the 'wife or woman of Lapidot'. But as *lapidot* means 'torches' or 'fire', it could also translate as 'Torch Lady' or 'Fire Woman', an apt name for the woman who was to set her nation aflame.

Petitioned by the people, Deborah sent for Barak, the captain of the armies of Israel. This name, which meant 'lightning', also suggests that Deborah was harnessing the forces of natural energy to send renewal crackling through the land. She ordered Barak to gather all the tribes, a force of 10,000 men, to draw Sisera and his mighty host down to the river in the valley. If he raised the army of the Israelites, she promised Barak, she would deliver Sisera into his hands.

Barak was not convinced. Sisera had his phalanx of iron chariots and an army of 'multitudes', while he had a random assembly of different tribes, men more accustomed to abuse than aggression. Like any hardened officer, he tested his commander's appetite for the battle to come and her strength of will. 'If you'll go with me', he declared, 'I will go. If you will not go with me, I will not go'.

Deborah did not flinch. Instantly she agreed to go with him, but added a wry warning that the battle would bring him no honour: the glory of the day and the downfall of Sisera would lie in the hands of a woman, not in his. She directed him to place all his troops on the high ground of Mount Tabor, forcing Sisera to occupy the river valley below: soft ground, ill-suited to his heavy iron chariots.

As soon as all her army was assembled, Deborah gave the order to attack. 'Up!' she commanded Barak, 'For this day, the Lord hath delivered Sisera into thy hand!' As Barak's motley host flew down the mountain, the Canaanites

'Blessed above women shall Jael be ... so let all thine enemies perish, O Lord!': Deborah sings the praises of her fellow Israelite for killing the Canaanite commander Sisera. From an 1865 illustration by the French engraver, Gustave Doré.

The world's first recorded 'honey trap' operative, Delilah won undying notoriety when she ensnared Samson for the Philistines, as described in the

DELILAH
c. 1049 BC

Delilah cutting the hair of her lover Samson before betraying him to his enemies: detail from a painting by the Italian Renaissance artist Caravaggio.

Book of Judges, chapters 13–16. Samson was the greatest of the Israelites, a prodigious fighter who had been a judge of Israel, like Deborah, for 20 years between 1069 and 1049 BC. The secret of his strength lay in his long hair, which his mother had never cut, following a revelation that her son, if unshorn, would deliver his people from the Philistines, the tribe that had oppressed the Israelites for 40 years.

Yet for a man chosen by God to be Israel's deliverer, the great Israelite seemed only too eager to put himself into Philistine hands, taking Philistine lovers and harlots and even a Philistine wife before falling in love with Delilah. For the leaders of the Philistines, it was a chance too good to miss. Each of them promised her 1100 pieces of silver to betray her lover, the enemy of her race.

Delilah set to work to wheedle out of Samson the secret of his great strength. He fobbed her off three times, but yielded to her pressure in the end. Delilah then lulled him to sleep and called for a barber to shave his head. Waking him with the taunting cry 'The Philistines be upon thee, Samson!', she handed him over to his enemies.

Delilah was only one of several women spies and undercover agents in the Bible. The modern-day Israeli, Cheryl Bentov, followed in Delilah's footsteps when she used the same trick nearly 2,000 years later. An Israeli army soldier recruited as a spy, Bentov sprang a 'honey trap' in 1986, when she targeted the Israeli whistle-blower Mordecai Vanunu, and delivered him into the hands of a Mossad snatch squad.

For betraying Israel's top-secret nuclear activity, Vanunu was jailed for 18 years. Bentov retired, and subsequently divided her time between a suburb in Israel and Florida, where she became a pillar of Orlando's Jewish community.

panicked. War machines and men were bogged down, and those who could took flight rapidly.

Foremost among them was their once-feared captain, the cruel Sisera. As Barak set about destroying the vast Canaanite host and hunting down the survivors, Sisera leapt from his lordly chariot and 'fled away on his feet'.

Against all the odds, the Israelites had triumphed over the Canaanites at the battle later called Taanach. Deborah had prophesied a victory and victory was theirs. Defeated, Sisera took flight, running for his life. Exhausted and alone on the vast plain beyond the river, he made for the only place of safety he knew, the solitary tent of Heber, a Canaanite ally and friend of Jabin, his king.

But when the shattered Sisera arrived, Heber was not at home. In her husband's absence, his wife Jael saw the fugitive approaching, went out to meet him, and welcomed him in. 'Turn in, my lord, turn in to me', she coaxed him: 'Fear not.' Half-dying of thirst, Sisera begged her for water, but Jael gave him milk – food and drink in one. Then she covered him with her mantle and promised to watch at the opening of the tent and give warning if Barak or any of the defeated leader's enemies approached.

> ## *'Up! … For this day, the Lord hath delivered Sisera into thy hand!'*
>
> DEBORAH BEFORE THE BATTLE OF TAANACH

Nursed with warmth, comfort and milk, Sisera was soon asleep. Trusting to Heber as his king's friend and supporter, he overlooked the fact that Jael was a staunch Israelite, and loyal to Deborah as her supreme judge. She obeyed her tribal allegiance, not her husband's manoeuvring, when she wooed his ally and drew him to his doom. As Sisera slept, Jael picked up a tent peg and a mallet and drove it through his temples so hard that she nailed his head to the ground. 'And so he died', recorded the ancient chronicler.

By the time Barak arrived, Jael was once again at the door of her tent. As Deborah had prophesied, Sisera was indeed delivered into his hand, but not by his hand. That triumph belonged to a woman, a doughty warrior in Deborah's motley force.

Deborah's last act on that day was to raise a mighty song of victory, which survives as the biblical Book of Judges, chapter 5. Like the Greek poet and warrior Telesilla (see pages 24–27), she celebrated the triumph of the Israelites in an extempore poem, which she sang and performed with Barak, her faithful second in command. In it she reflects on her long career of making war and bringing peace to the land and the wretched sufferings of the people 'until that I, Deborah, arose, till I arose a mother in Israel'.

After the celebrations, the Israelites pressed on to subdue the king of the Canaanites and lift the threat of oppression for the children of Israel. Deborah's bold action ushered in 40 years of peace. Her story is proof that a woman could hold high command over all the male leaders and war commanders of the tribes of the time, leading her army to victory and even more surprisingly, ensuring a lasting peace.

Like Boudicca, the Assyrian queen Sammu-Ramat has gone down in history by the name Ancient Greek chroniclers gave her: 'Semiramis'. And like the Celtic queen again, from her birth Sammu-Ramat was revered as divine, the daughter of the Great Goddess on Earth, and many legends arose and clung to her.

Sammu-Ramat
Ninth Century BC

Sammu-Ramat's achievement was to carve out a role for herself as a woman ruler in a strong line of kings. She established her right to rule by linking herself with the powerful goddess Astarte (Ishtar), the Queen of Heaven, and like any leader from Genghis Khan to Hitler, she consolidated her power by making war.

Assyria itself was the most northerly of the ancient countries occupying the great Mesopotamian plain, the region watered by the rivers Tigris and Euphrates and the cradle of European civilization. Its political importance lay in its location as a buffer between the Semitic tribes of the Mediterranean and Persia (Iran), and like most of the region throughout history until the present day, it was subject to constant war.

Sammu-Ramat originally claimed descent from Derceto, the Great Goddess in her incarnation as a fish, but from her earliest appearance she proved herself a mistress of manoeuvres on land. She married Onnes, an Assyrian general, and travelled with him to besiege the city of Bactra, capital of Bactria, where her swift grasp of the situation and shrewd advice shortened the siege and delivered the city into her husband's hands.

What became of Onnes is unknown. One story has Sammu-Ramat catching the eye of King Ninus of Assyria at the siege of Bactra. Struck by her bravery and military ability, he decided to marry her, at which the general obligingly killed himself. Widowed or not, Sammu-Ramat certainly married Shamsi-Adad V, who ruled Assyria from 824 to 810 BC and who is commonly identified by historians with Ninus. During his reign, Queen Sammu-Ramat rose to national prominence and with him founded the legendary city of Nineveh ('abode of Ninus'). She held supreme power during Shamsi-Adad's lifetime, and reigned alone after his death, which some accounts claim she arranged in order to consolidate her power.

With such a compliant husband, it is unlikely that Sammu-Ramat would have needed to kill the king. Steeped in the worship of goddesses, most of the tribes of the ancient world had little problem with power in the

In this painting by the Neapolitan baroque artist Luca Giordano (1634–1705), Sammu-Ramat (Semiramis) appears as a majestic figure riding a charger and driving her enemies away from the gates of Babylon.

Tahm-Rayis, queen of the Massagetae, was a warrior leader of one of the hard-riding tribes who for centuries roamed the vast steppes of Scythia, north of Ancient Greece. During her reign, the freedom of her horse-loving nomadic people in what is now southern Russia and modern Ukraine was under constant threat from the most powerful of the neighbourhood kings, the founder of the Persian empire, Cyrus the Great.

Cyrus planned to annex the territory ruled by Tahm-Rayis and to marry her by force. Tahm-Rayis refused his rough proposal, warning him that she: 'would quench his thirst for blood.' She then sent her army under the command of her son, Spargapises, to oppose the invading troops. Spargapises defeated Cyrus, but fell into a trap when the Persians feigned a retreat and left behind a vast store of wine. When the Massagetae had drunk themselves into a stupor, the Persians counter-attacked, massacred their opponents and took Spargapises prisoner.

Spargapises then tricked Cyrus into removing his shackles and committed suicide rather than allow himself to be used as a bargaining tool against his mother. Denouncing Cyrus as a treacherous coward, Tahm-Rayis led the remainder of her army against the Persian emperor and won a massive victory. According to the Greek historian Herodotus, when Tahm-Rayis defeated Cyrus, she had him killed to avenge her son. She then ordered the corpse to be decapitated and the head dropped into a wineskin of human blood, in fulfilment of her threat. Thereafter she kept the skull with her at all times, and drank wine from it until her own death.

The story of Tahm-Rayis was well known in the ancient world, and her fame lives on. Modern Kazakhs revere her as a great queen and independence fighter, and her name, in its modern spelling, Tomiris, remains popular in Kazakhstan.

In a bloodthirsty scene reminiscent of the biblical account of Salomé, Herod's stepdaughter, demanding the head of John the Baptist as a gift, Tahm-Rayis supposedly revelled in the decapitation of her enemy, Cyrus of Persia. Detail from a work by the Italian 17th-century painter Mattia Preti.

hands of a woman: other ninth-century BC female rulers include Queen Athaliah of Judah and Queen Dido, the founder of Carthage. Five years later, in 805, there was no opposition when Sammu-Ramat assumed the regency on behalf of her son, King Adad-nirari III, who died in 772 BC.

From the outset, Sammu-Ramat proved herself an early mistress of 'spin', fostering the many legends that grew up around her in her lifetime stressing her divinity and supernatural powers. Abandoned by her mother and exposed at birth, as she claimed, she was fed by a flock of doves, the messengers of the Great Goddess, who saved her life until human help arrived. By nature, though, she was more hawk than dove, as her aggressive programme of military expansion proved.

In her own time, Sammu-Ramat was renowned as an outstanding war leader, fighting many campaigns with her husband. Together they made conquests in neighbouring regions of Asia, subduing the warlike Bactrians of central Asia. When the king was fatally wounded by an arrow in this battle, Sammu-Ramat assumed command to push the expedition to a successful conclusion.

As sole ruler, Sammu-Ramat then led her forces in many military campaigns to increase her territories. She is said to have commanded 300,000 foot soldiers and 5,000 horses, along with war chariots, pack animals, camels and cameleers. In her time she successfully expanded landlocked Assyria's borders to touch not one sea, but four. She penetrated as far as India, then conquered Ethiopia, which she added to the Assyrian empire. Along the way she successfully repulsed attacks by the world's greatest military commander of the time, Alexander the Great.

After conquering Babylon, the queen is said to have erected the legendary Hanging Gardens there as a memorial to her success, a visionary construction still famed as one of the Seven Wonders of the Ancient World. Covering about 1.6 hectares (4 acres), this was a tower or pyramid-like structure consisting of a series of terraces, each supported by arches resting on hollow pillars up to 90 metres (almost 300 ft) high. Each terrace was planted with trees, shrubs, flowers and trailing plants so that the whole edifice resembled a series of gardens hanging in the air. On each level were fountains, reception areas and banqueting halls. Water from the Euphrates was pumped up to a reservoir on the top, from which it irrigated all the gardens below. Later historians question Sammu-Ramat's connection with this unique monument, attributing it instead to Nebuchadnezzar, one of the greatest of the region's ancient kings, who ruled Babylon from 604 to 561 BC. Many of her other achievements have also been dismissed as 'semi-mythical', reflecting the age-old dilemma of traditional historians in accepting daring and successful women leaders either in peace or war.

But miraculous as the gardens may have seemed, Sammu-Ramat proved herself elsewhere to be a bold and prolific builder. She is credited with the restoration and rebuilding of Babylon, which she then completely encircled with a high defensive brick wall. She founded and fostered many cities as well as Nineveh, and some of the great architectural works of the East are still ascribed to her. It is not known how, where or when Sammu-Ramat died, although one account states that she was killed by her son. Another legend links her with the supreme Babylonian female deity, Astarte, who turned her into a dove at her death. The dove was thereafter held sacred and Sammu-Ramat herself was worshipped as a goddess.

The world's first known female captain of a naval fleet, Artemisia was a queen of the royal house of Caria in Asia Minor. Named after the Greek deity, Artemis, the goddess of hunting – one of the incarnations of the Great Goddess and known as Diana to the Romans – she ruled the small kingdom of Halicarnassus (modern Bodrum, on the coast of Turkey). In her younger days she had been married and had at least one child, a son, but by the time of the great Battle of Salamis, which made her famous, she reigned alone. Her territory also included the Greek islands of Nissiros, Kos and Kalimnos, which she held as a vassal of the Persian emperor Xerxes I, Kheshayar Shah, 'the Great King, King of Kings', who ruled from 486 to 465 BC.

Artemisia
Fifth Century BC

Artemisia was bound by her oath of allegiance to Xerxes when 'the Great King' undertook a military expedition against the city states of Greece in 480 BC. The Persian invasion was halted by the heroic and immortal courage of the Spartan soldiers under the command of their king, Leonidas, at the battle of Thermopylae, when a force of 300 held countless thousands of Xerxes' men at bay. When they were at last betrayed and slaughtered to a man, Athens was captured and the Greek allies driven back to their last line of defence on the Isthmus of Corinth.

Xerxes now resolved to attack the Greeks by sea. Artemisia, who had provided five ships under her command to support her overlord, advised against it. Far better to pursue the Greeks on land, she argued: another victory like Thermopylae would scatter the random assortment of allies to defend their own city-states, and make them easier to pick off one by one. Also, the Greeks were known to be good sailors, while the Persian fleet contained allies whose seamanship was notoriously weak.

Artemisia was the only female among Xerxes' naval commanders, which did not offer her a position of strength. In the age-old conventions of the sea, a ship is always female. Phrases like 'maiden voyage' to describe a ship first being sailed, and the ancient naval superstition that any female on board is a 'jinx', all combine to reinforce the myth that the command of boats and sailing itself must be an all-male affair.

In fact, Artemisia is only one of the countless women who have been sailing and commanding from earliest times. In the classical world, their best chance lay in command, since the motive power of sailing ships

A 19th-century painting by Spanish artist Raphael Monleon Y Torres depicting Greek triremes typical of those used during the Battle of Salamis.

when the wind failed, whether merchant vessels or warships, was provided by oarsmen.

Three banks of oars, each one so heavy that it took a bench of men to move it, powered the trireme, the standard Mediterranean warship of Artemisia's day. Eight was finally deemed the maximum number of men who could efficiently handle a single oar. Given the demands this made on the muscular strength of the shoulders and upper arms, few if any women would ever have been able to row as strongly as men.

But they could still command, as Artemisia did. Utterly fearless in battle and always in the forefront of the action, as the Greek historian Herodotus recorded with great admiration, she was already renowned for her bravery and skill. Despite being old enough to have a grown-up son, she never held back. In addition to her outstanding physical courage, she showed judgement, wisdom and caution when she boldly counselled 'the King of Kings' to play to his military strength on land, not his weakness at sea.

> ## 'Truly, my men are becoming women and my women, men.'
>
> XERXES AT THE BATTLE OF SALAMIS

Xerxes ignored her advice. Lured on by a cunning message from the wily Greek commander, the great Thucydides, on 29 September 480 BC, he attacked the Greek fleet with disastrous results. Forced to fight against her will, Artemisia threw herself and her ships into the forefront of the action, and fought with such ferocious skill and daring that the Athenians put a bounty of 10,000 drachmas on her head.

When Xerxes' brother, an admiral of the fleet, died in combat, Artemisia succeeded in retrieving his body from the enemy. Her own ship was then targeted for hostile attention, and as she took evasive action, she found herself blocked by one of her allies. Trapped, she rammed and sank the other Persian ship, and made her escape. Watching this bold and brilliant manoeuvre, Xerxes commented: 'Truly, my men are becoming women and my women, men.'

But Artemisia's daring was not enough to save the fleet. The Persians suffered a catastrophic defeat at the Battle of Salamis, and were never again able to threaten the Greeks. The battle lost, Artemisia counselled Xerxes to immediate flight, sound advice that 'the Great King' finally decided to take. Loyal to the last, she transported members of his family to safety, lodging them in the sanctuary of her namesake, the goddess Artemis (Diana), at Ephesus.

The record of Artemisia's military service ends here. But the end of the war was to bring her no peace. Falling madly in love with a younger man who showed no interest in her, she consulted an oracle for advice. Whatever that was, it offered her no hope. Having survived so many fierce battles at sea, she chose to die at last in the embrace of the waves. She ended her life tragically at the scene of so many of her triumphs, throwing herself off a cliff into the Aegean Sea.

A formidable sea captain with her own fleet, Bouboulina proved that the tradition of fearless female Greek sailors did not die with Artemisia, but survived for 20 centuries after her death. An intrepid freedom fighter in the Greek War of Independence against the hated Ottoman Turks, she lived through civil war and internal exile, only to die in a vicious family feud.

Bouboulina was the daughter of a Greek sea captain who fought against the Turks in the failed revolt of 1769–70 and died soon after her mother gave birth to her in the jail where he was held. Mother and daughter then moved round the Greek islands until her mother married again.

Bouboulina herself married twice, and had six children. When her second husband died in 1811, she expanded his mercantile business, building four more ships. But the Turks were still the enemy. Bouboulina became the only female member of the Philiki Eteria ('The Friendly Society'), an underground organization dedicated to overthrowing Ottoman rule.

When the Greek War of Independence broke out in March 1821, Bouboulina, by then aged 50, raised a flag of defiance on her own ship, the mighty 18-gun *Agamemnon*, built at her own expense the year before. At the outbreak of hostilities, she sailed with her ships to mount a naval blockade of the key port of Nauplia (modern Nafplion).

In September 1821 Greek forces broke the siege of Tripolis, a key Turkish stronghold, and Bouboulina led her own sailors into the town. Mass slaughter followed the Greek victory, but Bouboulina single-handedly prevented the rape and massacre of the women in the Ottoman commander's harem. In the factional fighting that scarred the struggle for Greek independence, Bouboulina was exiled to her mother's island of Spetses, where she was killed by a stray shot during a family feud, four years before the Turks finally granted independence to Greece.

A modern statue of Laskarina Bouboulina looks out to sea from the harbour on Spetses, off the Peloponnese. It was erected to commemorate the achievements of the island's most famous daughter.

Telesilla won fame for arming the women of the Ancient Greek city-state of Argos and inspiring them to defend their city when many of their men had been killed in battle, or were fighting elsewhere. Like Artemisia, she was praised by Herodotus, the leading historian of the Ancient Greeks, and also won the admiration of his Roman counterpart, Plutarch. One of a number of real-life Amazons in the classical world, she contributed to the myth of the fearsome tribe of female warriors. However, like the seventh-century Islamic woman poet and warrior El-Khaansa, a contemporary of Muhammad, Telesilla was also renowned for her creative skills.

Telesilla
Fifth Century BC

Telesilla was first known as a poet, and nine fragments of her *Hymns* survive, three addressed to the sun-god Apollo and six to the hunter goddess Artemis (Roman Diana), the deity worshipped as 'the Lady of Wild Things'. In her early life, as the Roman historian Plutarch recounts, she 'was the daughter of a famous house, but sickly in body'. Keen to regain her health, she consulted an oracle for advice, and received a divine instruction to devote her life to the service of the Muses.

To the Ancient Greeks, the Nine Muses were minor deities, each one embodying the sacred spirit of one of the intellectual pursuits with which men and women could enrich their often sad and short human lives. They were: Calliope (epic poetry), Clio (history), Erato (lyric poetry), Euterpe (music), Melpomene (tragedy), Polyhymnia (choral poetry), Terpsichore (dance), Thalia (comedy) and Urania (astronomy). All nine were female, and the most important were poetry, literature, music and dance. By devoting herself to poetry and music, Plutarch noted, Telesilla 'was quickly relieved of her trouble' – possibly depression, an illness that was widely recognized in the ancient world under its Greek name, *melancholia*, or 'black bile'.

Telesilla's talent was soon recognized, first by her female admirers: 'she was greatly admired by the women for her poetic art', Plutarch said. Her fame later spread across the classical world: Antipater of Thessalonica, a Greek writer and wit who flourished from about 11 BC to AD 15, listed her among the nine greatest women lyric poets of Greece, and hailed her as 'renowned' even among 'the divinely-inspired tongues of these women reared on Helicon, the home and inspiration of the Muses themselves'.

In Greek mythology, the Nine Muses were thought to be the offspring of the supreme deity Zeus and the titaness Mnemosyne ('memory'). This Roman bas-relief carving, dating from AD 150–160, shows the muse of comedy Thalia, who holds a comic mask.

Telesilla's fame took on a new dimension in 494 BC, when her home state of Argos was attacked by the Spartan leader, King Cleomenes. Intent on subjugating the free-thinking, music-loving Argives to his martial rule, he crushed the troops of Argos in the field with a massive loss of life. When the survivors took sanctuary in a sacred grove, Cleomenes lured some out to their deaths with the false promise of a truce, and set fire to the grove in order to burn the rest alive. He then marched on the city itself.

Impulsive, daring, and by common belief divinely inspired, Telesilla used her heroic poetry to rouse all the able-bodied women of Argos to resist. Raiding the temples and private houses to gather all the weapons she could find, she armed herself and her troops with anything that came to hand. Then together they took a stand on the battlements in such numbers that they occupied the fortifications all the way round. This impressive show of force astonished the Spartans, who had thought that the city was ripe for the taking after the slaughter of so many of its men.

According to the majority of accounts, Cleomenes and his soldiers succeeded in penetrating the city, possibly even the citadel itself. Facing defeat, Telesilla drove her female army to a frenzy by reciting, chanting and singing warlike verses, until they fell upon the enemy in such a fury that they drove them out of the city of Argos.

A 17th-century painting by the Flemish artist Pauwel Casteels titled *The Battle between the Amazons and the Greeks.*

FIGHTING WOMEN OF ANCIENT ROME

Telesilla and her companions were real-life Amazons (see pages 8–11), the tribe of warrior women whose exploits were known throughout Ancient Greece. But fighting women were found everywhere in the ancient world. Written records of Rome from its earliest days offer scattered but abundant evidence of women under arms. One such was the Roman fighter Camilla, whom the poet Virgil portrayed in his account of the founding of the city of Rome, the *Aeneid*, which was written in around 20 BC.

A daughter of the royal house of the Volscians, Camilla was dedicated by her father at an early age to Diana, the Roman goddess of hunting, and trained in the use of weapons and the mastery of horses and dogs. She spent several years as a hunter before joining the forces of Turnus, king of the Rutulians in central Italy. At the time, Turnus was at war with the neighbouring kingdom of the Etruscans, and Camilla died in the fighting, killed by the Etruscan warrior Arruns.

In creating Camilla, Virgil drew on the life of another famous woman fighter, Harpalyce, daughter of Harpalycus, king of the Amymonei in Thrace, northern Greece. Her father brought her up as a warrior after her mother died. She fought at his side in battle, and once saved his life. After his death and the loss of his kingdom, she became a brigand, and was finally captured and killed. Despite her lawlessness, Harpalyce was given civic honours after death. Her tomb became a place of pilgrimage, and the rituals celebrated at her graveside included a mock fight.

During the Roman empire, individual women warriors fought in the public arenas, both as free women and as slaves. They competed in the games that marked the opening of the Colosseum in AD 80. According to the Roman satirist Juvenal, it became fashionable for women of the nobility to train and fight in the arenas until AD 200, when the Emperor Alexander Severus issued an edict banning all women from gladiatorial combat.

Another version of the story has Telesilla manning the battlements with all the men, boys and slaves who had been too young, old or infirm to fight. Giving the illusion of a garrison, she then led the women out of the city to ambush the Spartans at a place she knew would put them at a disadvantage. Meeting the enemy head-on, the women fearlessly stood their ground, undeterred by the blood-curdling Spartan war cry and the ferocity of their attack. In the resulting battle, many of the women were killed. But Cleomenes and the Spartans were repulsed with great losses, Telesilla and her troops won the day, and the city was saved.

The women who fell in the battle were buried close to the Argive Road, and the survivors were granted the privilege of erecting a statue of Ares, the god of war, as a lasting memorial to their outstanding courage. They then celebrated their victory with a tremendous party, during which Telesilla composed a battle hymn in honour of the event. In gratitude, her fellow citizens raised a memorial to her in the temple of Aphrodite, which was placed at the feet of the statue of the goddess herself. The stone carving represented Telesilla with her volumes of poetry scattered round her as she prepares to don a helmet, ready to give battle, a fitting tribute to both aspects of her undying achievement.

Cleopatra, wrote the French poet Théophile Gautier in 1845 'is a person to be wondered at ... whom dreamers find always at the end of their dreams'. In reality this famous sexual icon was an astute but ultimately unsuccessful power-monger, a hook-nosed and heavy-jawed ruler who remained celibate for over half her adult life and led her country to war by land and sea.

Cleopatra VII
69–30 BC

Born in Alexandria, Cleopatra was the third daughter of King Ptolemy XII, a descendant of Alexander the Great. Though she probably spoke Egyptian, if only to her officials and servants, Cleopatra was a Greek. Her family had ruled Egypt since 323 BC, but the failure of earlier leaders had made Egypt a puppet of Rome. When her ineffectual father died in 51 BC, the 18–year-old Cleopatra succeeded, along with the brother forced under Egyptian custom to be her husband too, the 12-year-old Ptolemy XIII.

Cleopatra at first attempted to govern alone. She was then ousted by a cabal of courtiers, tried and failed to raise a rebellion, and was forced to flee. When civil war broke out between the siblings, Ptolemy sought the aid of Julius Caesar, currently holding supreme power in Rome. Caesar's response was to seize Alexandria and claim the right to decide between the rival claims of the young king and his sister-queen.

Encountering Cleopatra when she had herself delivered as a present for him inside a rolled-up carpet, Caesar abandoned his plans to annex Egypt and backed Cleopatra's claim to the throne. Ptolemy XIII was drowned in the Nile, and Cleopatra was restored to the throne with a younger brother, Ptolemy XIV, as co-regent. Cleopatra bore Caesar a son, dubbed 'Caesarion', who accompanied his mother to Rome in 47 BC, where she lived in one of Caesar's villas. Although many Romans disapproved of her as Caesar's mistress, he installed a golden statue of her in the Temple of Venus Genetrix, the ancestress of his own family. After Caesar's assassination in 44 BC, she returned to Egypt, where Ptolemy XIV unexpectedly died. With another brother successfully despatched, Cleopatra resumed her position as queen, reigning as co-sovereign with her son, Ptolemy XV.

Two years after Caesar's death, now the undisputed monarch of Egypt, she was summoned to meet one of Rome's ruling triumvirate, Marcus Antonius (Mark Antony). As one of the three men who governed the mightiest empire the world had ever seen, Mark Antony's task was to judge Cleopatra's loyalty to Rome. Cleopatra so expertly turned the tables that

Cleopatra VII, lover of two Roman war leaders, has often been portrayed down the ages as a sultry, exotic *femme fatale*. The portrayal (right) of Cleopatra by Vivien Leigh in the 1945 film *Caesar and Cleopatra* has been described as 'alluring and fiery'.

her inquisitor was persuaded to abandon his former life, including his Roman wife, and to live with her in Alexandria. Over the course of the affair, she bore him three children, and married him by Egyptian rites.

In Rome, Anthony was now reviled as a man who had betrayed his Roman integrity and sunk into Eastern depravity and excess. To restore his dignity, Cleopatra financed a series of disastrous military campaigns in which he lost the greater part of his army. This did not prevent them from celebrating with a triumph in Alexandria, where Cleopatra and her children were declared rightful rulers of both the Roman and Egyptian empires. Mark Antony now planned to found a new imperial dynasty whose power base was to be Alexandria rather than Rome. Cleopatra would be Isis to Antony's Osiris, a notion that did not endear him to his enemies in Rome.

In 32 BC the Senate was persuaded to declare war on Cleopatra – in effect a move against Antony, who would not desert her. The Roman poet Horace gloated that Cleopatra would be dispatched 'as swiftly as the hawk follows the feeble dove'. The conflict was decided by the Battle of Actium, fought at sea off the west coast of Greece while substantial land-based hosts looked on. Of the 400 warships under Antony's command, Cleopatra had provided 200.

A silver tetradrachm with the head of Cleopatra VII. During her association with Mark Antony, double-headed coins were struck showing them as joint rulers.

Caesar's great-nephew and adopted son and heir Octavian, another of the three triumvirs, prudently delegated operational command of the Roman fleet to his competent lieutenant Vipsanius Agrippa. Mark Antony was able to break through Agrippa's battle line, but lost the day and fled to Egypt with Cleopatra, who had been present at the battle to inspire her own fighting men.

As Octavian's armies closed on Alexandria, both Antony and Cleopatra committed suicide. The ancient sources assert that Cleopatra killed herself with the bite of two poisonous asps, which she pressed to her arm, although it is possible that she ended her life with a poisoned hairpin. Her son Caesarion was captured shortly afterwards and put to death. Thus ended the line of the Greek rulers of Egypt, and with it the line of the pharaohs too. Cleopatra's children by Mark Antony were spared, and reared in Rome by his wife Octavia.

As Caesar Augustus, Octavian remodelled the constitution and carried Rome into a new age. Cleopatra was demonized by Horace as 'the wild

Like Cleopatra, Hatshepsut came to power as co-ruler with her husband and half-brother, Thutmose II, then took command as soon as Thutmose died. Nominally the regent for Thutmose's six-year-old heir, Hatshepsut assumed the title of pharaoh, and became the first supreme woman ruler of Egypt for 2,000 years.

HATSHEPSUT
1503–1482 BC

To consolidate her rule, she led her armies in a number of military campaigns, fighting at the head of her troops in Nubia and elsewhere. She also recognized the importance of sea power, building a great navy, which she later used for both commerce and war.

Hatshepsut had other battles to fight at home, as she tussled for power with bitter rivals within the royal hierarchy. To strengthen her position, she claimed divine birth, a manoeuvre also employed by Sammu-Ramat (see pages 16–19). Another tactic was to have herself depicted as a man, wearing men's clothing, headgear and even a false beard cut in the wedge-shaped style of a male pharaoh.

Making war did not distract Hatshepsut from the business of peace. She fostered commercial ventures and foreign trade, sending an expedition over the Red Sea to bring back spices, ivory and ebony, and exotic animals and plants. Nor did she neglect her subjects' spiritual needs. Hatshepsut herself rated bringing several huge obelisks to the temple at Karnak as one of her most important achievements.

In her lifetime, Hatshepsut successfully combined the roles of man and woman, war leader and enabler of peace. But when she died, her former ward Thutmose III, now a man, had the statues of her ruling as pharaoh defaced and smashed. Her tomb in the Valley of the Kings was left unfinished, and every effort was made to consign all traces of her to the shifting, whispering sands of the desert from which she sprang.

Head from a statue of Hatshepsut in the guise of the deity Osiris, from her funerary temple at Deir el-Bahri near Luxor. She is shown wearing the dual crowns of Upper and Lower Egypt and the false beard that traditionally signified kingship.

queen' who had plotted the ruin of the Roman empire. In spite of the collapse of all her own plans, Cleopatra nevertheless became a legend, reworked in countless paintings, poems and plays and, since 1908, movies. She lives again as the baleful silent diva Theda Bara's kohl-stained temptress of 1917; as Claudette Colbert's Art Deco sex kitten in 1934; and in the well-upholstered Elizabeth Taylor, dripping with diamonds and diaphanous nightwear, as she conspicuously consumes Richard Burton's Mark Antony in the 1962 blockbuster *Cleopatra*.

Dubbed by the Romans 'The Killer Queen', Boudicca became the ultimate symbol of the fighting Amazon with only the briefest of military careers to her name. She leaps into history for one short campaign, blazing like a comet across the sky with her enduring cry of 'Death before slavery!' before falling into oblivion. But in the space of a few months, she gave the Romans one of the greatest shocks their vast empire had ever suffered, driven to make war by a series of insults and cruelties so savage that all the tribes of East Anglia rose in rebellion and flocked to her side.

Boudicca
d. AD 61

Boudicca's tragedy was to face the invading Romans as a Celtic woman ruler in a society where women had high status, and queens ruled in their own right. In Rome, women belonged to their male relations, who had the legal right to inflict any punishment on them, including death. Barred from public life, they spent most of their lives confined to the women's quarters at home.

Faced with Celtic queens, the Romans always tried to deal with their men. Boudicca ruled the Iceni tribe with her husband, Prasutagus, who weakly signed a treaty accepting the rule of Rome as a client king. By Roman law, when a client king died, his kingdom with all its wealth passed into the rule of Rome. Prasutagus attempted to circumvent this by willing half the kingdom to the Roman emperor Nero, and leaving half to his two daughters.

But Roman law did not permit inheritance to be passed down the female line. When Prasutagus died in 61, the Romans claimed the kingdom and pillaged the royal households, richly stocked with cattle, grain, jewellery, gold and salt. Boudicca tried to defend her family and home, but was hauled out to be publicly flogged. She was then forced to watch as her daughters were first flogged, then raped.

As co-heirs of their mother, the girls shared the divinity that was attached to her. Rape robbed them of their supernatural attributes, and debarred them from claiming priestess status or inheriting her semi-divine role, breaking the 'mother right' of matrilinear descent, as the Romans intended. But Boudicca and her daughters did not go unavenged. The neighbouring tribe of the

Trinovantes hastened to her side, and she summoned all other Celts to come to her aid.

They came in their tens of thousands, as the entire region exploded into revolt. 'The whole island [of Britain] now rose up under the leadership of Boudicca, a queen, for Britons make no distinction of sex in their appointment of commanders', wrote the Roman historian Tacitus. Boudicca's divinity may explain the passion of her followers and their readiness to follow her

Bronze statue of Boudicca in a war chariot by the Victorian sculptor Thomas Thornycroft, which stands on the Thames Embankment in London. Boudicca was the queen of the Iceni tribe, whose lands covered much of modern East Anglia.

wherever she led. She also cut a striking figure 'tall, terrifying to look at, with a fierce gaze and a harsh, powerful voice', commented the Roman historian Dio Cassius. 'A flood of bright red hair fell down to her knees; she wore a golden necklet made up of ornate pieces, a multi-coloured robe and over it a thick cloak held together by a brooch. She grasped a long spear to strike dread in all those who set eyes on her.' He also recorded, with typical Roman condescension, that she was 'possessed of greater intelligence than is usually found in the female sex'.

Boudicca rapidly moved her army south, sacking the city of Camulodunum (modern Colchester) where she destroyed a huge and hated Roman temple, and routed the Roman relief force. Londinium (London) and Verulanium (St Albans) were next. According to Tacitus, 70,000 died at the sack of Londinium, with the Roman women meeting a particularly cruel fate. They were rounded up, taken to a grove dedicated to the Celtic war goddess Andraste, and tortured to death in revenge for the rape of Boudicca's daughters.

To the patriarchal Romans, the worst of this disaster was that it was inflicted by a woman 'which caused them the greatest shame'. The Roman governor Gaius Suetonius Paulinus, now moved against Boudicca with a force of about 10,000 legionaries and Britons friendly to Rome. He brought Boudicca's much larger army of about 230,000 to battle somewhere in the English Midlands, possibly Warwickshire. The Roman commander heartened his soldiers to fight against such overwhelming odds by telling them that they had nothing to fear from Boudicca's army, as it consisted of more women than men.

In Book XIV of his *Annals*, Tacitus describes Boudicca driving in her chariot with her daughters, making the rounds of all the tribes to deliver a fiery speech: 'We British are used to women commanders in war … but I am not fighting for my kingdom or my wealth [but for] my lost freedom, my battered body and my violated daughters … Consider what you are fighting for, and why. Then you will win this battle, or perish. That is what I, as a woman, plan to do. Let the men live in shame and slavery if they will!' She then released a live hare between the two armies, an animal sacred to the Great Goddess, and dedicated it to the war goddess, Andraste, in a fervent but ultimately futile hope of victory.

'We British are used to women commanders in war … but I am not fighting for my kingdom or my wealth [but for] my lost freedom, my battered body and my violated daughters … '

BOUDICCA RALLIES HER FOLLOWERS TO TAKE UP ARMS AGAINST THE ROMAN OCCUPIERS

Boudicca was only one of many Celtic fighting women of pre-Christian Europe. The Roman historian Ammianus Marcelinus (330–395), who fought against the Celts in Gaul, reported that: 'a whole troop would not be able to withstand one Celt in battle, if he calls his wife to his aid. [She is] stronger than he by far … especially when she swells her neck and gnashes her teeth and swinging her huge white arms, begins to rain down blows mixed with kicks, like the shot from a catapult.'

These women fighters sprang from an even older tradition in which, according to ancient chronicles, the best of them ran their own training schools, or 'war colleges', where women instructors taught men how to fight.

The epic Irish hero Cu Chulainn is told to seek training from the mighty woman warrior Scathach if he wants to be great, and drives his spear through her door to display his strength.

Taken on by Scathach, Cu Chulainn has to fight her enemy, Princess Aife: 'the hardest woman warrior in the world.' Before the contest, Cu Chulainn discovers that Aife's greatest love in the world are her two horses, her chariot and charioteer.

IRISH 'WAR COLLEGES'
pre-Christian era to AD 697

Losing the fight, he shouts out that they have all crashed into a valley and been lost. Aife thus distracted, he knocks the breath out of her and spares her life at the point of a sword, promising to rape her again and again until she gives him a son.

Aife's subjection foreshadowed a greater defeat. Christianity's onward march in the British Isles involved wholesale suppression of rights and freedoms enjoyed by Celtic women from the earliest days. In 697 a church law known as *Cain Adamnan* prohibited women from fighting, bearing arms or taking any part in war. This law, which stripped women of the right to fight for their families or defend themselves, was presented as an act of kindness to women, relieving them of the obligation to train for war, a clear indication that this had previously been the norm.

This image of a Celtic Amazon comes from 'The True Picture of a Woman Picte' by the 16th-century Flemish engraver Theodor de Bry.

But though a charismatic commander, Boudicca had no battle plan, meeting Suetonius on an open plain where Celtic fervour proved no match for Roman discipline. Suetonius, a veteran of mountain warfare, fought with a forest at his back, forcing the Celts to charge headlong up a slope to meet Roman javelins. When they had exhausted themselves, the Romans counterattacked, driving them back onto their wagons where their families waited, and where all were killed. In the bloody mêlée of defeated warriors, women, children, pack animals and baggage, Tacitus estimated the British dead at 80,000, compared with 400 Romans. In his account, Boudicca took poison, although others assert that she was taken prisoner after the battle and died in captivity. What became of her daughters is unknown.

A contemporary of Boudicca, Cartimandua was a queen who, whenever she could, chose to negotiate rather than to fight. Nevertheless as ruler of the Brigantes – the largest tribe in Britain whose northern territories reached the Scottish border and stretched from coast to coast – she also had to prove herself as a war leader on many occasions during her long reign.

Cartimandua
First Century AD

Cartimandua's early relations with the Roman conquerors were friendly, and by coming to a working accommodation with the invaders of Britain, she preserved the peace of her people and her own throne. Overcoming the deep-seated Roman resistance to women in power with very considerable skill, she negotiated a treaty with the Roman commander Claudius, by which she protected the northern borders of the Roman colony in Britain, and the Romans allowed her to continue her rule as an independent ally.

In AD 51 Cartimandua divorced her consort Venutius, and replaced him with a younger man. A man of noble birth, Venutius was infuriated by Cartimandua's choice of his replacement, Vellocatus, a youth who had been his armour-bearer, and raised a substantial force to attack Cartimandua and usurp her throne.

Cartimandua then seized Venutius' close relatives to hold as hostages, and civil war broke out. The queen turned to the Romans for their aid, and their commander took the opportunity to declare the whole of the vast Brigantine territory a Roman protectorate. At this tense juncture, a rebel Celtic king, Caradoc, the long-time war leader of the Welsh tribes in the resistance to Rome, was finally defeated in 51. Regardless of Cartimandua's obligation to the Romans, Caradoc fled to her hoping for sanctuary, and she had no option but to hand him over to his mortal foe. The Romans too honoured the terms of the treaty, and sent troops to help her quell Venutius.

But they were powerless to contain the inter-tribal war. Venutius, fighting with all the fury of an older consort cast off in favour of a younger man, roused so many of the tribes against Cartimandua that after a long and often victorious campaign, she was forced to flee. With Vellocatus in tow, she sought refuge in the massive fort at Camulodunum (Colchester), where they spent the rest of their days under Roman protection. She had held power for 12 turbulent years, and unlike many of her fellow Celtic rulers, lived to tell the tale, and die in her own bed.

Nevertheless, the impulse to turn Cartimandua's survival into disaster has a long history. Stories of all the Celts found their way back to Rome, and Roman mothers were wont to hold up Cartimandua as an example to their daughters of the fate of women who descended into adultery and lust, unaware that there was no such thing as adultery in the Celtic world: unlike Roman and Christian wives, Celtic women never became the possessions of men in marriage. Historians have also contrasted Cartimandua adversely with Boudicca, portraying her as a traitor who betrayed a fellow Briton and a famous patriot,

No sooner had the Romans begun their conquest of Gaul, in the late second century BC, than they encountered the phenomenon of Celtic warrior women. This detail from a frieze of a temple in Civita Alba, depicting a Gaulish woman in battle, dates from around 110 BC.

Women fighters were a continuous element of Celtic culture from the dawn of the race into recorded history. Warrior queens like Boudicca and Cartimandua became legendary in their own times, often taken as goddess figures in the pre-Christian world for their exceptional strength, courage and skill.

The Celts had many war goddesses, two of which Boudicca invoked for victory over the Romans, Boudiga and Andraste. She herself enjoyed divine status: her name, which derives from *bouda* ('victory'), invested her with all the force of the goddess in her warlike incarnation as Boudiga, 'the Lady of Victory'. Boudicca may not even have been the tribal queen's personal name, but her royal or religious title, which would make her, in the eyes of her followers, the goddess made flesh.

Cartimandua too held similar status within her tribe the Brigantes, whose lands spanned the northern half of England, enjoying full sovereignty as the incarnation of the goddess and the spirit of the land. A Celtic queen was thus part Druidic princess, part-priestess, part-goddess. All Celtic women had the right to choose their own husbands and to change them at will, along with the right to show 'thigh-friendship' to any man of their choice. Their queens in particular had exceptional freedom, power and prestige. They were seen as embodying the spirit and sovereignty of the land, and their royalty was only a step away from the divinity of the Great Mother Goddess, who was worshipped everywhere.

Boudicca, Cartimandua and other warrior queens also commanded the allegiance of Celts beyond their own tribe. Their prowess is commemorated in

CELTIC WARRIOR QUEENS AND GODDESSES
pre-Christian era

coins struck by the Redones and the Turones, two tribes of northwestern Gaul, showing images of naked female riders and charioteers brandishing weapons and displaying shields. They may represent war goddesses or the Great Goddess herself rather than individual fighters or queens, but the image of the powerful, fearless woman warrior is unmistakable.

This relief, from the Saarland region on the borders of France and Germany, shows Epona, the Gaulish patron goddess of riders, horse-breeders and carters. The Celtic world had an extensive pantheon of female deities.

'We can picture the couple, she now having lost her looks and he his ambition to be king, declining into bitterness and regret, perhaps bickering through the long nights over glasses of cheap army wine ... '

WRITER JOHN KING IMAGINES CARTIMANDUA'S FINAL YEARS

while the warrior queen of the Iceni, only a decade later, was prepared to die for her tribe, her country and her goddess beliefs.

This urge to stigmatize Cartimandua persists. As late as 2000, the writer John King commented on Cartimandua's later years living with Vellocatus under Roman protection: 'We can picture the couple, she now having lost her looks and he his ambition to be king, declining into bitterness and regret, perhaps bickering through the long nights over glasses of cheap army wine ... .' We may equally well picture the couple enjoying a life of peace and retirement after the terrors of war and rebellion, toasting each other in the admittedly unreliable wine, and continuing the vigorous relationship which sexually interested older women usually turn to younger men to provide.

Future historians may well look more kindly on Cartimandua. In a comparison with Boudicca, she was considerably the more impressive of the two. Her territory was many times greater and held a more complex mixture of tribes than anything Boudicca had to deal with, and the length of her rule is proof of her political skill. While Boudicca stormed into battle with her famous red hair aflame, dying in a matter of months as her star burned out, Cartimandua stayed the course. Fighting against Venutius (a longer and far more tricky campaign than that of Boudicca against the Romans), she outmanoeuvred him on a number of occasions, reinforcing her positions with some impressive military results. Having made a treaty with the Romans, she remained true to it, unlike other Celts who would make and break such undertakings in an afternoon.

Caractacus, too, survived his capture and defeat. Taken to Rome to face a Roman triumph and certain death, Caractacus so impressed his captors with his honour and dignity that he was reprieved. Reunited with his family, he lived on in Rome, a famous prisoner-guest like Zenobia (see pages 44–47) for the rest of his life.

Cartimandua's career is conclusive proof that British women of the first century AD were able to hold supreme authority, enter into treaties with foreign powers, lead their own armies into battle and dispose of unwanted husbands at will, rights denied to any Roman woman of the time and indeed to all Italian women for the next 2,000 years, until divorce finally became legal in Italy at the end of the 20th century.

In Vietnam the Tru'ung Sisters, known individually as Tru'ung Trac and Tru'ung Nhi, were two women leaders who for three years led a successful rebellion against the Chinese Han dynasty (202 BC – AD 220) and are today revered as national heroines.

The Tru'ung Sisters
C.AD 12–42

'When war comes, even women have to fight.'

VIETNAMESE PROVERB DATING BACK TO THE TRU'UNG SISTERS, WHO DROVE THE CHINESE FROM THEIR HOMELAND, VIETNAM, IN THE YEAR 40

The sisters were born in the Vietnamese countryside, the daughters of a magistrate and military man who acquainted them with the art of soldiering and filled them with a loathing of their Chinese overlords. The Chinese executed Tru'ung Trac's husband, Thi Sach, for advocating resistance to Chinese rule, and raped his widow, a punitive measure which parallels the harsh treatment meted out to Boudicca by the Romans. Tru'ung Trac and her sister responded by raising an army, consisting principally of women, to avenge the death of Thi Sach.

They enjoyed some success. In the Chinese book *Biographies of the Southern and South-Western Barbarians*, Tru'ung Trac is described as a 'ferocious warrior' who 'captured 65 cities and claimed to be queen'. The territory over which she briefly held sway stretched from the city of Hue in the south to the Chinese border in the north. The Chinese Emperor Guangwu despatched a large and well-equipped army to bring the insurgents to heel.

Tru'ung Trac had many fanatical female supporters, among them Phu'ung Thi Chinh who, despite being heavily pregnant, plunged into battle against the Chinese and gave birth, pausing only to strap her baby onto her back before hacking her way out of the mêlée. Legend has it that the Vietnamese army was unnerved by the Chinese tactic of going into battle naked. The female Vietnamese warriors, thus shamed, fled the field, leaving their male colleagues vastly outnumbered and overwhelmed.

Knowing that defeat by the Chinese would mean certain death at the hands of the victors, the Tru'ung sisters protected their honour and saved themselves from ridicule by drowning themselves in the River Hat. The noble Phu'ung Thi Chinh also took her own life and that of her baby, born so recently in the heat of battle. The victorious, and more practical Chinese general, Ma Yuan, then proceeded to win Vietnamese hearts and minds by constructing networks of canals for irrigation and by simplifying the

Modern relief of the Tru'ung Sisters in the Women's Museum in Hanoi. A district of the city is named Hai Bà Tru'ung ('the two ladies Tru'ung') in their honour.

'I only want to ride the wind and walk the waves, slay the big whales of the Eastern Sea, clean up frontiers, and save the people from drowning. Why should I imitate others, bow my head, stoop over and be a slave? Why resign myself to menial housework?'

QUOTATION ATTRIBUTED TO THE THIRD-CENTURY SEMI-MYTHICAL VIETNAMESE FEMALE WARRIOR TRIEU AU

onerous Han legal system that had been forced upon their country. The Chinese account fails to mention the suicides of the Tru'ung sisters. Nor indeed does it record the murder of Tru'ung Trac's husband or the sending of men into battle unclothed. This shock tactic seems unlikely, as Ma Yuan was a noted disciplinarian.

Nevertheless, the Tru'ung sisters earned their place in Vietnamese history as the leaders of the first resistance movement after nearly 250 years of subjugation. Many temples are dedicated to them and every February the anniversary of their deaths is observed by many Vietnamese. Streets and schools are named after them, and they are often depicted riding into battle on elephants.

Another Vietnamese female warrior frequently depicted riding into battle on an elephant is the third-century heroine Trieu Au, a semi-mythical figure who, like the Tru'ung sisters, made a courageous stand against the Chinese oppressors of her people. The mythical Trieu Au supposedly stood 2.7 metres (9 ft) tall and sported pendulous breasts. She also possessed a voice that rang like a bell and could walk 500 leagues (1,500 miles/2,400 km) in a day. With serene indifference, the Chinese sources chose to ignore this imposing figure. In 248 the real woman, often known as the 'Vietnamese Joan of Arc', raised an army of 1,000 men to fight against the Chinese. When her brother remonstrated with her, she rebuffed him with the famous words: 'I only want to ride the wind and walk the waves, slay the big whales of the Eastern Sea, clean up frontiers, and save the people from drowning. Why should I imitate others, bow my head, stoop over and be a slave? Why resign myself to menial housework?'

Like the Tru'ung sisters her campaign against the Chinese got off to a promising start, forcing the Chinese – according to Vietnamese sources – to resort to the last-ditch measure of stripping down to the buff before battle. Once again defeat was followed by suicide. Even after her death, however, her lingering spirit of defiance obliged one Chinese general to seek 'voodoo' protection by decorating his door with cartoons of dozens of penises. The Vietnamese, though, continued fondly to remember Trieu Au charging into battle, defiantly tossing her yard-long breasts over her shoulders.

A later example of a consummate woman warrior of the Far East, versatile with many different weapons, Tomoe Gozen was a legendary fighter at the time of the Genpei War (1180–85), a period that witnessed the birth of the samurai tradition in Japan.

The sources differ on the details of her life. She was either the wife, concubine or female attendant of the Japanese commander, Minamoto no Yoshinaka. Skilled in the martial arts and fearless in battle, she was one of Yoshinaka's senior officers in the struggle for the control of Japan between the Taira and Minamoto clans. The title 'Gozen' is not a surname, but an honorific applied principally to women.

Tomoe Gozen's beauty and prowess are described in the *Heike Monogatori* ('Tales of the Monogatori'): 'Tomoe was especially beautiful, with white skin, long hair and charming features. She was also a remarkably strong archer, and as a swordswoman she was a warrior worth a thousand, ready to confront a demon or a god, mounted or on foot. She handled unbroken horses with superb skill; she rode unscathed down perilous descents. Whenever a battle was imminent, Yoshinaka sent her out as his first captain, equipped with strong armour, an oversized sword, and a mighty bow; and she performed more deeds of valour than any of his other warriors.'

Minamoto no Yoshinaka's ambition to head the Minamoto clan eventually led to his downfall. The clan chieftain Minamoto no Yoritomo decided to nip his cousin's designs in the bud, and despatched his brothers to kill him. Yoshinaka did battle with Yoritomo's forces at Awazu in February 1184, where it was said that Tomoe Gozen decapitated at least one of the enemy. With only a few of his soldiers left standing, Yoshinaka ordered Tomoe Gozen to quit the field. One account has her remaining and meeting death at Yoshinaka's side. Another has her surviving to become a member of a religious order. In yet another she casts herself into the sea, clutching Yoshinaka's severed head.

Japanese manuscript illustration of Tomoe Gozen, one of the very few female samurai recorded in the country's history.

Zenobia (Znwbya bat Zabbai) has gone down in history as the military partner of her husband Odenath, a vassal king of the Romans who had colonized their city-state of Palmyra in modern Syria around AD 17. Zenobia never accepted the Roman invasion, nor the invaders' right to rule. Consistently described as beautiful, intelligent and virtuous, she also proved supremely strong and athletic, and chose a life of action from an early age. King Odenath was a renowned and fearless fighter, but the chronicles report that Zenobia was as daring and effective as her husband in combat, dubbing her 'the better man of the two'.

Zenobia
c.240 – d. after 274

Zenobia and Odenath made many conquests together, and may even have captured the legendary treasure of the Persian emperor. Historians of her own era record that Zenobia was more reckless in war than Odenath, able to keep pace with her foot soldiers on the march, and to drink with them without getting drunk. Her voice was clear and strong, useful for rallying the troops. She also refused to let her husband sleep with her except rarely, seeing no point to sex unless she could get pregnant. She rode with Odenath on many campaigns against the Persians and the Goths, and when he was assassinated, took up the reins of government on behalf of herself and her infant son Vaballathus.

Riding into battle was an important element of Zenobia's success. A warrior woman on horseback is a powerful inspiration to her troops, a ploy used also by Queen Isabella of Spain and Elizabeth I of England. Presenting herself as a goddess, Zenobia tapped into the same ancient tradition of Arabia and the Middle East previously exploited by the Assyrian queen Sammu-Ramat (Semiramis, see pages 16–19), the pre-Islamic belief in the Great Goddess in her incarnation as the Lady of Victory.

Zenobia always claimed to be descended from the ruling house of Ptolemy in Egypt, specifically from Cleopatra VII (see pages 28–31), and she certainly spoke Egyptian as well as Greek, Latin and Aramaic, and displayed a strong predisposition towards Egyptian culture. She had nothing to lose by associating herself with a glorious woman warrior and powerful queen of the past. Her Egyptian heritage may also have emboldened her to lay claim to Roman territory there in 269, when she marched her armies into upper Egypt after Odenath's death.

She also moved into Roman territories in Arabia and Asia Minor to expand Palmyra's trade, and may have hoped that the Romans would turn

Portrait of Zenobia by the British 19th-century painter Sir Edward John Poynter. The Victorian artist chose to portray her as a romantic heroine, captive and in chains, but still radiating a quiet regal dignity.

Zenobia was a direct descendant of the Amazons described by Homer in the *Iliad*, his account of the Trojan War. Written in around 750 BC, Homer's epic contains the first literary reference to the Amazons, described as 'women the equal of men'.

Before the establishment of modern frontiers, lands, rivers, cultures and tribes flowed in and out of the territory that runs from modern Russia in the north to India and Arabia in the south. For these tribes, it was common practice for women to fight alongside men. Numerous Iron Age burial sites throughout the region from around 600 BC contain women buried with swords, spears, armour and all the trappings of war. Proof that these were women and not boys or slender men lies in the distinctly female grave goods also found in their tombs: mirrors, cosmetics and spindles for spinning wool into yarn – women's work since time immemorial in every culture under the sun.

FIGHTING WOMEN OF THE CENTRAL PLAIN
prehistory to early Christian era

At one site, the body of a girl aged between ten and twelve was found buried in full-body chain mail, which suggests that she was already trained for combat and considered fit to fight. Some of these women warriors had exceptionally high status, as their graves also contained the remains of a male servant and a horse, to maintain their dignity in the afterlife.

Most famous after Zenobia, say the records of the time, was the Syrian queen Mawiyya, who became sole leader of the Tunukh tribe when her husband Alexandra-Halawi, its last king, died in 375. Like her indomitable predecessor, Mawiyya led a rebellion against Roman rule that drew in many of the tribes of the region, riding at the head of her army into Phoenicia and Palestine. She repeatedly defeated the Romans, until they begged to have her as their ally, not their foe. Driving a hard bargain to secure terms of peace, she died in her husband's tribal lands in 425.

a blind eye to this. Her thriving city-state was a vital Mediterranean trading link between Phoenicia, Emesa (now known as Homs in western Syria), Damascus and Egypt itself, and any new wealth would benefit the Romans as much as the Palmyrenes.

But by 269, Zenobia had secured most of Egypt and annexed vast swathes of Syria. Soon she had forged a vast empire out of tiny Palmyra. She then defeated one Roman expedition sent against her, proclaimed her son Vaballathus 'Augustus' (Emperor), and declared independence from Rome by minting her own coinage with her image on it. To the Roman emperor Aurelian, this was a rebellion so grave that he personally took command of the campaign to crush Zenobia and her son.

Zenobia commanded a large army with heavily-armoured cavalry, and confronted Aurelian and his force near Antioch. She was seen in the forefront of the battle, galloping alongside her troops, shouting orders and controlling events. Aurelian instructed his cavalry to flee, luring the Palmyrenes to give chase until the weight of their armour exhausted both horses and men. Then the Roman horsemen turned on their opponents and cut them down.

Having lost the battle amid horrible slaughter, Zenobia fell back into Antioch, claiming victory and keeping the city loyal by the device of leading through the city in chains a man who resembled Aurelian, as if she had defeated him in the fray. But at the next engagement, the seasoned

Roman legions prevailed again, and Zenobia was forced to flee. Setting out by camel to seek help from the Persians, she was overtaken by Aurelian's horsemen and captured on the banks of the River Euphrates.

Aurelian displayed a Roman magnanimity towards the vanquished citizens of Palmyra, sparing their lives and contenting himself with seizing all the city's wealth. But he executed most of Zenobia's adherents, including the philosopher Longinus, famed as 'a living library and walking museum', one of a number of Greek intellectuals whom Zenobia had attracted to her court.

Facing Aurelian armed with her beauty, intellect and sexual allure, Zenobia demanded immunity on the grounds of her sex. One tradition claims that she then committed suicide like her ancestor, Cleopatra, who also fell into the hands of the Romans and died rather than suffer the ignominy of being forced to parade in a Roman triumph. But Latin sources state that she was brought to Rome in safety, and led through the streets of Rome in Aurelian's triumph of 274, shackled in golden chains. Disdaining her royal right to ride in a chariot, she walked defiantly with Aurelian's other conquests, defeated Goths and Vandals and a band of Scythian fighting women the Romans called Amazons.

After a Roman triumph, captives were normally killed or sold into slavery. Zenobia survived. Granted a pension by the Roman Senate and a villa on an estate near Tivoli, she married a Roman senator, and settled down to country life. From there she faded into history like her son Vaballathus, who was not exhibited in Aurelian's triumph and must have died before then.

But Palmyra had not forgotten its queen. Two years later the citizens rose up against the garrison Aurelian had left there, and installed her father as their emperor. Aurelian marched back to Palmyra and quelled the second rebellion. What happened to Zenobia's father is not known.

Palmyra lay at an oasis in the Syrian desert and became prosperous as a key trading city on the route from the Persian Gulf to central Asia. Under Roman control from the reign of Tiberius, the revolts by Zenobia and her father saw the city razed to the ground in 273 and its trade relocated north to the cities of Mesopotamia.

Chiefly remembered for her hideous death, Brunhilde deserves more credit for her long and eventful life. As a warrior queen and stateswoman, she displayed indomitable courage and formidable skill throughout 40 years of continuous war. Thrown into the bearpit of Frankish politics as a young bride, she ruled until she became regent for her great-grandchildren, and was almost 70 by the time she died.

Brunhilde
fl. 567–613

Born Princess Bruna, the daughter of Athanagild, king of the Visigoths in Spain, Brunhilde was noted for her intelligence and beauty from an early age. Her tragedy lay in her entanglement with the warring rulers of the Frankish empire when she was old enough to marry. Once the domain of the powerful Clothaire I and covering most of modern Europe, on his death in 561 the vast empire had been split between Clothaire's four sons. Six years later Brunhilde married the youngest of these, Sigebert, ruler of Austrasia, the Eastern Frankish kingdom that covered most of modern western Germany and a portion of northeastern France.

Sigebert was already at odds with his older brother, the cruel and worthless Chilperic, who ruled the neighbouring kingdom of Neustria, consisting of most of northern France. Brunhilde already had cause to doubt Chilperic, who had taken one of his slaves, Fredegund, as his mistress, and had yielded to her persuasion to set his wife aside, and later to have her killed. But Brunhilde was powerless to stop her father from forcing her younger sister Galswintha into marriage with Chilperic, despite his vicious reputation. To the king of the Visigoths, the importance of this strategic alliance outweighed any concerns about his prospective son-in-law's notorious depravity, or his daughter's future happiness: Galswintha is recorded as weeping, lamenting, and begging for her freedom every step of the way from her home in Spain.

The marriage did not last. Brunhilde soon learned that her sister was dead. Once again, Chilperic had been induced to dispose of an inconvenient wife, when Fredegund persuaded him to have Galswintha

This Dutch woodcut of c.1480 vividly conveys the agonizing death suffered by the Austrasian queen Brunhilde, pulled to pieces by being strung between four horses.

strangled in her bed not long after the wedding. Brunhilde's grief and rage were intensified when the less-than-grieving widower made his murderous mistress his new queen, marrying Fredegund only a few days later.

This barbarous act earned Brunhilde's undying enmity, and triggered a long and bloody war. Vowing vengeance for her dead sister, she turned to her husband Sigebert, Chilperic's younger brother, and with his help, made war upon the killers. Despite some early successes, Brunhilde and Sigebert were beaten at last. Brunhilde herself narrowly escaped with her life in 575 when Fredegund defeated the couple in battle and had Sigebert assassinated. Brunhilde was captured and imprisoned, but set free by Chilperic's son Merovaeus, who fell in love with her, a move that cost the infatuated young man his life.

Returning to her own kingdom, Brunhilde found herself at war again. Her young son was now established on his father Sigebert's throne, and Brunhilde took up the reins of power on his behalf. The rule of a woman was anathema to a strong political party of noble seigneurs (lords), who raised an army against her. Brunhilde met them clad as a soldier and dressed for battle, but with a message of peace, appealing to them not to plunge the kingdom into civil war. Her overtures were contemptuously rebuffed, and in a grim foreshadowing of her eventual fate, she was warned: 'Depart from us, lest our horses' hooves trample you underfoot.' Undeterred, Brunhilde led her forces into battle, and won the day. Confirmed in power, she was able to rule openly on behalf of her still youthful son Childebert.

Meanwhile the war between her kingdom and that of Fredegund dragged on. At Childebert's majority, Brunhilde stepped down, but when he and his wife were poisoned, probably on the orders of Fredegund, she took up arms again, ruling on behalf of their two young sons. Her bitter rivalry with Fredegund only deepened in 584 when Fredegund had her own husband Chilperic killed, and seizing power, began to rule in her own right. Brunhilde and her grandsons were now in constant danger of assassination, and Fredegund made more than one attempt to have them poisoned. The threat from Fredegund only ceased when the great murderess died unexpectedly in 597, leaving a son, Clothaire II.

But Brunhilde's wars were not over. Her former enemies among the Frankish nobles now persuaded the older of her two grandsons to seize power and banish her. Brunhilde fought back with the aid of the younger brother and her opponent was defeated and killed, but the victorious grandson died suddenly at the age of 26, leaving four young sons.

Approaching 70 years of age, Brunhilde found herself regent again, this time for her great-grandchildren. But she was no longer able to contain the rapacious ambition of her noblemen. Her enemies turned in secret to Fredegund's son Clothaire II, and offered him the kingdom if he would remove the queen. Clothaire accepted. Betrayed by the leader of her own countrymen, Brunhilde was imprisoned by her enemies and handed over to her former rival's equally cruel son. The accounts of her death vary, but all agree that she was subjected to three days of appalling humiliation and torture in front of Clothaire and all his army, before finally being torn to pieces by horses.

One of the most bloodthirsty and sadistic women in history, Fredegund achieved power through her husband and used it to keep his kingdom in a state of war for over 40 years. A queen of the vast empire of the Franks, a territory covering most of modern Europe, Fredegund was also an early exponent of 'dirty' warfare, and relied heavily on poison and other covert operations to despatch her foes.

Fredegund began her rise to power as a slave at the court of the Frankish emperor Chilperic. Catching his eye, she became his mistress and soon displaced his wife, persuading Chilperic to have her killed. A second wife, the sister of Brunhilde, was murdered in the same way. During the ensuing war, Fredegund claimed another victim in 575, when she sent assassins posing as peace envoys to knife Brunhilde's husband Sigebert.

Sigebert's death and Brunhilde's capture ended this phase of the war. But Fredegund's victory was shortlived, when her stepson Merovaeus fell in love with Brunhilde and set her free. Fredegund then hounded Merovaeus to his death, which he chose to seek at the hands of a faithful servant rather than fall into the clutches of his wicked stepmother.

Fredegund pursued Brunhilde all her life. Brunhilde's son and his wife were poisoned, forcing Brunhilde to take up the regency of the kingdom on her grandsons' behalf, thereby making them too the target of Fredegund's uncontrollable rage. Fredegund even had her own husband Chilperic murdered in 584, when he discovered one of her many affairs, and ruled alone as regent for her son.

Despite many attempts, all Fredegund's covert operations against Brunhilde and her grandchildren failed. She was still directing both open and covert warfare, involving her favourite weapons of knife and poison, when she died unexpectedly in 597, leaving her kingdom to her equally cruel and murderous son Clothaire II.

Another of Fredegund of Neustria's victims was Praetextatus, bishop of Rouen, who was stabbed by an assassin acting on the queen's orders. Below, detail from Fredegund by Praetextatus' Deathbed *(1861) by Sir Lawrence Alma-Tadema.*

Many fighting women are known to have taken arms in the religious struggle that followed the seventh-century birth of Islam. One honoured battle heroine and war leader of the early Islamic era was Salaym Bint Malhan, who although pregnant, fought in the ranks of Muhammad and his followers with an armoury of swords and daggers strapped round her swollen belly. Another, El-Khaansa, also a contemporary of Muhammad, was renowned both as a warrior and a poet. A warrior called Safiyya bint 'Abd al-Muttalib is reported on the battlefield at Uhud, one of Muhammad's early and important engagements, lashing about her with her weapon in her hand.

Women Fighters of the Arab World
Seventh Century

An Ottoman Turkish miniature of 1594–95, from a history of Islam illuminated for Sultan Murad III, depicts the decisive victory of the Muslims over Quraishi (Meccan) forces at the Battle of Badr in 624. The Quraishi woman warrior Hind al-Hunnud acquitted herself well at this engagement.

But the most famous female warrior of the period is the Ansari woman Nusayba bint Ka'b, also known as Umm 'Umara. Armed with sword and bow and arrow, she fought at the battles of Uhud and al-Hudaybiyya in 625 and 630; she was still active at Khaybar, Hunayn and al-Yamama in 633–34.

At Uhud, fighting (alongside her mother, according to some accounts) against the forces from Mecca, Umm 'Umara valiantly defended Muhammad when the tide began to turn against the Muslims, sustaining severe injuries in the process. Her opponent, the Makkan warrior Ibn Qumi'a, had loudly proclaimed that he would kill the Prophet, and Umm 'Umara later made the proud boast that she had succeeded in cutting through the ranks and striking him. But her heroic attack was all in vain, she complained, because 'the enemy of God had on two suits of armour'. Umm 'Umara would later lose a hand at al-Yamama during the battle against the false prophet Musaylima after the fall of Mecca in 630. But her achievement was recognized by Muhammad himself, who is recorded as saying: 'On the day of Uhud, I never looked to the right nor to the left without seeing Umm 'Umara fighting to defend me.'

In other reports, Umm 'Umara joined Muhammad's holy war or *jihad* with her sister, her husband and two sons, who all fought together in the Battle of Uhud. Always in the thick of the action, she suffered many wounds – no fewer than 11, the chronicle recounts – and lost an arm.

'On the day of Uhud, I never looked to the right nor to the left without seeing Umm 'Umara fighting to defend me.'

THE PROPHET MUHAMMAD ON THE FIGHTING PROWESS OF UMM 'UMARA

The Prophet's own female relatives were also active in his *jihad*; his young wife 'Aish'ah was at the forefront of the Battle of the Camel in 656, while his granddaughter Zaynab bint Ali fought in the Battle of Karbala, the momentous engagement in 680 in modern-day Iraq between supporters of Muhammad's grandson Hussein ibn Ali (Shi'ites) and forces of the Umayyad caliph Yazid I (Sunnis). Another woman, Umm Alexandra Dhouda Bint Mas'ud, fought so magnificently at the Battle of the Khaybar in 629 that the Prophet allotted her a share of the spoils equal to that of a man. Other women were recognized for their presence on the battlefield to tend to the wounded, and for encouraging their men to fight for the triumph of Islam.

Not all women accepted Muhammad's cause, however. Many fought against Islam as it set out to replace the existing faith in the Great Goddess with the insistence on one father God. Countless women who worshipped 'the Lady', 'the Queen of Heaven' and 'the Mother of Life and Death' – all titles by which the Great Goddess was known – took up arms to resist. Foremost among them was the Arab leader, Hind al-Hunnud. Described as peerless, 'the Hind of Hinds', she led the opposition of her tribe, the wealthy and powerful Qu'raish, to the forced imposition of Islam.

The climax of her campaign came at the terrible Battle of Badr in 624 in the Hejaz region of western Arabia, where she succeeded in engaging directly with Muhammad himself. Hind fought valiantly and ended the day alive, but her father, uncle and brother were killed. For a time she directed a guerrilla war of vengeance, but was eventually outnumbered, surrounded, forced to submit and to convert to Islam. In her heyday, Hind had been not only a warrior and war leader, but a priestess of the Goddess in her incarnation as 'the Lady of Victory'. After she submitted to the will of Allah, nothing more was heard of this brilliant and unusual woman.

Despite such defeats, the tradition of women fighters in the Arab world was slow to die out. The 12th-century memoirs of the Syrian notable, Usama bin Munqidh, describe the women combatants of his own day, including his mother. In 15th-century Yemen, the Zaydi chieftain Sharifa Fatima, daughter of an imam, conquered the city of Sana'a, and as late as the 18th century, Amira Ghaliyya al-Wahhabiyya led a military resistance movement in Saudi Arabia to defend Mecca against foreign incursions.

But the tide of repression had long been turning against women warriors and their freedom to fight. Islamic authorities began to question the martial activities of their own women warriors who had helped Muhammad to victory, and later chroniclers (such as the Egyptian Mameluke biographer Ibn Hajar, d.1449) made much of the case of an obscure woman 'Companion of the Prophet' by the name of Umm Kabsha, who is said to have been refused permission to accompany Muhammad in battle. This was taken to mean that the earlier permission given to women to participate in battles, either as active combatants or as providers of humanitarian services, had been withdrawn.

As the oppression of women under Islam gathered strength, male religious authorities concluded that women could take no part in *jihad*. For centuries, albeit with a few rare exceptions, the women in the East were denied basic physical freedoms and autonomy, and subordinated to the control of men, destroying the heritage of women fighters at its source. With the encouragement of generations of misogynists and fundamentalists, the insistence that only men could fight or participate in a holy war hardened into dogmatic certainty. This view has recently been revised, after male Islamist radicals in Israel, Iraq, Chechnya and elsewhere realized the potential of the burqa-clad female body to carry explosives undetected, and so to advance their cause as suicide bombers.

During a fierce fight against the Byzantines in the early struggles of Muhammad, the chronicles report that the wavering forces of Islam were rallied by a tall knight muffled in black, and fighting with ferocious courage. After the victory, the 'knight' was reluctantly exposed as the Arab princess Khawlah.

AL-KIND'YYA, KHAWLAH BINT AL-AZWAR

seventh century

Even defeat in battle could not break Khawlah's spirit. Captured at the Battle of Sabhura, near Damascus in Syria, she rallied the other female captives with the challenge: 'Do you accept these men as your masters? Are you willing for your children to become their slaves? Where is your famed courage and skill that has become the talk of the Arab tribes as well as of the cities?'

A woman called Afra' Bint Ghifar al-Humayriah is said to have returned the wry reply: 'We are as courageous and skilful as you describe. But in such cases a sword is quite useful, and we were taken by surprise, like sheep, unarmed.' Khawlah's response was to order each woman to arm herself with a tent pole, form them into a phalanx and lead them to victory. 'And why not?' the narrator of their story concluded, 'if a lost battle meant their enslavement?'

This question betrays the mixed feelings of Arab and Islamic commentators about the women warriors who were an established feature of pre-Islamic culture in the Middle East. As a fighter, Khawlah was exceptionally gifted and strong, but she was far from unique. For centuries, Muslim women in different struggles and communities joined men on the front lines of war, fighting and dying at their side, as they still do in some regions to this day.

Wu Chao was the daughter of a general, from whom she may have derived both her warlike temperament and her outstanding tactical skills. Given to the emperor of China at the age of 13 to be the youngest of his concubines, she fought her way out of this powerless position of ritualized prostitution and child abuse to make herself the supreme ruler of the entire empire, using and taming its military as she saw fit. She held total power for over 50 years, wielding it with a piquant blend of cultured enlightenment and primeval savagery, and in 696 had herself proclaimed 'Supreme God'.

Wu Chao
625–705

Wu Chao's path to divinity began when she caught the eye of those who supplied the 'little lotus blossoms', or child concubines, to the household of the T'ang emperor, T'ai Tsung. The connection was probably through her father the general, who had served the first emperor of the T'ang dynasty, Kao Tsu, in the wars to establish the dynasty. Prostituting his daughter to the man regarded as the imperial 'God on Earth' would have struck the general as a likely stepping stone to much higher things.

Wu Chao was a beautiful young girl, and like all successful war leaders, she was lucky, too. A prophecy had foretold that a woman would sit on the emperor's throne, and when Wu Chao appeared, a soothsayer immediately bestowed the accolade on her. Her first successful battle came when she secured the favour of the emperor, her second when she captured the heart of his son and successor, Kao Tsung. As the new emperor's favourite concubine and the mother of his four sons, Wu Chao easily defeated his wife, the childless empress, and took her place.

Soon she supplanted the weak and ailing emperor too. Kao Tsung doted on her and allowed her to run the government. She used her power to get the country's military leaders on her side, and only appointed government officials who would be loyal to her. She was thus in a prime position to seize supreme power in 660 when Kao Tsung was disabled by the first of a series of strokes. With the aid of the military, she swiftly brought a successful conclusion to the ongoing war between China and Korea, and continued to use the army to back up her claim to power.

Wu Chao's command of the armed forces was crucial to her survival, especially after Emperor Kao Tsung died in 683. The new emperor was Wu's own eldest son, but like another self-appointed sole ruler, the Russian empress Catherine the Great, Wu Chao's appetite for power was far

Wu Chao, China's only female emperor, from an 18th-century album of portraits of 86 Chinese rulers. She was ruthless in her pursuit and retention of power.

stronger than any maternal instincts, and she would not give up the throne. She swung the army into action to depose her son, and eventually exiled him and his ambitious wife. For a while she continued to govern through her second son, but in 690 she abandoned this pretence, and usurped the throne.

Despite her family and dynastic wars, Wu unified the Chinese empire and presided over a long era of peace and prosperity. But there was no quarter for her enemies, imagined or real. Any concubines who might pose a threat to her were summarily dispatched, and all opposition was ruthlessly eliminated, including members of her own and the imperial family. Despite her innate violence and cruelty, her reign is still remembered for its many outstanding achievements in culture, art and architecture. She also ushered in major social reforms, dismantling the hereditary power of the ancient military aristocracy in favour of a scholarly and meritocratic bureaucracy, selected by open examination.

Fired-clay figurines of court women from the Han Dynasty. In the rigid hierarchy of the Chinese court, Wu Chao had to fight her way up from the lowest ranks; when she first entered the palace, she was designated a 'wife' of the third class.

Formally known as Empress Shunlie (literally 'the kind and accomplished empress'), Liang Na was an empress during the Han Dynasty and the wife of Emperor Shun. She later acted as regent for his son, Emperor Chong, and the two subsequent emperors selected from collateral lines, Emperor Zhi and Emperor Huan. As empress dowager and regent, she appeared to be diligent and honest, but she placed too much trust in her violent and corrupt brother Liang Ji.

Liang Na's father was Liang Shang, the marquess of Chengshi, who was also related to consort Liang, the mother of Emperor He. As a young girl, Liang Na was said to excel at needlework and to be devoted to the Confucian classics. In 128, when Liang Na was 12, she was selected to be Emperor Shun's imperial consort and became his favourite. In 132 Emperor Shun made her empress.

As empress, Liang was modest and refrained from interfering with her husband's court. As a result, Emperor Shun trusted her relatives, promoting her father to Grand Marshal and her brothers to high office. In 144, as the emperor's health was failing, he made Liu Bing, his only son and a small child, crown prince. Emperor Shun died four months later, and Empress Liang became empress dowager and served as regent.

Empress Dowager Liang continued to rely on trusted officials to advise her on important affairs. However, she also had great faith in her brother Liang Ji, who used her position to consolidate his own power. In 145 the young Emperor Chong died. Liang Ji convinced Empress Dowager Liang to make another child, the seven-year-old Liu Zuan, Emperor Zhi, so that he could easily control him, while Empress Dowager Liang continued to serve as regent.

In 146 Liang Ji killed the young emperor by poison because the latter offended him by openly calling him 'an arrogant general'. Liang Ji persuaded Empress Dowager Liang to replace him with another 14-year-old, Emperor Huan; Empress Dowager Liang remained as regent. In 147 Emperor Huan married Empress Dowager Liang's sister and made her empress.

In 150 Empress Dowager Liang announced that she was stepping down as regent and returning imperial power to Emperor Huan. She died later that year and was buried alongside her husband, Emperor Shun. However, her corrupt brother remained in power. In 159 Emperor Huan finally grasped the nettle and overthrew Liang Ji before slaughtering his entire clan.

Reform of the military weakened her support, and Wu Chao was unable to resist the rising tide of unrest as she grew older. Dissatisfaction centred on her choice of favourites, in particular a pair of Chinese eunuchs, whose influence over her enraged all, leading to their deaths and her downfall. In 698 Wu Chao was forced to agree to their execution, and to recall her eldest son Chung, but she continued to cling to whatever power she could. She resisted her opponents for a further seven years, when she was finally persuaded to retire to her summer palace, where she died at the age of 80.

Some 1,400 years later, Wu Chao's career remains a phenomenal achievement in a country where women were explicitly forbidden to hold power, where female infanticide is still rife, and where today's 13-year-old girls have yet to gain more than nominal equality with males. She is regarded as one of China's strongest and most successful leaders, along the lines of England's Elizabeth I, and remains the only woman in Chinese history to have ruled exclusively in her own name.

An intrepid war leader and ruler, Aethelflaed was the daughter of England's founding king, Alfred the Great of Wessex. She was born into war from her childhood, as her father fought to free his emerging country from the constant invasions of the warlike Danes. In one account, the ferocious invaders even attacked Aethelflaed and her party as she rode to her wedding, bent on preventing the union of a princess of Wessex with the kingdom of Cumbria.

Aethelflaed
d.918

But Saxon women were made of stern stuff, and Aethelflaed was determined to resist these incursions. She refused to be bullied out of the kingdom her father was forging from a mess of warring tribes. A bold tactician and an outstanding commander, she played a major part in driving out the warriors, raiders and thugs known as the Vikings, who regularly pillaged the eastern coast of England from the plague-ridden and famine-prone German and Scandinavian countries across the North Sea.

Aethelflaed followed in a long line of Saxon queens like Bertha, who died in 616 after introducing Christianity into pagan England, and the eighth-century Queen Cynethryth of the Mercians, the only woman in the Europe of the time to mint her own coinage showing a likeness of herself. Aethelflaed also paved the way for another Saxon queen involved with the Danes, the fatal Aelfgifu (see page 62), whose arrogance and cruelty contrast strongly with Aethelflaed's undoubted diplomatic skills.

One of King Alfred's greatest achievements was his insistence on the establishment of the English language and the education of his people, high and low. Despite the cares of office, he also maintained a lifelong interest in philosophy. It is therefore highly likely that Aethelflaed was taught to read, write and think, in an age when almost all, even high-born men and women, were illiterate. As a Saxon woman, albeit a princess, Aethelflaed also enjoyed more freedom in choosing a husband than the females of other tribes and cultures of her day. She married Aethelraed, *ealdorman* [lord] of the kingdom of West Mercia, and ruled it with him, though she was the controlling force from early on.

West Mercia, the country around Stratford-on-Avon in the modern English Midlands, was a first-rate strategic base for a woman of Aethelflaed's vision and scope. There she created around her a military household that she dominated totally. Aethelraed died in 911. After his death Aethelflaed ruled alone, using her military might to advance her kin.

Statue of Aethelflaed, queen of the Mercians, in Tamworth, where she died of unknown causes in 918. The contemporary *Anglo-Saxon Chronicle* records how she upheld her father's policy of building fortresses to repel attacks by the Danes.

The imperious warrior princess and queen Aelfgifu was a Saxon noblewoman who had the luck to catch the eye of Prince Cnut (Canute) of Denmark in the 11th century, when he was raiding England as a young man. When Cnut successfully claimed the English throne in 1016, she became his consort and remained his closest companion all his life, bearing him two sons, despite his later marriage to another princess, Emma of Normandy (confusingly also called Aelfgifu in Anglo-Saxon).

As king of England and Denmark, Cnut made the eldest of his sons, Svein, the king of Norway in 1030 and appointed Aelfgifu to rule as regent in the young man's stead. Her reign there was so harsh, her military manoeuvres so ill-judged and her use of force so cruel and indiscriminate that she provoked an uprising that drove her from the country in 1035. She is still remembered in Old Norse sagas for the savagery of the taxation she imposed, which reduced the Norwegians to starvation, until they were eating the fodder of

QUEEN AELFGIFU
b. *c.*980

their own cattle and 'living like goats, on husks'.

Deposed, Aelfgifu fled with Svein to Denmark, where he died shortly afterwards from an arrow wound sustained in the fighting.

Aelfgifu took power in Denmark, but when Cnut died in England in 1035, she swiftly returned to the country and persuaded the nobles to recognize her second son by Cnut, Harold 'Harefoot', as his father's heir, against the claim of Cnut's son by his French wife, Emma of Normandy. Harold became king of England 1037. No records of his formidable mother exist after that date, but Aelfgifu is generally assumed to have ruled England on behalf of Harold until her death. She thus remains the only woman in history to have held supreme power and military command in three different countries.

A manuscript illumination recording a presentation of a golden cross to a church by Cnut and Emma of Normandy in 1031.

When her brother Edward succeeded her father as king of Wessex, she threw her forces into his battle against the Vikings, who had not abandoned their raids on England's eastern flank. Her shrewd intervention turned the tables on the invaders, and helped to complete the task that her father had begun. Her unique status and importance by this time are reflected in the title by which she became known, 'The Lady of the Mercians'.

Aethelflaed's sense of strategy went beyond defensive campaigns. Marching the length of England and carrying her campaign into Wales, she fortified key strongholds such as Chester in the north, where she repaired the walls. Returning south, she created a new fortress at Warwick in the English Midlands and at Stafford to the northwest, boosting both peace and local commerce as they soon became important centres of trade.

By 917, still battling for her brother Edward, the queen was ready to launch a major attack on the Vikings who continued to harry England's shores. She was also developing wider territorial ambitions, and led her army to a major victory over the town of Derby. When she reached Leicester, her reputation as a war leader was such that the inhabitants surrendered without a fight.

From what we know of her manoeuvres and campaigns, Aethelflaed now seems to have been intent on uniting most of England under a single rule. Both Derby and Leicester were far north of what had been her father's original kingdom, now under Edward's sway, and of her own home territory of Mercia. She had already succeeded in dominating parts of Wales to the west, and of Northumbria on the border of Scotland. In 918 she was in another town in the north Midlands, Tamworth, planning campaigns further north still. She had already achieved the capitulation of the Viking stronghold in the northern capital city of York when she unexpectedly died.

Aethelflaed's sudden death in June 918 raised the spectre of the plague, a dreaded summer visitor of which England was not completely free until the 19th century. Her brother Edward took over her territories in 919 and proved a capable ruler, but never displayed Aethelflaed's matchless drive and flair. By uniting as much of England as she did, she became one of the few women permanently to change the course of English history. A towering figure in England's island story, who knows what she would have achieved had she survived?

Aethelflaed's success is highlighted by the downfall of another warlike female ruler, her direct contemporary, the eighth-century Byzantine empress Irene. The first woman to rule the Byzantine empire alone, Irene embarked on numerous military expeditions which eventually cost her the throne. She came to power as the wife of the Emperor Leo IV, and like the empresses Wu Chao of China (see pages 56–59) and Catherine II of Russia (see pages 136–139), refused to step down in favour of her son Constantine VI when her husband the emperor died. Not content with ruling as regent during Constantine's adolescence, she eventually had the feeble youth blinded in 797, and seized power in her own right.

Now installed as *basileus* ('king'), and always addressed by this title, Irene used her power to resolve deep-seated social and political tensions, particularly the vexed question of the worship of icons in the Orthodox church. But her touch deserted her when it came to war. Her penchant for throwing the empire into one ill-judged conflict after another seriously drained the imperial treasury, and in 802 a rebellion of her ministers swept her from the throne. Banished into exile, she died the following year.

Matilda was the right-hand woman of Pope Gregory VII in the struggle between the papacy and the Holy Roman Empire. Her spiritual adviser, Anselm of Lucca, later Pope Alexander II, observed that she combined the will and energy of a soldier with the mystic and solitary spirit of a hermit. Fighting for the Supreme Head of the Church of Rome provided Matilda with the opportunity to fulfil both the spiritual and martial sides of her indomitable nature.

Matilda of Tuscany
1046–1115

Matilda was the daughter of the margrave Boniface, whose citadel was the impregnable Apennine fortress of Canossa, and Beatrice, the daughter of the duke of Upper Lorraine. Her father was assassinated in 1052, and the death of her siblings left her to inherit some of the richest lands in Italy.

As a child, she was taught to ride like a lancer, spear in hand, and to wield a battleaxe and sword. Writing about her in 1666, Ludovico Vedriani noted that she disdained: 'with a virile spirit that art of Arachne [spinning], she seized the spear of Pallas.' She was strong and tall and clearly able to bear the heavy weight of armour. She also liked needlework, and sent an embroidered war pennant to her contemporary William the Conqueror. Her mother supervised her education, and she was unusually well schooled for the time, fluent in German, French, Italian and Latin, and able to write letters without the assistance of a clerk.

Matilda's introduction to the turbulent power politics of the 11th century came in 1059, when she accompanied Beatrice and her stepfather, Godfrey of Lorraine, to the Council of Sutri, at which noble families vied for the papal succession following the death of Pope Stephen IX. It is likely that Matilda's first appearance on the battlefield came two years later, at her mother's side, as Alexander II battled against the schismatics who challenged his succession to the papacy after the Council of Sutri. A contemporary account describes the young Matilda 'armed like a warrior' and carrying herself with 'such bravery that she made known to the world that courage and valour in mankind is not indeed a matter of sex but of heart and spirit'. It is also possible that she was present at the Battle of Aquino (1066) in which Godfrey of Lorraine defeated the Roman and Norman supporters of a rival pope.

The death of Godfrey in 1069 marked a turning point in Matilda's life. Aided at first by her mother, who died in 1076, she began to exercise her own authority in Italy in the absence of her husband, her step-brother

A 12th-century depiction from the Italian School of Henry IV asking Matilda of Tuscany to intervene in the conflict with Pope Gregory VII.

EX ROGAT ABBATEM·/ MATHILDEM SUPPLICAT ATQ

Godfrey the Hunchback, whom she had married in 1069. Matilda controlled Tuscany, parts of Umbria and Emilia-Romagna and encouraged the economic power of the Florentine guilds.

In February 1076 Godfrey the Hunchback was killed campaigning in the Low Countries, and her mother died in the following April. Marriage to Godfrey had left Matilda with no heir – their children had died in infancy – and she was free to take up arms for the papacy of Pope Gregory VII in his struggle with the Holy Roman Emperor Henry IV.

A firm believer in the centralization of the Church, Gregory had long acted as a power behind the throne during the pontificate of Alexander II. The new pope believed that the Church was tainted by the practice of laymen buying and selling its offices, and in 1075 prohibited the practice under pain of excommunication. That Christmas, Gregory was seized at Mass, assaulted and then abducted with the intention of spiriting him away to Germany. He was only saved by a spontaneous uprising of the people of Rome.

THE CASTLE AT CANOSSA

The remains of Matilda's fortress are to be found in the province of Reggio Emilia in northern Italy on the slopes of the Apennines. It was built in the mid-tenth century by Adalberto Atto, on the summit of a rocky hill, and was protected by a triple line of walls. In 950 Adelaide of Italy, the widow of King Lothair II, took refuge in the fortress and withstood a three-year siege.

In the Middle Ages it was one of the strongest castles in Italy, lying at the heart of a region which bristled with forts and strongpoints. However, in 1255 the castle and its church were destroyed by the local peasantry. Today the remains of the citadel are perched on a massive rock which towers over the surrounding countryside. The citadel looming at its peak is all that remains of a vast fortress system which contained barracks for its garrison, lodgings for the lord and his retainers, an imposing church and monastery, storehouses, stables, workshops and all the associated buildings of a medieval castle.

The penitence of Henry IV was played out in the castle courts overlooked by the citadel while his reception by the pope took place in the citadel itself. Matilda was a worthy inheritor of the magnificent castle. She led her own troops into battle, armed with sword and cuirass and in faithful service of her papal master. Until the early 17th century, two strong suits of mail were preserved at Quattro Caselli, reputedly worn by Matilda herself in battle.

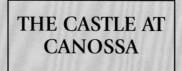

Canossa Castle, site of Henry IV's humiliation in the Investiture Controversy. A 'walk to Canossa' is an idiom in German and Italian meaning 'to eat humble pie'.

In January 1076, at the Council of Worms, Henry IV renounced obedience to Gregory, whom he denounced as a 'false monk' and declared effectively deposed. Gregory responded by excommunicating Henry. The terms were worked out at Matilda's stronghold at Canossa. Henry was given 12 months to make penance. If he failed to do so, his subjects were no longer obliged to obey him and he was personally stripped of all civil rights. Henry's vassals saw the pope's strictures as a signal for insurrection. The scene was set for one of the great dramas of the medieval world.

Gregory was only able to call Henry's bluff because of the military backing of Matilda. In January 1077 Henry was received by Gregory as a penitent at Canossa, which now bristled with men-at-arms, prelates and members of the German priesthood, desperate to escape anathema themselves. The emperor was obliged to stand for three days in the bitter winter cold outside the castle, barefoot and clad only in a woollen robe, before he was allowed in to beg forgiveness. Matilda made her presence felt, and some accounts suggest that even Gregory grew more than a little vexed by her interventions.

On the fourth day, the wretched emperor was allowed into the fortress to throw himself at the pope's feet and receive his mercy, an absolution which was granted him as a man not as a king (although subsequently Gregory referred to him as a monarch). This spectacular triumph was shortlived. Gregory was driven from Rome and into exile, dying in 1085. The emperor's allies preyed upon Matilda's possessions and their efforts, although grievously undermining her strength, provoked the occasional stinging riposte. Her castle at Sorbara, a softer target than Canossa, was besieged in 1084, only for the attackers to be driven off by an audacious sortie launched under the cover of darkness, and personally led by Matilda wielding her father's sword and standing in the stirrups of her steed.

The election of Pope Urban II in 1088 saw an improvement in Matilda's fortunes. However, papal politics required her, at 43, to marry the 17-year-old Welf V of Bavaria and thus bring the callow teenager into an alliance with the See of Rome. It was a marriage of convenience that lasted six years, and gave no pleasure to either partner, but it enraged Matilda's old enemy Henry IV. Eventually she made peace with Henry's son Henry V, who declared: 'in the whole earth there could not be found a princess her equal.' She died in her 70th year leaving him her lands, despite the fact that she had already made them over to the papacy. Much confusion and wrangling between the pope and the emperor ensued.

In the 17th century, the body of the woman dubbed the 'pope's handmaid' was re-interred in St Peter's Cathedral in Rome. On her tomb is a reference in Latin to Penthesilea: 'This warrior woman disposed her troops as the Amazonian Penthesilea is accustomed to do. Thanks to her – through so many contests of horrid war – man was never able to conquer the rights of God.'

One of the most powerful women in medieval Europe, Eleanor inherited the duchy of Aquitaine and Poitiers from her father William X in 1137 at the age of 15 and immediately married Louis VII, the king of France. Four years later, she knelt in the cathedral of Vézelay at the feet of the abbé Bernard of Clairvaux to offer him thousands of her vassals to fight in the Second Crusade.

Eleanor of Aquitaine
1122–1202

On 11 June 1147 Louis, accompanied by Elcanor, was at the Abbey of Saint-Denis to receive from Pope Eugenius III the Oriflamme, the royal banner of France, together with the pilgrim's wallet, and was commended to God's keeping on his enterprise, the Second Crusade.

The crusading army that marched overland to Constantinople aiming to link hands with the German forces of the Holy Roman Emperor Conrad, was led by Louis. But Eleanor enthusiastically joined the expedition herself, accompanied by 300 women, among them the countesses of Flanders and Toulouse, who were pledged both to fight and to tend the wounded. Before they left, they are said to have distributed white distaffs (spindles) to the fainthearted, a medieval anticipation of the stigmatic white feathers of the First World War, the message being: 'If you're too afraid to fight, sit at home and spin.'

The women affected armour and lances, and 'kept a martial mien, bold as Amazons', but never saw action. Rather, their presence on the crusade, and that of hundreds more of their camp followers, attracted fierce criticism. More trouble followed when Eleanor arrived in the city of Antioch, in Asia Minor, and rekindled a romantic attachment to her uncle, Raymond of Poitiers, who had been appointed prince of the city, a suitable base for launching operations against the Saracens. Raymond, a dashing, cultivated man, cut a more attractive figure than the glumly pious Louis.

A clash over strategic priorities ensued: Eleanor supported Raymond's plan to recapture Edessa, which had fallen to the Turks in 1144, while her husband's eyes were fixed on Jerusalem. When Louis demanded that Eleanor accompany him to the Holy City, she responded with the fanciful charge that their marriage was no longer valid, as they were related in the fourth and fifth degrees, a technical matter of canon law which had proved no hindrance to their marrying.

Louis won the strategic argument, but many losses followed. Both the marriage and the expedition foundered, and in 1149 the couple returned to

France in separate ships. On the return journey, Eleanor received the news that Raymond had fallen in battle and his severed head had been delivered to the caliph of Baghdad. Her marriage to Louis was annulled in March 1152, and her two daughters by Louis were taken away from her to be brought up in the French court.

Two months later she married Henry of Anjou, 11 years her junior but a dynamic man of equally fierce temperament In 1154 Henry became King Henry II of England after his rival for the throne, Eustace the son of King

Tomb effigy of Eleanor of Aquitaine at Fontevraud Abbey near Chinon in France. She was interred there beside her former husband Henry II and near to her son Richard I.

Stephen, choked to death while devouring a dish of eels. On 19 December Eleanor and Henry were crowned in Westminster Abbey. Henry was 21 and Eleanor was 32 and in those years she had packed in more than a lifetime's experience. Moreover, she was now queen of England, duchess of Normandy and Aquitaine, and countess of Poitou and Maine. Her experience ranged far beyond domestic concerns to include entanglements with the German and Byzantine emperors, the politics of the crusade, relations with the Norman king of Sicily and Pope Eugenius. She had travelled across France, through Germany and the Balkans to Constantinople and through what is now modern Turkey into Asia Minor, Palestine and Jerusalem, returning by way of Sicily and Italy.

In 13 years Eleanor bore Henry three daughters and five sons; two of the sons, Richard and John, would become kings of England. All this time, she combined child-bearing with high-level political intrigue, and lost none of her warlike spirit. In 1173, at the age of 50, she led her three sons in a rebellion against Henry, was captured attempting to return to Aquitaine and imprisoned for 15 years until her husband's death in 1189.

With the death of Henry in 1189 from an old ulcerated wound, and the accession to the throne of her son Richard I, Eleanor's fortunes were once again in the ascendant. On her release, Eleanor made a triumphal progress through the kingdom, dispensing amnesties and ensuring the country's loyalty to her son. When Richard was absent on the Third Crusade to the Holy Land, she ruled as regent and personally arranged the ransom that secured his release when he was captured while making his way back to England. After Richard's death in March 1199, wounded by a crossbow bolt in a minor siege southwest of Limoges, she lost no time in aggressively ensuring the succession, on 25 May, of his brother John.

A restless traveller in her old age, she kept a wary eye on family interests, cannily cementing alliances with the marriages of her five daughters. At the same time she established a brilliant court in Poitiers, where she encouraged troubadours and the writers of Breton romance cycles. She fought her last military campaign in 1201, thwarting the designs of Arthur of Brittany on her possessions in Anjou, Aquitaine and Mirebeau.

But Eleanor's formidable powers were now ebbing away. She retired to the abbey at Fontevrault, where her husband Henry is buried and died

' ... an incomparable woman, beautiful yet virtuous, powerful yet gentle, humble yet keen-witted, qualities which are most rarely found in a woman ... still tireless in all labours, at whose ability her age might marvel.'

CHRONICLER RICHARD OF DEVIZES ON ELEANOR OF AQUITAINE

ELEANOR OF PROVENCE
1223–91

Eleanor of Provence, the queen of Henry III of England, was his loyal marriage-partner for 36 years. Strong-willed, ambitious and practical, she played a major role in steering the kingdom through the turbulent 13th century. She remains a largely forgotten figure because Henry's reign was marked with so many miscalculations and disasters that not even a strong helpmeet could have averted them. If Eleanor had been a reigning queen instead of a queen consort, it might have been a different story.

As daughter of Count Raymond of Provence, Eleanor grew up in the sunny, pleasure-loving culture of southern France. When she married Henry, she brought from her birthplace her taste for the good life and her familiarity with many influential players on the European stage. Eleanor also installed her relatives in important offices in England, a move that did not endear her to Henry's barons or to the English people, who mistrusted foreigners.

Henry was an ambitious but ineffective king. But Eleanor more than made up for his lack of willpower. Like her two predecessors on the English throne, Isabella of Angoulême and Eleanor of Aquitaine, Eleanor of Provence was fiercely ambitious for her children and supremely self-confident in the exercise of power.

She played an important role in Henry's military campaigns. These included excursions to France to fight for the Continental lands over which the French and English had been squabbling for decades. At home, Henry and Eleanor were faced with rebellious barons. When Henry was captured by his own barons and forced to agree to reforms on their terms, Eleanor went to France and raised a formidable army to free her husband. But her invasion fleet was wrecked before it reached England. Her son Edward (later Edward I), a man as combative as his mother, defeated the rebels and rescued his father.

After Henry died in 1272 Eleanor became queen dowager, but she never relinquished her active role in promoting the royal family's interests. Only after 14 years did she take off her crown and don the veil at the nunnery of Amesbury. There she lived a quiet, pious life until her death in 1291. She was beautiful, resourceful and clever but also unpopular. Her foreign airs and entanglements, her influence on her husband and her imperious manner did not endear her to the English. The chronicler summed up her contradictory qualities after her death: 'the generous and devout virago.'

During her lifetime, Eleanor of Provence was renowned not just for her beauty but also for her learning, cleverness and skill at writing poetry.

there in 1204. A contemporary, the chronicler Richard of Devizes, remembered her as: 'an incomparable woman, beautiful yet virtuous, powerful yet gentle, humble yet keen-witted, qualities which are most rarely found in a woman … still tireless in all labours, at whose ability her age might marvel.'

He concluded, nevertheless, with a word of caution: 'Many know what I would that none of us knew. This same queen, during the time of her first husband, was at Jerusalem. Let no one say any more about it; I know it well. Keep silent!'

Dubbed 'King of Kings and Queen of Queens' by her subjects, Tamara presided over an all too brief golden age in the history of Georgia, a trans-Caucasian kingdom on the very edge of the medieval Christian world. Canonized by the Orthodox Church and, with scant regard for history, characterized by the 19th-century Russian writer Mikhail Lermontov as a 'sprite from hell', she enlarged Georgia's boundaries to their greatest extent in its history while mounting numerous military expeditions and quashing a series of rebellions in a reign of perpetual campaigning.

Tamara
1160–1213

Georgia first emerged as a regional power during the reign of Tamara's great-grandfather, David Afghmashenebeli – sometimes known as 'David the Builder' – who expelled the Seljuk Turks from his kingdom and established the capital city of Georgia at Tbilisi. By the time of his death in 1125, his empire stretched from the Black Sea in the east to the Caspian Sea in the west.

In 1178 David's grandson, George III, declared his 19-year-old daughter Tamara his co-ruler and heir apparent. Proclaiming Tamara to be the 'bright light of his eyes', he hailed her as queen with the assent of Georgia's patriarchs, bishops, nobles, viziers and generals. Seated on George's right hand and wearing purple robes trimmed with gold and silver, she was given her official title, 'Mountain of God', while a crown encrusted with rubies and diamonds was placed on her head.

On George's death in 1184, Tamara became sole ruler, although she was placed under the guardianship of her paternal aunt, Rusudani. The Georgian nobility, anxious for her to produce a male heir, rushed Tamara into a marriage with George Bogolyubski, a debauched Russian prince who had won fleeting popularity with two expeditions against Muslims in the south. He lasted two years before Tamara, wearying of his overbearing and truculent behaviour, sent him into exile. Her second husband, David Sosland, an Ossetian prince and a notable horseman, fathered a son and a daughter, Giorgi and Rusudani, both of whom would later ascend the Georgian throne.

The mural in the cave monastery of Vardzia in southern Georgia (12th–13th centuries). Queen Tamara and her father George III can be seen in the bottom right hand corner.

With the succession secure, Tamara was now free to embark on a policy of military expansion, which also had the advantageous by-product of distracting the Georgian nobility from their favourite pastimes, namely frustrating the influence of the monarch and pursuing power at home.

Commands were distributed among the different branches of the nobility, the better to bind them to her side. However, she had first to deal with Bogolyubski, who in 1191 attempted to woo the Georgian nobility and wrest the kingdom from her. She defeated him twice in the field, took her former husband prisoner and, displaying notable forbearance, chose to exile him for a second time rather than execute him.

She then turned her attentions to the Seljuk Turks, fulfilling the roles of queenly figurehead and active strategist in her campaigns. The prosecution of war became her favoured method of binding together the many fissiparous elements in Georgia. For the next 20 years, Tamara pursued a ferocious policy of aggression – eloquent testimony to the internal problems that faced her at every turn. In the rare intervals between campaigns, she maintained control with compulsory field sports, 'riding into battle' behind her hounds, her court streaming after her.

In the field with her military, she always addressed her troops before they went into battle. At Cambetch in 1196, she urged them on with the words 'God be with you!' to which the army responded with cheers of 'To our king Tamara!' Eight years later, Tamara marched barefoot at the head of the army to make camp on the eve of the Battle of Basiani. The next day she gave the order to mount before taking up a position to watch from a safe vantage point the Georgian rout of the Turks under the Seljuk sultan of Rum.

' ... ploughmen sang verses to her while they tilled ... Franks and Greeks hummed her praises as they sailed the seas in fair weather.'

GEORGIAN CHRONICLER ON POPULAR GRIEF AT TAMARA'S DEATH

The campaign of 1204 took her troops to Trebizond, on the southern shore of the Black Sea, which became a Georgian protectorate. Tamara exercised a loose sway over Muslim semi-protectorates on her southern marches, while on her northern borders the people of south Russia paid her tribute. In 1210 she launched a furious response to an incursion by the sultan of Ardabil, who in the previous year had crossed the Arak mountains, slaughtering and pillaging as he went. Ardabil was seized in a surprise attack and, on Tamara's orders, the emir and thousands of his subjects were put to the sword. The rampage surged deep into northern Persia, and her army returned laden with booty. Her son Georgi was appointed the ruler of Kars.

Tiflis, her capital, now boasted a population of some 100,000, while Georgia traded not only with its immediate neighbours but also with Russians, Armenians, Persians and Turks. The extravagant and unfulfilled ambitions of her great-grandfather David the Builder had been more than fulfilled. A contemporary saying ran: 'One knows a lion by its claws and Tamara by her actions.'

THE AGE OF QUEENS

c.980   The Saxon princess Aelfgifu born, who, as mistress of Cnut of Denmark, regent of Norway, and mother of King Harold 'Harefoot' of England, ruled in three countries.

1028   Zoe became empress of the Byzantium in her own right.

1028   Asma, the ruling queen of the Yemen, succeeded by Queen Arwa, her daughter-in-law, bypassing the sultan, Al-Mukkaram, with his consent.

1105   Melisande born, later queen of Jerusalem.

1136   Agnes of Courtenay born. From Melisande's girlhood to the death of Agnes in 1185, these two women ruled as crusader queens of Jerusalem, governing its development for virtually the entire century.

1226   Blanche of Castile, queen of France, became regent for her son, St Louis, and dominated European politics for the next 25 years.

1454   Caterina Corner born, later to rule as queen of Cyprus.

1461   Anne of Beaujeu born, princess of France, later queen of the Bourbons and *de facto* ruler of France for her weak brother Charles VIII.

1477   Anne of Brittany born, ruler of her own territories from the age of 11 and later – through her marriage to two ineffectual kings – of France as well.

1530   Grainne Mhaol (Grace O' Malley) born, Irish princess, war leader and naval commander in the struggle against the English.

1533   Amina, Nigerian queen and war leader born. As her father's heir, she became a warrior, refused all husbands and extended her country by conquest.

1571   The Persian Nur-Jahan born, later Mogul empress of India, ruling alone for her opium-addicted husband.

1582   Njinga born, ruling queen of Angola, Endongo and Mattamba for over half a century of successful resistance to Portuguese invasion.

These actions were not confined to making war and taking life. During Tamara's reign, Georgian culture flourished alongside martial glory. Shota Rustaveli's epic poem, *The Knight in Panther's Skin*, was dedicated to her, and she sponsored the building of many churches. Tbilisi, situated athwart busy trade routes, prospered. When Tamara died, a chronicler wrote: 'ploughmen sang verses to her while they tilled … Franks and Greeks hummed her praises as they sailed the seas in fair weather.' Yet her achievements would not stand the test of time. Twenty-five years after Tamara was laid to rest in the tomb of her ancestors at Gelati, her daughter Rusudani, who after the death of the dissolute Giorgi had been proclaimed 'King of Kartli', was driven from Georgia by the Mongols, and Georgia descended into chaos. The great days of Georgia were over. In the words of Rustaveli: 'Their tale is ended like a dream of the night. They are passed away, gone beyond the world. Behold the treachery of time; to him who thinks it long, even for him it is a moment … .'

Isabella, a French princess given in marriage to King Edward II of England, earned her nickname, the 'She-Wolf of France', for raising the war that cost her husband his throne and his life. Her military prowess owed much to her lover, Roger Mortimer, earl of March, but her skill in winning the propaganda war against the king was all her own.

Isabella of France
1292–1358

The marriage in 1308 had been ill-starred from the first. Despite the fact that she was a beauty, the 15-year-old Isabella held no charms for the openly homosexual Edward, who treated her with neglect, if not contempt. Although he performed his dynastic duty and fathered a son by her, the king reserved all his enthusiasm for his male lovers. This aroused the murderous hatred of his young wife, who sought revenge on her husband and his religious and political cronies, all under orders from the king to reduce her income and curb her power.

Edward's way of life provided Isabella with an opportunity she was not slow to take. In the devout Roman Catholic temper of the time, homosexuality was regarded as a mortal sin, as well as being a capital offence. Not for a king, however, who was beyond the reach of the law. Edward's behaviour thus alienated huge swathes of his subjects, who loathed not only Edward's gay lifestyle but also his mistakes in running the country, squandering money on his favourites while England's overseas territories were being steadily re-annexed by the French. Playing upon this, Isabella secretly won to her side most of the powerful men of England, including the dashing Mortimer, later earl of March, who became her lover.

In this manuscript illumination of 1470, Isabella presides over the execution of Hugh le Despenser, a favourite of her husband, in 1326.

Isabella then travelled to France to raise an army and returned in 1326 to invade England with Mortimer at the head of her troops. Drawing near to London, Isabella subjected its citizens to a charm offensive, claiming she had come to put an end to the tyranny of her husband and to bring a return to the good old English freedoms of ancient days (with which, although she was a Frenchwoman born and bred, she claimed to be deeply familiar).

She also played the 'battered wife' card to great effect, declaring Edward had sworn: 'that if he had no other weapon, he would crush her to death with his teeth.' But, she loudly complained: 'the King carried a knife in his hose to kill the Queen.' Reference to what Edward carried in his hose [i.e. in his trousers] was a crude attempt to stir up hatred for him on the grounds of his homosexuality, and it worked very well in turning public opinion against the now fugitive king.

As the invasion progressed, Isabella received a parcel containing the head of one of her greatest enemies, Bishop Stapledon, whose crime had been to carry out Edward's orders restricting the queen. It was only the first of several such grisly tributes, as Isabella's men hunted down Edward's supporters. Edward was finally captured and forced to abdicate in favour of his young son, Edward III, and Isabella declared herself and Mortimer regents for the boy.

The next year, 1327, she saw to it that the king was killed in captivity. Intent as ever on winning over public opinion, she ordered his body to be publicly displayed to show that there was no mark of violence upon it, claiming that he died from natural causes in his bed. This did nothing to allay the widespread belief that he had been murdered, since Edward was a man of famously good health, with a strong constitution and a lineage of legendary longevity. The display of the unblemished body merely gave rise to the rumour, sniggered over by every English schoolboy ever since, that Edward had met his end through a red-hot poker being thrust up his anus, which the mores of the period would have considered poetic justice for his sins.

With her husband dead, her son a boy, and her lover at her side, Isabella was riding high. The death of the king secured Isabella and Mortimer from further plots on his behalf, but the stench of adultery and murder created a strong backlash against them, and shortened their prospects of remaining in power. Isabella made a final attempt to deflect criticism and shore up her authority by the time-honoured tactic of planning another war against the Scots. But Parliament would have none of it. Her power was ebbing away.

What is more, the 'She-Wolf' was losing her touch. She took no heed that Mortimer's arrogance had now made them both as detested as Edward had been, if not more. But as she found to her cost, she was not the only plotter in the family. Three years later in 1330, her 18-year-old son Edward

A vital pawn of Queen Isabella in her campaign to overthrow her husband King Edward II, Philippa was one of five daughters of William III, count of Hainault in the Low Countries. Desperate to raise an army from 1325 onwards, Isabella offered to marry her son, the heir to the throne, to one of the daughters, in return for a large dowry and as many fighting men as the count could provide.

The count accepted. Primed with the cash and a fighting force of 'Hainaulters', widely admired as among the best mercenary soldiers in Europe, Isabella overthrew her husband and had him killed. So when the 15-year-old Philippa was married in 1328, her bridegroom was no longer heir apparent, but King Edward III.

Philippa was to bear Edward 12 children, seven sons and five daughters, but still remained involved with all the wars of the realm. Her life was dominated by her husband's incessant battles, principally against the Welsh and the Scots, and between her confinements she was required to accompany him on his many campaigns. Edward's reign also saw the start of the cruel and useless Hundred Years' War between England and France, in which Philippa was constantly engaged. Her pre-arranged intervention in 1346, when she begged her husband on her knees to spare the life of the burghers of Calais, has passed into history.

But although compliant and renowned for her patience with Edward's compulsive womanizing, Philippa was no mouse. In 1348 she persuaded him to refuse a proposal of the Electors of Germany to make him Holy Roman Emperor, which she rightly saw as a quagmire of new enmities, especially in her own native Flanders. Edward valued her opinion, and sincerely mourned her when she died from the Black Death in 1369.

Statue of Philippa of Hainault by the 19th-century Danish sculptor Herman Bissen. Philippa was careful not to alienate the people of her adopted country by bringing a large retinue of foreigners to the English court.

repeated her own strategy of using the nobility to turn the tables on a hated administration, and had both her and Mortimer arrested. Mortimer was swiftly hauled out to be hanged, drawn and quartered, while Isabella was imprisoned in Castle Riding in Norfolk. But Edward bore no long-term grudge against his mother, restoring her to court and giving her an honoured place before she died – unlike both her husband and her lover – in her old age, at peace and in her own bed.

Isabel, countess of Buchan, a daughter of the ancient Scots house of Fife, was a devoted supporter of King Robert the Bruce in his war against the English, and paid for it in a peculiarly horrible way. Her loyalty to Robert was a part of her inheritance, since the house of Fife was second only in importance to that of the Bruce, the Scots monarchy of the day, and by tradition none other than a hand of Fife could perform the coronation of the king of the Scots.

Isabel of Fife
14th Century

When Robert the Bruce raised an army to rid Scotland of the overbearing English rule and the tyranny of Edward I, Isabel immediately declared support for him, even though this meant leaving her husband, who opposed Robert and favoured keeping in with the English king. Isabel rode to the Bruce's side on her husband's favourite charger, joining the faithful band of women who always supported him: his wife, his sister and his young daughter.

Robert then proclaimed himself king, and Isabel was called upon to play a vital role. The current earl of Fife was no more than a 16-year-old boy, and a ward of the English king, a prisoner in effect. In his absence, acting as the senior member of her noble house, on 26 March 1306 Isabel led Robert by the hand up to the throne of Scotland, seated him on the ancient Stone of Scone, and placed the gold circle on his head.

This readiness to abandon her husband and her position in support of the Bruce gave rise to the rumour that she was Robert's mistress, a slander uncritically repeated by later historians who did not understand the power of the immemorial link between the house of Fife and the royal house of Scotland. Isabel conferred the mystique of that link on Robert the Bruce, strengthening his cause in the eyes of all true Scots. But to the English king, this was a gross act of treason he could not forgive.

Later that same year, Edward exacted his revenge. Robert the Bruce was defeated in a major battle and his womenfolk captured. His daughter's youth meant that she was merely confined to a nunnery. But for Isabel, Edward devised a special punishment. She was put into a cage and hung outside the walls of the tower of Berwick Castle high above the town, exposed to the elements and to the eyes of one and all. Her only refuge from the Scots weather and from the public gaze was to retreat into the privy through which she had been thrust out, which was no more than a stinking hole in the castle wall, winter and summer through.

Early 20th century painting by Stewart Carmichael of Isabel of Fife inside the cage from which she was hung outside the walls of Berwick Castle for four years between 1306 and 1310.

Known as 'Black Agnes' because of her magnificent head of dark hair, the countess of Dunbar was related to the Bruce and Stewart royal dynasties of Scotland through both her parents. Her father was Sir Thomas Randolph, the first earl of Moray, who became regent after the death of his uncle Robert the Bruce. Agnes's mother was Isabel Stewart, a cousin of Walter, the High Steward of Scotland, who married Marjorie Bruce, whose son became Robert II, the first of the Stewart monarchs. Thus Agnes could trace her descent through two famous Scottish fighting clans, but her coolness under fire was a personal quality.

By her marriage in 1320 to Patrick Dunbar, Agnes became countess of Dunbar and March. In 1338 Dunbar came under attack during the conflict that followed Edward Balliol's attempt, with English backing, to seize the Scottish throne from David II, the son of Robert the Bruce. Agnes's husband was away when the castle was besieged by an English force under the command of the Earl of Salisbury, one of the most formidable soldiers of the day. Left alone, Lady Agnes had only her retinue of servants and a few soldiers to defend the family seat.

Agnes brushed aside Salisbury's demand that she surrender Dunbar Castle with the ringing declaration: 'Of Scotland's King I haud [hold] my house, He pays me meat and fee, And I will keep my gude auld [good old] house, while my house will

AGNES RANDOLPH
c.1312–69

keep me.' Salisbury launched his assault by battering the castle's walls with boulders and lead shot launched from siege engines. Agnes's response was a studied insult to the English warlord; she appeared on the castle's outer walls with her maids, whom she commanded to pretend to dust away the damage with their handkerchiefs. When a battering ram was trundled up to the base of the castle wall, it was swiftly disabled by one of Salisbury's boulders, which was toppled from the ramparts and returned with interest. The frustrated Salisbury then captured Agnes's brother, the third earl of Moray, and paraded him under his sister's eyes with a rope around his neck, threatening to hang him. The redoubtable Agnes urged him to go ahead, because the earldom would then pass to her. This cool display of brinkmanship saved her brother's life, and the hapless Salisbury was obliged to abandon the siege after five fruitless months. He is said to have observed ruefully: 'Cam (came) I early, cam I late, ther(e) was Agnes at the gate.' Agnes succeeded in peaceful fashion to her brother's estates when he died in 1346. Sir Walter Scott said of her: 'From the record of Scottish heroes, none can presume to erase her.'

Illustration of 'Black Agnes' defending Dunbar Castle against the English. From The Book of History *(London, 1914).*

The same fate befell Robert's sister Mary Bruce, imprisoned in a similar cage at Roxburgh on the express orders of Edward I, whose savage punishments were now bordering on dementia. Robert's queen, Elizabeth, had the good fortune to be the daughter of one of Edward's powerful allies, so she was never caged nor forced to endure the Scottish winters out of doors. But she was locked up in a bleak Scots royal manor, denied furniture, bed and bedding and even clothing, and attended by women jailors deliberately chosen for being ugly, old and harsh.

Isabel and Mary remained in their cages for four years. They were not brought down until 1310 when Robert began making headway against Edward, and both women became more valuable as state prisoners or bargaining counters rather than as an awful warning to one and all. Isabel

was allowed to leave Berwick for confinement in a Carmelite convent, and Mary was removed to conditions of easier imprisonment in Newcastle.

Four years later, Robert's success in battle against the English allowed him to ransom his queen, and Elizabeth returned to the arms of a husband she had not seen for eight years. Although middle-aged, she was to bear the king two more daughters and a son, an heir for the newly-enfranchised Scottish throne. Robert's sister Mary Bruce came home at the same time.

But Isabel of Fife did not return. The ransom documents make no mention of her name, and her fate is unknown. With victory on his side, and given the ancestral bond of loyalty between Bruce and Fife, it is inconceivable that King Robert would not have ransomed Isabel too. She must have died in captivity, after her years in the cage.

The legendary heroine of the bitter Hundred Years' War between England and France, Joan of Arc (French: Jeanne d'Arc) has inspired generations of schoolgirls as the epitome of female courage and patriotism, going into battle at the head of her troops clad in shining armour like a man. In reality, her value to the French rested more on her usefulness as a propaganda tool than on any military prowess, and her war career ended without her dispatching even one of the enemy.

Joan of Arc
1412–31

Almost all the concrete details we possess of the real-life Joan of Arc have been gleaned from the records of the two trials she underwent – one at the end of her life and the other after her death. In the first, orchestrated by the English but presided over by French judges, the aim was to prove the English claim that she was a witch, the most hated form of female life at the time (between the ninth century and the 19th, many thousands of women were hanged or burned as witches, with the persecution reaching its peak around Joan's time). During the second, posthumous process, which was held for the benefit of the king of France, the judges were under a different kind of pressure, to rehabilitate her as a divinely inspired national saviour and embryonic saint.

Joan was born to a prosperous peasant family of Domremy in Lorraine and led an apparently unremarkable life until 1425, when she was aged 13. In that year, which may have coincided with the onset of puberty, she claimed that she had had visions of St Michael, St Catherine and St Margaret, all of whom told her that she had been chosen to free France from the English and ensure the coronation of the *dauphin* (heir apparent) Charles, later Charles VII. However, it was not until four years later in 1429 that she succeeded in persuading the commander of the local castle in the neighbouring town of Vaucouleurs to escort her to Charles at Chinon.

Dressed in male attire – she later explained that 'for a virgin, male and female clothes are equally suitable' – she was able to pick Charles out of the crowd at Chinon (he had made a deliberate attempt to disguise himself) and, after careful inspection, her virginity was confirmed. Charles decided that the striking young woman might prove useful, and had a suit of armour made for her, complete with lance and shield. An excellent horsewoman, she quickly mastered the basics of combat. Under the watchful eyes of two marshals of France, she was assigned to the French

During the 19th century, Joan of Arc was elevated to the status of national heroine. Her native village was renamed Domremy-la-Pucelle ('the virgin') in her honour, and the neoclassical painter Dominique Ingres completed a famous portrait of her (right; 1854) in armour at the coronation of Charles VII.

INGRES J.A.Dominique 1780-1867
Jeanne d'Arc au sacre de Charles VII

English cannon and bowmen in siege towers batter the walls of the French city of Orléans in 1429. Scene from a contemporary manuscript illumination.

army as it struggled to lift the English siege of Orléans, the key to Charles's continuing hold on territory south of the River Loire. Joan's role was to despatch threatening letters to the city's English besiegers, to participate in councils of war, and to play a part in skirmishing, where her powerful voice could be heard over the din of the fighting, in which she was twice wounded. Although she had no official standing with the French troops, her bravery and coolness – remarkable for an uneducated peasant girl – earned her instant respect. The siege was lifted after nine days of fighting, and Joan was present at Charles's coronation at Rheims on 17 July 1429.

When the French launched an unsuccessful bid to regain Paris in August and September of that year, Joan was wounded a third time. By the time she joined the attempt to relieve Compiègne, which had been besieged by the Burgundians, she was famous throughout France and rode into battle in a sumptuous cloak of red and gold. But this proved her last moment of glory. She was captured by the Burgundians and treacherously ransomed to the English. Her captors imprisoned her in Bouvreuil Castle and subjected her to a lengthy interrogation, after which she was tried for witchcraft and fraud by an ecclesiastical court whose task was to show that her mission was inspired not by God, but by the Devil himself.

Joan bore her captivity with equanimity, remained calm when threatened with torture, made a bold, physically gruelling but unsuccessful attempt to escape, and declined parole on the condition that she would not try to escape again. She also refused to promise her captors that she would not take up arms again. She signed an 'abjuration', but recanted two days later. She was eventually found guilty and convicted of wearing male clothes, an offence against the Church and, because of her recantation, of having fallen into 'various errors and crimes of heresy, idolatry [and] invocation of demons'. She was burned at the stake in Rouen marketplace on 30 May 1431. She died of smoke inhalation and her body was burned a second time. A third fire was required to reduce her organs to ashes, which were reportedly thrown into the River Seine. Her active career had lasted barely 18 months and although she had seen action, she confessed before she died that she had never killed anyone.

In 1456 the judgment was reversed by an ecclesiastical court, and her legend began to grow. She was dubbed 'd'Arc' in the 16th century, became a French national heroine in the 19th century and was canonized in 1920. During the Second World War, both Vichy France and the Free French forces claimed her as a symbol of their cause.

There is a curious footnote to her story. In 1867 ashes that were said to contain the remains of Jeanne d'Arc were found in the loft of a Parisian apothecary and were transferred to a museum in Chinon. In 2007 scientific tests revealed that the 'holy relics' were in fact part of an Egyptian mummy at least 2,000 years old and their age was confirmed by carbon dating. There have been many movies about Joan of Arc, the most memorable being the 1927 silent classic *The Passion of Joan of Arc*, starring Renée Falconetti in the title role and directed by the Danish master Carl Dreyer.

ALEXANDRINE BARREAU
1773–1843

Barreau was born in Semalens, in the department of Tarn, northeast of Toulouse. In 1792, accompanied by her father and her brother, she enlisted in the 2nd Battalion of the Tarn Grenadiers, a volunteer unit that augmented the French Republic's regular army in the wake of the Revolution.

The Grenadiers were considered élite soldiers and were always thrown into battle where the fighting was at its most fierce. A British officer who fought against them in the Peninsular War (1808–14) observed: 'They were the finest I ever saw, most beautifully clothed and equipped. They made a most formidable show in line. They were the first that were charged by our regiment and a proper example was made of them, they have hardly a man left to tell the story.'

In 1793 Barreau fought with the Western Army in the Pyrenees. At the storming of Alloqui, held by a strong Spanish force, her father and brother were both wounded alongside her, and Barreau exhausted her ammunition. She then drew her short sword and rallied her exhausted comrades. She was the third French soldier into the Spanish positions, and the enemy was put to flight. She then returned to tend her father and brother.

Barreau married a soldier, one Layrac, and when he was wounded in action she led his section into battle. She served until 10 September 1793 and thereafter was forced to petition for a pension. The petitions, supported by doctors' certificates, are testimony to the hardships she had to endure on campaign and the toll they had taken. She suffered from migraines, poor sight, growing deafness and crippling rheumatism.

In January 1819 the 'Tarn grenadier' was granted an annual pension of 100 francs. In 1832 she and her husband entered the Hôtel des Invalides in Avignon, where she died aged 69.

Learned and fierce, and as devoted to politics as she was to the pleasures of the chase, Margaret was a true product of the clever and cruel house of Angevin. But her courage and ruthlessness in the opening exchanges of the Wars of the Roses availed her little, and she died in poverty and isolation.

Margaret of Anjou
1430–82

Margaret was the daughter of René I of Anjou, titular king of Naples and Sicily, and was raised by her energetic and learned mother, Isabella of Lorraine, and then by her grandmother, Yolande of Aragon. Margaret was considered a great royal catch, and in 1445 she made an arranged marriage with the 24-year-old Henry VI of England as part of the provisions for the Truce of Tours. She brought no dowry with her, and the truce provided for the cession by the English to France of Maine and Anjou, a move that would prove unpopular in England and as a result was kept secret.

Once in England, the spirited 15-year-old allied herself with the 'King's Party', led by William de la Pole, duke of Suffolk, and later Edmund Beaufort, duke of Somerset, against Richard Plantagenet, duke of York, and successfully negotiated an extension of the Truce of Tours. Where her husband was pious, passive and indecisive, Margaret was, in spite of her youth, active, decisive and engaged. Henry was happy to be led by her, and she assumed responsibility for the administration of England, raising taxes and match-making for the offspring of the nobility. In 1448 she founded Queens' College, Cambridge, in emulation of her husband, who had founded King's College, Cambridge, in 1441.

Nevertheless, by 1447 Henry's inertia, the troubled state of the royal finances, growing lawlessness at home and a disastrous military campaign in France led to the exile and murder of Suffolk and a shortlived rebellion in which London was occupied by forces under the command of a former soldier, Jack Cade. In August 1453 Henry succumbed to the bi-polar disorder that ran in his family. It so disabled him that he failed to respond to the welcome news in 1453 that, after nearly ten years of marriage, Margaret had borne him a son. In 1454 the duke of York was named regent as Protector of the Realm, Margaret was promptly sidelined and Somerset detained in the Tower of London.

On Christmas Day 1454 Henry regained his senses and Margaret moved quickly to reassert her control over his affairs. She persuaded Henry to dissolve parliament and raised an army to crush their enemies.

Hostilities in what was later called 'The War of the Roses', fought between the houses of York and Lancaster, began with the first Battle of St Albans (1455), in which Somerset was killed. Both sides recoiled from full-blown civil war, Henry suffered another nervous collapse and the duke of York was briefly reappointed Protector before being despatched to Ireland by Margaret in a move that anticipated the many twists and turns the conflict would take over the following 30 years.

At the Battle of Northampton (1460), Henry was captured and taken to London while the duke of York pressed his claim to the throne of England. Margaret massed an army in the north of England which carried the day at the Battle of Wakefield (1460), in which the duke of York and his son were killed. Their severed heads were later displayed on the gates of the city of York.

Margaret then hurried to Scotland, from which she returned with an army she could not afford to pay. It marched south, plundering and looting as it went, and defeated the Yorkist forces at the Second Battle of St Albans (1461), after which her distracted husband was found, abandoned by his captors, wandering helplessly in a wood.

Statue of Margaret of Anjou and her son Edward in the Jardin de Luxembourg, Paris. An inscription on the plinth reads: 'If you cannot respect an exiled queen/Respect an unhappy mother' – an allusion to the fact that her son died before her, the only English heir apparent ever to fall in battle.

Portrait of Margaret's husband, Henry VI (*c.*1535) by an unknown artist. The only son of the warlike Henry V, his susceptibility to bouts of insanity rendered him periodically unfit to govern.

Margaret did not follow up her success at St Albans, but fell back on the north and saw her army routed in a driving snowstorm by the Yorkist forces, under the duke of York's son, now Edward IV, at Towton (1461) in Yorkshire, the bloodiest engagement ever fought on English soil. Of the 80,000 men who took part in the battle, some 20,000 were killed in the rout and pursuit. Henry and Margaret fled to Scotland, whence Margaret embarked to seek help in France. She returned with a small force provided by King Louis XI, but by the autumn of 1463 she was back in Europe with a begging bowl.

In 1470 the influential Richard Neville, earl of Warwick ('Warwick the Kingmaker') broke with his cousin Edward IV and was reconciled with Margaret and Henry. Warwick returned to England, defeated the Yorkists in battle and restored Henry to the throne. A lethargic and vacant-looking Henry was paraded through London, a sad contrast to the vigorous Edward

IV. Again, indecision cost Margaret dear, and her tardy arrival in England, in April 1471, was on the day when the Kingmaker was killed at the Battle of Barnet. Edward IV now moved quickly to fall on Margaret's small army at Tewkesbury (1471), and her son was killed in the battle. Margaret remained Edward's prisoner until 1475, when Louis XI obtained her release. Her husband had been imprisoned in the Tower of London, where he was murdered on 21 May 1471. She retired to Anjou, where she lived in reduced circumstances until her death.

BRILLIANA HARLEY
1598–1643

Brilliana Conway was the daughter of Viscount Conway and third wife of Sir Robert Harley, who served as her father's aide in the English parliament when the latter was Secretary of State.

During the English Civil War, in December 1642, in the absence of her husband and sons, her home, Brampton Bryan Castle in northwest Herefordshire, was threatened by royalist forces. The gentle and modest Brilliana was torn but determined to do whatever her husband would want her to do. She wrote to her son Ned that: 'I never was in such sorrows.'

The siege of Brampton Bryan began in earnest in July 1643. Brilliana was requested to surrender by the royalist commander, Sir William Vavassour, to prevent 'further inconvenience' to her. Brilliana protested that she had 'the law of nature, of reason, and of the land on my side'. The royalist response was to bombard her walls and to slaughter her livestock.

Earthworks were thrown up around the castle, close enough for the shocked Brilliana to hear the unfriendly besiegers. The language of the royalist soldiery: 'infected the air; they were so completely

Portrait of Lady Brilliana Harley. Hundreds of her letters survive, giving a picture of a highly educated and devoutly Puritanical woman.

inhuman, that out of their own mouths, and the mouths of their guns, came nothing else but poisoned words and poisoned bullets.'

On 24 August Charles I despatched a letter to Brilliana, urging her to avoid further 'effusion of blood', but the defender of Brampton Bryan would not surrender, as she had received intelligence of the approach of parliamentary forces. She prevaricated, and protested when the royalists stole some bells. She gave the orders to open fire, telling Ned: 'we sent some of His Majesty's subjects to old Nick for their sacrilege.'

Brampton Bryan was relieved, but not for long. As autumn approached it was again under threat. Brilliana took to her bed with a heavy cold, and within days had succumbed to 'an apoplexy and defluxion of the lungs'. One of the defenders of Brampton Bryan noted that in place of the thunder of guns, Brilliana's death was greeted with 'volleys of sighs and tears'. Later the castle was destroyed by the forces of Prince Rupert of the Rhine, although Sir William Vavassour prevented the slaughter of its inhabitants.

Isabella was a warrior monarch who, during the re-conquest of Spain, often appeared on the battlefield 'superbly mounted and dressed in complete armour'. This tactic, aimed at infusing her soldiers with loyalty and rousing their intense feelings of chivalry, was employed by a number of queens in time of war, notably Elizabeth I.

Isabella I of Spain
1451–1504

The daughter of Juan II of Castile and Isabella of Portugal, Isabella was three years old when her father died. Until the age of 13 she was brought up by her mother before being taken to the court of her ineffectual half-brother Henry IV, king of Castile. Although Isabella became the focus of opposition in the corrupt and febrile court, she avoided entanglement in conspiracy and in September 1468 was eventually recognized as the heir to the throne of Castile. Unlike Elizabeth I, she had received little formal education, and it was only later that she set herself to learn Latin, the language of diplomacy and statecraft in order to deal with foreign dignitaries. She was subsequently very careful to ensure that her own daughters, including Catherine of Aragon, who married Henry VIII, received comprehensive tutoring from distinguished teachers.

She married Ferdinand of Aragon, her second cousin and own choice, in 1469. In 1474, on the death of Henry IV, Isabella swiftly arranged to be crowned 'Queen Proprietress' of Castile instead of Juana, Henry's illegitimate daughter and his final choice as heir. At Isabella's coronation, which took place in Ferdinand's absence, Isabella ordered that the unsheathed sword of justice be carried before her, an ancient practice but one which had never previously accompanied the coronation of a female monarch. When Ferdinand received the news, he declared: 'Tell me, you may have read so many histories, did you ever hear of carrying the symbol of life and death before the queens? I have known it only for kings.'

The king of Portugal invaded Spain in support of Juana, but was defeated in 1479. Juana was confined to a convent and in the same year Isabella's husband Ferdinand succeeded to the throne of Aragon as Ferdinand II. In 1480 the intensely austere and pious Isabella allowed the establishment of the Inquisition in Andalusia, principally as a measure to deal with Jews and Muslims who had converted to Christianity, but whose loyalties she did not trust. Both Ferdinand and Isabella were later given the title 'the Catholic' by the pope in recognition of their 'purification' of the Catholic faith. To the pontiff, they were 'the athletes of Christ'.

Although Isabella and Ferdinand appeared to govern independently, they shared a single mind. They resembled two mighty oaks, below whose spreading canopies the roots were inextricably entwined. Nowhere was this more evident than when the two muscular Christians came together to expel the Moors (Muslims) from the territories in Spain that they had occupied for eight centuries.

The *Reconquista* lasted ten years and was completed in 1492 with the conquest of the kingdom of Granada. Isabella played a prominent part in the campaign, travelling with her five children, and involving herself in every detail of the military establishment. She founded the Queen's Hospitals, consisting of six large hospital tents staffed with physicians and surgeons, which trundled across

A 19th-century colored woodcut titled *The Surrender of Granada*, which depicts Isabella I of Spain and Ferdinand of Aragon with representatives of the defeated Moors.

the landscape from siege to siege. The *Reconquista* was primarily a war of sieges, during which the arrival of Isabella in her chain mail was guaranteed to stimulate such enthusiasm in her troops that the beleaguered citadels quickly fell. When in late 1488 she arrived before the walls of Baza, mounted on a spirited horse with flowing mane, her appearance sent a clear message that the siege, thus far unsuccessful, was to be prosecuted with renewed vigour. The cry was raised by the troops: 'Castile, Castile, for our King Isabella.'

Sometimes her appearances were carefully choreographed and ceremonial rather than tactical. At Seville, the army was drawn up for review in full battle array. Battalion after battalion lowered their standards as the queen passed by on her mule, seated in a saddle-chair embossed in gold and silver, before she raised her hat to her husband and the two monarchs bowed to each other. When not on duty, Isabella's tastes were more modest, a contrast to those of Elizabeth I. She confided in her confessor that she preferred a 'simple dress of silk with three gold hem bands'.

> **' ... they went by the roads and fields with much labour and ill-fortune, some collapsing, others getting up, some dying, others giving birth, others falling ill, so that there were no Christians who were not sorry for them ... '**
>
> CHRONICLER ANDRÉS BERNÁLDEZ ON THE *RECONQUISTA*

This practical cast of mind underlaid Isabella's invaluable qualities as a quartermaster-general. She oversaw the recruitment of thousands of pioneers to build roads, which eased the passage of the cannon in her siege train and also engaged Don Francisco Ramirez, dubbed *El Artillero*, to deploy them at their destination under the direction of her husband.

Her personal interventions, however sincere, were always carefully stage-managed. When Ronda was captured, the emaciated and filth-caked prisoners who staggered from its dungeons were comforted by the queen herself. The royal entry into Moclin was accompanied by a Te Deum sung in the royal chapel. These devotions were accompanied by faintly audible noises from underground beneath the chapel, indicating the presence of Christian captives long held underground and now awaiting deliverance.

The year of her final victory over the Moors, 1492, was a busy time for Isabella, which also saw the expulsion from Spain of all Jews who refused to convert to Christianity. Isabella, while often commanding in war, was scrupulous to heed the bigoted advice of her (male) confessors. The results were not always happy. According to the chronicler Andrés Bernáldez: 'They [the Jews] went out from the land of their birth – boys and adults, old men and their children, on foot, and riding on donkeys and other beasts and in wagons ... They went by the roads and fields with much

In 1567 King Philip II of Spain despatched troops to pacify his possessions in the Low Countries. The Dutch mounted a stern resistance which lasted until 1579 and the formation of the united provinces.

In 1573 the town of Haarlem, a dozen miles south of Amsterdam, was besieged by Frederick of Toledo, the son of the duke of Alva, at the head of a force of some 12,000 men. Haarlem was defended by 4,000 fighting men and 300 women who had been raised by Kenau Hasselaar, a woman in her late 40s, who ran a timber yard. Hasselaar could be seen on Haarlem's walls at the head of her women, shoring up breaches and building new defences. She tended the wounded, helped Haarlem's cannoneers, stiffened the morale of those who looked like giving up and brought up water to the defenders. Even the Spaniards who had invested the town accorded her grudging respect.

Don Frederick had predicted that the siege would last no more than seven days, but it dragged on for seven months. Its defenders held out because Haarlem proved very difficult to isolate, the preliminary to starving out its population. For many weeks, fresh troops and provisions could be brought across a large lake, the Harlemmermeer, adjacent to the town, to sustain its defenders.

Haarlem surrendered on 13 July 1573. Its citizens were allowed to live, at a price of 240,000 guilders, but the garrison was put to death, with the exception of its German element, and some 40 of Haarlem's burghers were executed. This grisly task kept half a dozen executioners busy for a week. When their arms grew too heavy to lift their swords, they finished the job by tying the remainder up back-to-back and tossing them into the River Spaarne.

Hasselaar survived and her name is revered in Haarlem to this day. Many a Dutch warship proudly bore her name in later years, a name that in popular parlance was often used to denote a rambunctious and feisty woman.

KENAU HASSELAAR 1526–88

The redoubtable Kenau Simonsdochter Hasselaar, defender of Haarlem. A contemporary account calls her 'an extremely manly woman'.

labour and ill-fortune, some collapsing, others getting up, some dying, others giving birth, others falling ill, so that there were no Christians who were not sorry for them ... .'

Also in 1492, and after much prevarication, Isabella sanctioned a voyage of discovery to find a western passage to the East Indies, undertaken by the Genoese seafarer Christopher Columbus. In addition to sponsoring exploration, Isabella supported many scholars and artists, founded educational establishments and amassed a huge art collection. She left the throne of Castile to her daughter Joan, as she had been predeceased by her eldest son Juan and daughter Isabella. A portrait of Isabella shows her with a long nose and a glum expression. The surviving armour of the husband-and-wife architects of the *Reconquista* indicates that Isabella was taller than Ferdinand by as much as an inch. She was also a year older.

In a Papal Bull, Sforza was castigated as 'the daughter of iniquity' and in another described, equally bluntly, as 'the daughter of perdition'. In her early 20s she threw herself into soldiering, and when in command maintained an iron discipline with the aid of blood-chilling sanctions.

Caterina Sforza
1462–1509

Caterina was the illegitimate daughter of Galeazza Maria Sforza, who later became the duke of Milan and was assassinated in 1474. In 1477 Caterina was married by proxy to Girolamo Riario, the nephew of Pope Sixtus IV (there were persistent rumours that he was the pope's son). Well educated by the standards of the day, she was also athletic and a passionate hunter, favouring bloodhounds and setters. She was a handsome woman, but her beauty regime left little to chance. Lotions of nettle seed, cinnabar, ivy leaves, saffron and sulphur kept her golden locks in perfect condition. Her shining teeth received daily applications of charcoaled rosemary stems, pulverized marble and coral cuttlebone. Her blue eyes were bathed daily in rose water and unguents smoothed her breasts. Ironically, Caterina's feminine obsession with her looks was turned against her when she applied herself to the masculine pursuit of waging war.

Nevertheless her approach to war was characteristically stylish. In August 1484, on the death of Sixtus IV, Caterina was despatched to Rome to hold the ancient Castel Sant'Angelo (see page 98), a papal property, until it could be handed over to Sixtus's legal successor. At the time Caterina was seven months' pregnant and cut a striking figure in a gold satin gown, plumed hat, and belt from which dangled a bag bulging with golden ducats. The only martial touches to the ensemble were a curved sword and the ripe language that she employed to curse and cajole the soldiers under her command. Caterina held the castle until October 1484, when she surrendered it on her husband's order to the Sacred College of Cardinals.

On 14 April 1488 Riario was murdered by members of the rival Orsi family. His palace in Forlì was sacked and his children held as hostages. Caterina, who kept control of the citadel at Forlì, is said to have shouted to her enemies, 'Do you think, you fools, that I don't have the stuff to make more?', while hoisting her skirt to expose her genitals. More genteel historians maintain that she was pregnant when the threat to her children was made and, in a more decorous gesture, merely pointed at her swelling belly. History does record, however, that with the assistance of Lodovico il

Moro, duke of Milan, she was able to defeat her enemies, regain possession of her dominions and exact revenge on the murderers of her husband.

There were public executions and secret stranglings, but the most ghastly fate was reserved for the 80-year-old patriarch Andrea Orsi. Dressed in a vest, shirt and one sock, and with his hands bound, Orsi watched helpless as his house was razed to the ground and he was then dragged

Contemporary portrait of Caterina Sforza by the Florentine painter Lorenzo di Credi.

round a square by a horse before being disembowelled and dismembered while still alive. His limbs and organs were tossed to a baying crowd.

Clearly, Caterina was not a woman to cross. In August 1495 Giacomo Feo, the castellan of the citadel at Forlì whom she had secretly married in 1488, was murdered by spearing and mutilation, the result of a conspiracy in which her own family was involved. Feo was widely hated but Caterina, who was unaware of the conspiracy, was infatuated with him. Her revenge was swift and terrible. The murderer was done to death as an entrée before his wife and sons were flung down a deep well and left to die. The same fate overtook the wives, mistresses and children of the other conspirators.

She contrived to establish more friendly relations with the new Borgia pope, Alexander VI, and with the Venetians, whose ambassador, Giovanni

THE CASTEL SANT'ANGELO

An imposing cylindrical building in the heart of Rome, the castle was commissioned by the Emperor Hadrian as a mausoleum for himself and his family. Hadrian's tomb was built on the right bank of the Tiber between 135 and 139 and housed the emperor's ashes, those of his wife Sabina and his first adopted son Lucius Aelius. The remains of successive emperors were interred in the mausoleum, the last being those of Caracalla in 217. Hadrian was also responsible for the bridge, the Pons Aelius, facing the mausoleum.

The building was converted into a fortress at the beginning of the fifth century. In 410 Visigoth looters scattered the imperial urns and ashes, and in 537 most of the statuary went the same way at the hands of the Goths. The plundering continued until, in the 14th century, successive popes converted the mausoleum into a fortress. Pope Nicholas III connected the castle to St Peter's Basilica by a covered fortified corridor called the Passetto di Borgo. The fortress was the refuge of Pope Clement VII from the siege of Holy Roman emperor Charles V's *Landsknechte* during the sack of Rome (1527) in which goldsmith Benvenuto Cellini describes strolling the ramparts and shooting enemy soldiers.

Popes also used the castle as a prison. Giordano Bruno, the Dominican mathematician and astronomer, was held there for six years and subsequently burned at the stake. Executions were carried out in the small interior square. The castle also provided the setting for the third act of Puccini's opera *Tosca*, in which the eponymous heroine leaps to her death from the walls.

View of the Castel Sant'Angelo and the Pons Aelius. After defending the fortress in 1484, Caterina later found herself imprisoned there.

de' Medici, she secretly married in 1496. When he died two years later, in September 1498, the resourceful Caterina deterred the Venetians from seizing her lands by negotiating an alliance with the Florentines. However, she was less surefooted when she refused to allow her son Ottaviano to marry the pope's daughter Lucrezia Borgia.

The accession of Louis XII to the throne of France in 1498 brought further turmoil to central Italy. At Blois in February 1499 a secret deal was struck between France and the Borgias. Louis pledged to help that power-hungry clan drive the ruling families out of the Romagna. Their lands were to be absorbed by Alexander's son Cesare, while Louis was to be given a free hand in the pursuit of his own claims to Milan and the kingdom of Naples. At the beginning of March, Alexander VI promulgated a Papal Bull that characterized Caterina as the 'daughter of iniquity' and formally invested Cesare with Imola and Forlì.

In the winter of 1499 Cesare moved against Sforza with an army reinforced by 14,000 French troops. The castle at Imola held out until December 1499. Caterina clung on grimly at Forlì, sending Alexander VI letters impregnated with poison in the forlorn hope that dispatching the pontiff would save her. But she would have needed a very long spoon to poison a Borgia, and her plan came to nothing.

In a desperate move, she ordered the magazines in her stronghold to be blown up, but the order was disobeyed and the citadel taken in January 1500 after Cesare Borgia demanded *la bellicosa signora* be brought to him dead or alive. On taking her alive, he raped her, subjecting her to the same humiliations that had befallen the women of Forlì and boasting to his officers that she had defended her fortress more vigorously than her virtue.

Caterina was imprisoned for a year in the Castel Sant'Angelo. Thereafter she fled to Florence to escape persecution by the Borgias. When their baleful power collapsed with the death of Alexander VI on 18 August 1503, she attempted to regain control of her lands. She petitioned the new pope, Julius II, who initially favoured the restoration to the Riario family of Imola and Forlì. However, after the people of both cities declared that they did not wish to see her return, all ideas of restitution were dropped and the estates passed into other hands.

In her final years, Caterina found refuge in a convent, and consolation in training her son by Giovanni de' Medici, Giovanni della Banda Nera in the art of war. The 'Tiger of Forlì' succumbed to influenza on 28 May 1509. In June 1537, 28 years after Caterina's death, her grandson, Cosimo de' Medici, the sole son of her own son Giovanni, became duke of Florence and, in 1569, grand duke of Tuscany. Through him, Caterina was the direct ancestor of the later grand dukes of Tuscany, the dukes of Modena and Reggio and the kings of Spain and France. Caterina's other notable descendants included Marie de Medici, King Charles II of England and Diana, Princess of Wales.

The most celebrated woman to take part in the Spanish conquest of Central America, Malinalli, known as La Malinche, was an Indian of noble birth who became the mistress of the Spanish commander, Hernán Cortés. Her contemporary fame as a native conquistadora was later obscured by the contempt in which she was held in 19th-century Mexico, which earned her the derisory nicknames of La Vendida ('she who sells out') and 'The Great Whore'.

Malinalli Tenepal
c.1498–1529

Malinalli was born into a noble family in the Paynalla province of the Coatzacoalcos in the Veracruz region of southern Mexico. When her father died, her mother remarried and gave birth to a son. Although Malinalli was her father's firstborn and rightful heir, her mother and stepfather favoured the new baby. Having been born under an ominous sign portending disaster, she was handed over to merchants who sold her into slavery with the Mayan Indians of Tabasco, the Mayan-speaking region of Yucatán. After Hernán Cortés defeated the *cacique* (headman) of Tabasco in 1518, he was presented with 20 young women to serve his soldiers and cook for them. One of them was Malinalli, who was baptized and renamed Marina.

She was at first handed over to Cortés's aide Alonso Hernandez de Puertocarrero, but then advanced quickly in Cortés's service. She was a gifted linguist and soon became his interpreter, working with Jeronimo de Aguilar. When Cortés reached the Nahuatl-speaking tribes along the Gulf Coast, Marina would interpret between Nahuatl and Maya for Aguilar, who then conveyed information to Cortés in Spanish. Marina quickly learned Spanish, providing Cortés with vital information about the mindset and military tactics of the region's tribes. She was said to have been at Cortés's side in many battles, but never to have taken an active part in the fighting. This is possibly an acknowledgement of the role of women in ancient Indian warfare, in which females often accompanied their menfolk into the thick of battle, but only to advise and encourage them. Because Marina was invariably in the company of Cortés, and always spoke for him, the Indians dubbed him 'Marina's captain'. Cortés wrote in a letter: 'After God we owe this conquest of New Spain to Dona Marina.'

This was, perhaps, an overstatement. The major factors behind his success were the insatiable Spanish appetite for gold, the lethal smallpox epidemic that the Spanish bequeathed to the Indian population, and the firepower of the *conquistadoras*, which spectacularly offset their numerical

Modern mural in Tlaxcala showing the discussions between Hernán Cortés and the ancient city fathers. Malinalli is seen in a prominent position at this meeting. She was always anxious to avoid bloodshed, and the high point of her role as interpreter came when she accompanied Cortés to his face-to-face meeting with Moctezuma, the Aztec emperor who in 1520 was imprisoned and killed by the *conquistador*.

When Hernán Cortés landed on the Yucatán in 1519 at the head of 550 men, his small command was accompanied by 12 Castilian women who were following their husbands and fathers. Eight were white and four were black, a reflection of the increasingly multiracial nature of Spanish society in the early 16th century, the result of the number of African slaves and free individuals living in Spain.

Initially, Cortés was reluctant to let the women join the march on the Aztec capital, Tenochtitlán. He wanted to leave them at Tlaxcala, which he had captured after a hard fight. The women protested vehemently, declaring: 'Castilian wives, rather than abandon their husbands in danger, would die with them.' They joined the march, although their duties were at first confined to acting in a domestic role in the expeditionary force's camps. Inevitably Cortés's mission frequently exposed them to battle. The women were required to nurse the sick and wounded, to perform guard duties and, on occasion, to join the fighting alongside the men. At least 5 of the 12 died in battle.

The *conquistadoras* had sacrificed comparative safety for the rigours of campaigning and the tangible but dangerous rewards it offered – prestige, land, slaves and treasure. They fought hard to secure them. Two in particular, Beatriz Bermudez and Maria de Estrada, distinguished themselves by ferocious courage in battle, and lived to reap the rewards. When Cortés tried to billet them in a safe town as he pressed

on again to attack the Aztec capital, Tenochtitlán, all the *conquistadoras* defied him, and declared their willingness to face what lay ahead.

In the battles that followed, Bermudez and de Estrada fearlessly risked their lives and often outdid the men on either side. During the battle of Tenochtitlán, Bermudez donned men's body armour and brandishing a sword, rallied the flagging *conquistadoras* with the words: 'For shame, Spaniards, turn upon these base people, or if you will not, I will kill every man who attempts to pass this way!' Fired with the same spirit, Maria de Estrada also armed herself like a man with helmet, breastplate, weapons, sword and shield and rode into battle, running many of the Indian fighters through with her lance.

Years later, the Spanish women had not lost their appetite for a fight. Battling to take Morelos in 1522, Cortés announced that the soldier who led a charge against hostile Indians would be rewarded with a grant of land. This prompted de Estrada to mount up with lance and shield and beg her commanding officer to allow her to charge the Indians as proof of her valour. Cortés granted her request and Estrada charged, shouting 'Saint James, attack them!', driving many of the Indians into a ravine. As a reward, she was granted the towns of Telala and Hueyapan.

Page from the codex known as the Lienzo de Tlaxcala *('History of Tlaxcala'; c.1585) showing Cortés and 'Dona Marina' parleying with an Aztec chieftain.*

inferiority. Nevertheless, Marina played an important role, facilitating communication between Cortés and the many native American leaders he encountered, particularly the Tlaxcalans, who were seeking allies against the Aztecs, with their overbearing demands of tribute and their addiction to human sacrifices.

Marina also bore Cortés a son, Martin, who was much loved by his father and became his legitimate heir by papal decree. Thus Don Martin Cortés became the first *mestizo* of historical note. He eventually held a position in government, was a Commendator of the Order of St Jago, and in 1548 was accused of conspiracy against the Spanish viceroy and executed.

Cortés never married any of his Indian lovers, but in Marina's case he made her substantial land grants, and about 1524 arranged for her to marry one of his lieutenants, Don Juan Caramillo. Marina bore him a daughter,

Dona Maria. As the mother of both a son and a daughter of mixed blood, the blood that courses through the veins of most Mexicans, Marina could truly be considered the mother of the Mexican nation.

In all probability Marina died in one of the epidemics which, during the next century, killed some 98 percent of the native population. In 1542, in a dispute over the land granted to Marina, seven of Cortés's lieutenants testified to the governors of New Spain about the important role she had played in the Spanish conquest of Central America. Yet the conquest proved an unmitigated disaster for the region's native peoples, and in the 19th century the nationalist custodians of Mexico's past attempted either to vilify Marina or to write her out of history. Today Mexican-Spanish speakers use the word *malinchista* to mean 'one who prefers foreign things' and for many *Malinche* is synonomous with 'traitor'.

Mochizuke Chiyome made her entry into the annals of war in 1561, when her husband, the Japanese samurai Mochizuke Moritoki, was killed at the battle of Kawanakajina. Some of the women of the nobility undoubtedly trained and fought openly as samurai like their men, but Chiyome chose to work undercover with ninjas, 'the dark heart of the samurai', when she went to war on her late husband's behalf.

Chiyome
fl. 16th Century

For around 1,000 years, from the Dark Ages to early modern times, sworn brotherhoods of men known as 'ninjas' were employed by the warlords of Japan to take care of anything deemed below the dignity and honour of a noble samurai. Ninjas took care of all the covert or unethical operations of their feudal lords: spying, deception, disinformation, infiltration, kidnap and assassination. These techniques, later known as *ninjutsu*, 'the ninja's art of stealth', began to evolve around 600 and were codified into a new theory of secret warfare from the early 12th century.

From the start it was plain that women could gain entry where even the most skilful male ninja could not penetrate, and so were born the *kunoichi-ryu* or 'deadly flowers', as the female ninjas were known. *Kunoichi* worked as spies, going undercover to find out enemy plans, or spreading subversion to lower enemy morale. Trained as geisha as well as killers, they also acted as secret assassins, ready to take out either the political opponents of the warlord or rival samurais.

The original ninjas, or *ninjutsu-ryu*, originated in ancient China as a secret society dedicated to protecting its own chosen people through the covert arts of war. Reaching Japan around 715, it soon gained a lasting foothold among the mountain families who lived in regular conflict with each other and with the warlords of the surrounding areas.

By ancient tradition, ninjahood could only be passed down through the blood, and ninja families enrolled their offspring from generation to generation. These were mainly found in remote villages in the Iga and Koga districts of Japan, where the sons and a few daughters of mountain families and peasants of the plain studied eastern philosophy as well as the arts of war, favouring the Shinto belief in the harmony of nature and developing their own personal philosophy, *Toh Shin Do*, 'the way of the pure-hearted sword'.

For hundreds of years, these mysterious and often terrifying male-dominated bands of ninjas ravaged their neighbourhoods at the bidding of the local warlords or their own warring desires. But after the defeat and death of her husband in the mid-16th century, Chiyome set up a school to train female ninjas and hire them out to warlords for special operations. A former ninja from the Koga region, Chiyome saw the potential for empowering the *kunoichi* to act in their own right, not as adjuncts to men.

Chiyome herself was well aware of the reality of male power. The widow of one warlord, she was left under the protection of another, Daimyo Shingen Takeda, her late husband's uncle. In support of Takeda, a leader she considered worthy of her loyalty and theirs, she devised a plan

Woodcut of a samurai trained in *ninjutsu*, the martial art of guerrilla warfare. Originally evolving in small schools, ninjas came together as larger societies for each region, with women granted no more than associate status, whatever the importance of their contribution.

to create a band of fully trained female operatives who could act as spies, gather information and deliver coded messages to his allies.

Supported by Takeda and untroubled by husband or children, Chiyome set up her school in secret, where from around 1562 she began cultivating her own 'deadly flowers'. Flouting the hereditary principle of membership, she set up her operation in the village of Nazu in the Shinshu region and enrolled orphans, runaways and lost girls of the streets, victims of the civil war that engulfed the entire country. These young women were indebted to her for saving them, and Chiyome never let them forget it.

Under the guise of being a wealthy philanthropist dedicated to rescuing female waifs and strays, Chiyome educated her girls in the deadliest forms of martial arts. As a primary cover, the girls were all taught the skills of a *miko*, or shrine attendant, who could serve at any of the Shinto shrines across the land. This allowed them to travel anywhere without suspicion, looking demure and devout, while all the while being armed and dangerous. The *kunoichi* system was based on appearing vulnerable, thereby drawing the opponent into close range where the *kunoichi* could mount an unexpected and fatal free-hand attack focusing on the throat, eyes and hair.

The girls had weapons training too, learning the use of knives, swords, spears and the medieval battle-axe-with-spear, the halberd. Their main weapons were the *koshigatana*, or twin short swords, which could be deployed very swiftly and effectively because of their light weight and abbreviated blades. But Chiyome also specialized in teaching her girls the art of seduction and how to use their female wiles. Often they obtained access to their target clad in the finest and most formal court kimonos, when the unfortunate victim would discover that the ritual sash, or *obi*, wound around the female ninja's slender waist, concealed all manner of deadly instruments. Steel claws, blinding powder, throwing-blades shaped like stars and a range of knives all lay ready to hand inside the three-yard length of woven cloth. An alternative was to use the *obi* itself as a garrotte. And once the chosen 'mark' had been despatched, the female ninja could make her escape by using her *obi* as a climbing rope, or as a strapping or bandage in case of injury.

Survival was also prominent in the curriculum, and the trainees learned to shin up any tree, to hide under water, and in extremis to dislocate their joints to free themselves from being tied up or imprisoned in a very small space. For normal activity, the *kunoichi* wore the so-called 'cloak of darkness', clad head-to-toe in black. For other assignments they would don street clothes. Over time, Chiyome's female ninjas set up an extensive network that served Takeda well. The intelligence they supplied gave him the advantage over his opponents, and his *kunoichi* also disseminated black propaganda on his behalf, spreading rumours to foment rebellion or create panic.

A selection of concealable ninja weapons. As geishas, Chiyome's 'deadly flowers' were taught to kill with anything, especially women's weapons such as poisoned hairpins or razor-sharp ivory fans.

The work of the ninjas as sexual seductresses and honey-trap operatives goes back to the Old Testament time of Delilah and beyond. In the years before the Second World War, official Nazi policy was, in general, opposed to women working or holding positions of power. But there were always ways in which they could serve the interests of the Nazi state.

Although brothels were officially outlawed in the Third Reich, the *Schutzstaffel* (SS), the most powerful and feared arm of the Nazi regime, was authorized by its chief, Heinrich Himmler, to use prostitutes to gather intelligence. Himmler delegated the task to his deputy, Reinhard Heydrich, who established the Salon Kitty in Berlin's Giesebrechtstraße.

The SS took over an existing high-class brothel, whose madame, Kitty Schmidt, had been forced to cooperate by Walter Schellenberg, the SS man in charge of the Reich Security Service. Schmidt had been caught smuggling currency abroad and was presented with a stark choice – co-operation with the SS or a one-way ticket to a concentration camp.

The brothel was wired and equipped for surveillance on foreign diplomats and visitors, which enabled the assemblage of dossiers on the sexual peccadilloes of Nazi bigwigs and government guests. Additional girls were recruited by the Berlin vice

SALON KITTY
1930s

squad and received special training in the art of seduction, the better to prise out confidential information from their clients, as well as fat fees. Cameras were concealed in bedroom walls, and the luxurious bedheads were fitted with microphones to convey indiscretions, and energetic love-making, to a listening post in the basement.

A notable customer of the salon was Count Galeazzo Ciano, the Italian Foreign Minister, son-in-law of Benito Mussolini and by no means an unqualified admirer of the Third Reich, as his overheard remarks revealed. Sepp Dietrich, an old comrade of Adolf Hitler and the commander of the Führer's bodyguard, hired the girls for an all-night orgy, but let slip no secrets. Heydrich himself made a number of 'inspection tours' during which the microphones were switched off. Another regular at Salon Kitty was the British agent Roger Wilson, whose cover was that of a Romanian press secretary.

A bomb demolished much of the building in 1942 and within a year the project had been abandoned, leaving Schmidt to continue to run her business provided she kept her mouth shut. She survived the war and died in 1954. In 1976 the story of Salon Kitty was turned into a movie starring Helmut Berger as Heydrich's henchman Walter Schellenberg (renamed Walter Wallenberg) and Ingrid Thulin as Kitty Schmidt.

The work of female ninjas lasted long after Chiyome's time, and ninjas remained active in Japan through the Edo period (1603–1868), when the government in Tokyo finally overcame the last traces of the feudal warlords and unified modern Japan. What became of Chiyome herself is not known. Her enduring achievement lay in reversing most of the assumptions of conventional war, and adapting warfare itself to match her young female ninjas' physique. Eschewing armour, the *kunoichi* were protected by an illusion of weakness. Instead of a long spear or sword, they were armed with an arsenal of lethal concealable weapons or some, like the *obi*, which did not appear to be weapons at all. Instead of hiding in shadows, all the *kunoichi* moved freely through villages, towns, castles and temples. In a male-dominated world of war, they carved out their own unique place. Is it a modern tribute or a pitiful parody that the 21st-century female ninja or 'Warrior Woman' is now an established star of computer games, prancing through fatuous adventures clad only in wisps of chiffon designed to reveal her most un-Japanese Marilyn Monroesque hips and bouncing breasts?

Myth and legend swirl around the figure of O'Malley, like sea fret off the coast of County Mayo. But behind the legend lies an extraordinary swashbuckling life to match anything in fiction.

Grace O'Malley
c.1530–1600

O'Malley was probably born in County Mayo and sprang from a famous family of sea rovers who traded as far as Scotland and Spain in their fleet of caravels and galleys. Her parents were initially reluctant to let her go to sea with her father, telling her that her long hair would catch in the ship's ropes. She cut it off in protest, earning the nickname *Grainne Mhaol* ('Grace the Bald'). In all probability she received a formal education, since in 1593, during her celebrated encounter with Queen Elizabeth I, the two women were said to have conversed in Latin.

In 1546 she married Donal O'Flaherty, heir to the headship of a Galway clan and known as 'Donal of the Battles'. O'Malley bore him three children – Owen, Margaret and Murrough – and outdid her husband in the profession of piracy and tribal feuding. After her husband died, probably in a tribal battle, a rival clan, the Joyces, attempted to regain possession of an island castle that O'Flaherty had seized from them. It was successfully defended by O'Malley, winning the grudging respect of the Joyces, who gave the castle the nickname *Caislean-an-Circa*, the 'Hen's Castle'. She later defended it against the English, tearing lead from the roof, melting it down and sending it cascading over the heads of the attackers. She summoned help by despatching a man to light a pre-prepared beacon on the nearby Hill of Doon. Reinforcements arrived to drive off the English, who never returned

After O'Flaherty's death, O'Malley eventually returned to her family lands and established herself on Clare Island, from which she could monitor the busy shipping traffic and, with a private army of 200 followers, extract money from mariners in return for safe passage, or turn her pirates loose to plunder. By 1566 she strengthened her power base by marrying 'Iron Richard' Burke, who owed his name to a coat of mail inherited from his Anglo-Norman ancestors and held a castle at Rockfleet, County Mayo. 'Iron Richard' fathered her son, 'Theobald of the Ships' or *Tibbot-na-Long*. According to legend, O'Malley gave birth to Tibbot on a trading mission in which she overcame Turkish pirates, capturing their ship, dispatching the crew and adding it to her fleet. Tibbot was later knighted as Sir Theobald Bourke, and in 1626 was created 1st Viscount Mayo by Charles I.

A bronze statue of Grace O'Malley, by the artist Michael Cooper. Situated in the grounds of Westport House, County Mayo, Ireland, the statue was commissioned by Jeremy Altamont, 11th Marchioness of Sligo. The original owner of the house, Colonel John Browne (1638–1711), married the great, great grandaughter of Grace O'Malley.

By 1574 O'Malley was creating such havoc among English ships sailing out of Galway that her castle at Rockfleet came under siege. Once again, she and her private army prevailed. In 1577 O'Malley sought an alliance with the Lord Deputy of Ireland, Sir Henry Sidney, who described her as a 'notorious woman in all the coasts of Ireland'. A year later she was captured while raiding lands owned by the earl of Desmond and imprisoned for 18 months in Dublin Castle. Somehow, she talked her way out of prison and was allowed to return to Connaught, where she continued to foment mischief.

In 1586 O'Malley was arrested by Sir Richard Bingham, governor of Connaught, who confiscated her property, dismissed her followers and erected a gallows in anticipation of her execution. Although O'Malley was released when her son-in-law took her place, her own son Owen was murdered by Bingham's men. She returned to piracy and troublemaking, earning the title of 'nurse to all Rebellions in the province'.

Bingham retaliated by arresting her sons Murrough and Theobald and her half-brother Donal-na-Piopa, a move that prompted her to petition Queen Elizabeth I for their release. The letter, which survives, catalogues the injustices suffered by her sons, reminds Elizabeth of O'Malley's advanced age and ends with the request: 'to grant unto your said subject under your most gracious hand of signet, free liberty during her life to invade with sword and fire all your highness' enemies, wheresoever they are or shall be, without any interruption of any person or persons whatsoever.' Hardly the supplication of a frail old woman.

This led to an extraordinary encounter on 6 September 1593 between two of the most remarkable women of the age. It was a bold move on

Grace O'Malley, the 'Pirate Queen of Connacht' during the famous audience in September 1593 with Queen Elizabeth I of England at Greenwich Palace.

O'Malley's part, as Elizabeth was perpetually plagued by Irish rebellions. But the queen dearly loved a battler, female or male, and had encouraged the English privateers who had carried the fight against Spain to the New World. She was a very different woman from O'Malley, a master of statecraft rather than a buccaneer, but their boldness suggests striking similarities of temperament.

The two women met at Greenwich Palace. Elizabeth was surrounded by guards and members of her court; O'Malley refused to bow before her because she did not recognize Elizabeth as the queen of Ireland. Before the meeting got under way, Elizabeth's guards relieved O'Malley of a dagger that the unabashed corsair claimed that she carried purely for her own protection. She then further ruffled her English hosts by blowing her nose on a fine lace handkerchief proffered by one of Elizabeth's ladies-in-waiting before tossing it onto the roaring fire with the explanation that, in Ireland, a used handkerchief was always destroyed after use. It seems more likely that the gesture was a sly insult to her host. Nevertheless, the meeting produced a letter from Elizabeth to Bingham, ordering him to release O'Malley's sons and to provide her with a pension for life. When Bingham dragged his heels, O'Malley secured the release of the prisoners by threatening to return to England to inform the queen of his intransigence.

It was not long before O'Malley was at sea again, ostensibly privateering for Elizabeth, but closely watched by a sceptical Bingham. Eventually her luck ran out. Some say that she died in a sea battle while attempting to board a ship, others that she died in poverty at her castle at Rockfleet. She was subsequently immortalized in countless Irish tales and ballads.

'to grant unto your said subject ... free liberty during her life to invade with sword and fire all your highness' enemies.'

GRACE O'MALLEY PETITIONS ELIZABETH I

Another fighting Irishwoman, Christina Davies, also known as 'Mother Ross', achieved celebrity through the account of her eventful life written by Daniel Defoe. It was a classic tale of a woman disguising herself as a man to search for her husband who was campaigning in the Low Countries.

She was born in Dublin, the daughter of a brewer and farmer who in 1689 joined the army of James II, which was defeated by William of Orange (William II) at the Battle of the Boyne (1690). Having chosen to fight on the wrong side, her father suffered the confiscation of his land and effects. Christina went to live with an aunt, who left her the inn she owned.

Christina married her barman, Richard Welsh, with whom she had several children before he disappeared. A year later she discovered that he had been lured onto a ship, abducted and cast adrift in Holland, where he joined an infantry regiment. Christina decided to find her husband, dressed in his clothes and enlisted in Captain Tichbourn's company of foot. She soon found herself in Holland and in the middle of the Nine Years' War. At the Battle of Brabant (1693), the Allied army of William III was routed by the French, suffering some 19,000 casualties, one of whom was Christina Welsh, who was hit in the leg.

She was briefly a prisoner of the French, joined the 6th Dragoons after her release and served throughout the campaigning season of 1695. In 1701, after the outbreak of the War of the Spanish succession, she rejoined the 6th Dragoons, fighting with them at Nijmegen and the siege of Venlo. After receiving a musket wound, and once again avoiding detection, she encountered her husband, with whom she served as a fellow-soldier. They were never reunited as man and wife.

At the Battle of Ramillies, Christina was hit in the head by a mortar fragment and this time her sex was revealed in hospital. She later served as an auxiliary nursing the wounded and as a sutler selling provisions. Richard Welsh was killed at Mons in September 1709, prompting an outburst of grief and tender consolation from an officer, one Captain Ross, which prompted Christina's nickname 'Mother Ross'.

Returning to England, she astonished her fellow-passenger while travelling by stagecoach to Liverpool, overpowering and knocking out a highwayman and riding his horse to Coventry, where she was rewarded by the mayor with £16. She ended her days in London as a Chelsea Pensioner, along with her third husband, and was buried with full military honours in the churchyard of St Margaret's in Westminster.

A 1750 engraving of Christina Davies.

Queen Elizabeth I became the most famous woman in the world in 1588, when she led England to a stunning victory over the Spanish Armada. But fate had cast her as a major player in this long-simmering conflict before she was born. When still in the womb, she earned the undying hatred of the Most Holy Catholic Majesty of Spain, and when the mighty Armada finally put to sea, it bore down on the 55-year-old queen with all the force of an Islamic *jihad*.

Elizabeth I
1533–1603

Elizabeth's father, King Henry VIII, desperate for a son, had appealed to the pope for a divorce from his Spanish wife, Catherine of Aragon, in order to marry his pregnant mistress, Anne Boleyn. But the most powerful Catholic ruler in the world, King Charles V of Spain, was the nephew of the wronged queen, and under pressure from him, the pope refused.

Spain's fury at Henry's treatment of his queen only increased when Henry broke with Rome and set up his own Protestant church to marry Anne. His heir had to be legitimate: no bastard could succeed, and Anne was confidently expected to produce a boy. But Anne's child was a girl. Henry's rage and England's consternation knew no bounds, while universal rejoicing broke out in Spain. The baby Elizabeth, already anathematized as a bastard by the pope before she was born, was now stigmatized as a wrongful heir. In time, the rightful Roman Catholic ruler would be restored to England, aided by the watchful power of Spain.

From her earliest years the threat of Spain hung over Elizabeth, but she did everything she could to keep the foe at bay. For a woman who is revered as one of the greatest war leaders the British have ever known, Elizabeth was an extremely reluctant belligerent. Like Winston Churchill, Britain's prime minister in the Second World War, she infinitely preferred 'jaw-jaw to war-war', and never willingly went on the attack. She hated the chaos and ruinous expense of war.

Covert operations presented an alternative. Elizabeth had no scruples about encouraging privateers like Francis Drake and John Hawkins to wage a campaign of guerrilla warfare at sea. Secretly funding their expeditions to raid the great galleons of the Spanish Main, she greedily pocketed the lion's share of their loot while publicly condemning the privateers. For Elizabeth, this policy made sound strategic sense. Spain was Europe's major power, convinced of its rightness and driven by a moral crusade, while England, a much smaller country on the edge of the

During her long reign, Elizabeth, who was well versed in the art of propaganda, commissioned many portraits of herself as the 'Virgin Queen', a forbidding figure defending the integrity of her nation and the inviolability of the Protestant faith.

The scale of the disaster that had hit the Armada at the end of July was not immediately evident. In the following days, Elizabeth still anticipated a land invasion from the Low Countries, where the duke of Parma had assembled a fleet of 1,500 barges to ferry thousands of Spanish pikemen across the Channel.

Elizabeth rode out to hearten her army clad in armour previously made for her late brother Edward VI, who had died aged 16, as his silver breastplate was the only piece in the Royal Treasury small enough to fit her slender frame. At Tilbury, on the Thames outside London, she delivered the speech which has become world famous, declaring: 'Though I have the body of a weak and feeble woman, I have the heart and stomach of a king, yea and a king of England too.' She went on to heap insults on the enemy, in the long tradition of commanders pumping up the aggression of the troops: 'I think foul scorn that Parma or Spain or any prince of Europe should dare invade the borders of our realm!' she proclaimed, promising her soldiers cash rewards and 'a famous victory over the enemies of God, my kingdom and my people!'

The defeat of the Armada was secured by a combination of tactics and good luck. The summer of 1588 saw violent winds and unseasonable storms in the Channel, which caused havoc among the top-heavy Spanish galleons. The English fleet largely escaped damage. In this the Elizabethans saw the

hand of God. Once victory was certain, Elizabeth, image-conscious to the last, seized the opportunity for a worldwide anti-Spanish and anti-Catholic propaganda coup. She ordered a medal to be struck and widely distributed with the Latin slogan *Deus flavit, et dissipati sunt* – 'God blew, and they were scattered'. God was a Protestant, and he had shown his true colours by fighting on England's side. With a little help from England's rightful if not Holy Roman Majesty.

Elizabeth delivering her famous speech to her forces at Tilbury.

continent, had to take every chance to tip the balance against an overwhelmingly powerful enemy in its favour.

By 1588 the Spanish were determined to annihilate England and Elizabeth. The king of Spain, Philip II, embraced war against her as a religious crusade. The kings of Spain bore the title of 'Most Holy Catholic Monarch of all Europe', and Philip was intent on bringing England back into the Roman Catholic fold. He also claimed to be asserting the right to 'his' throne, having been proclaimed king of England by Pope Sixtus V.

In declaring war on England, Philip was also avenging a personal slight. At the start of her reign, he had proposed marriage to Elizabeth, and she turned him down. Now she would pay. One hundred and thirty warships, many of them standing seven stories high above the water, and armed with 2,360 cannon, set sail. They carried some 19,000 hand-picked fighting men, 8,500 sailors and 2,088 galley slaves. Confident of victory, the Spanish dubbed their invasion fleet the *Grande y Felicisima Armada* ('Great and Most Fortunate Navy').

Through the superb intelligence of her spymaster, Francis Walsingham, Elizabeth was apprised of the Spanish plans. As a war leader, Elizabeth showed her true genius. She rose to the crisis, she chose her commanders with great skill and then reined in her instinct to micro-manage, giving them their head. Above all, she remained at the helm, refusing to leave London despite the entreaties of her ministers, just as the British royal family stayed in Buckingham Palace throughout the Blitz of 1940–41. And Elizabeth's faith in her English fleet was fully justified. Although overtopped by the massive Spanish galleons, the English warships were more manoeuvrable, darting in and out of close combat like dogs baiting a bear. Among the English captains, Drake, Hawkins and others had the priceless experience gained through successful attacks against galleons on the Spanish Main.

> **'I sent the Armada against men, not God's winds and waves.'**
>
> PHILIP II RUES THE DEFEAT OF HIS ARMADA

The result was decisive. On 19 July the Armada, under the command of the duke of Medina Sidonia, a man with no experience of naval warfare, was sighted off the Lizard in Cornwall, heading towards Plymouth, where the English fleet, commanded by Charles Howard, 2nd baron of Effingham, was assembled. At first the English were frustrated by strong winds and currents and unable to get to grips with the Armada, which sailed up the English Channel towards its rendezvous with the invasion force, commanded by the duke of Parma, which was to be conveyed from Dunkirk to the English coast in a fleet of barges.

The English commanders were eventually able to put to sea, tracking the Armada as it entered the Channel. Small-scale encounters flared off Portland Bill on 23 July and the Isle of Wight two days later, but these did not break up the Armada's defensive crescent formation. On 27 July it anchored off Calais to await the arrival of Parma's barges. This presented Howard with the chance to send eight fireships into the crowded seaway. The Spanish captains were forced to cut their cables and sail away in some disorder. The rendezvous with Parma had been thwarted.

On 29 July the Spanish and English fleets clashed in an eight-hour battle off Gravelines. The English exploited their superior manoeuvrability to provoke the Spanish while remaining out of range. They then moved in, firing repeated broadsides into the Spanish ships. Five Spanish ships were lost and many others sustained serious damage, particularly those that had borne the brunt of the action.

On the following day the wind had backed southerly, enabling Medina Sidonia to sail north away from the French coast. The Armada was now forced to find a way back to Spain round Scotland and Ireland, where many ships were wrecked on those inhospitable shores. Only 67 of the proud 160 ships limped back to Spain.

Described by the Dutch leader of her bodyguard as a 'cunning virago', Jinga Mbandi led her forces in an ultimately unsuccessful war against a European power with designs on her kingdom. In the 21st century, she remains a popular heroine in Angola and a symbol of both national resistance and Pan-Africanism.

Jinga Mbandi
1580?–1663

Jinga Mbandi (also known as Njinga Mbande) was born in West Africa at a time when the two most powerful tribes in the region were those of the Kongo and Ndongo. In all probability, she was the daughter of the *ngola* (king) of the Ndongo, who in the mid-16th century had welcomed Portuguese missionaries. However, it was not the promise of Christian converts but the financial rewards of the slave trade that led the Portuguese to found Loanda (present-day Luanda, capital of Angola) in 1575 and to install a governor.

We first encounter Jinga in the early 1620s, when she negotiated with the Portuguese on behalf of her brother, who had become the *ngola,* but had been exiled to an offshore island by the governor. The *ngola* had become entangled in the murky politics of the slave trade, which in the early 17th century was booming. A Portuguese official boasted that the teeming population of the African interior would supply slaves 'to the end of the world' to work in the Brazilian plantations and mines. Local chiefs became an integral part of the trade, raiding rival tribes for valuable human cargo. Naturally enough, the Africans wanted to control the trade on their own terms, but the Portuguese begged to differ. The *ngola* had become a casualty of this brutal jostling.

Jinga's task was to secure the return of her brother and enlist the help of the Portuguese in expelling a rival tribe from Ndongo territory. To curry favour, Jinga shrewdly allowed Portuguese missionaries to baptize her and her two sisters, acquiring in the process the name Ana de Sousa. Her siblings became Dona Engrácia and Dona Bárbara. Her encounter with the governor was, if the legend is to believed, an indication of her composure. When he insisted that she remain standing while he was comfortably seated, Jinga summoned a slave, ordered her to go on all fours and settled on her back. Some versions claim that Jinga had the slave executed after the meeting, explaining that a queen never used the same chair twice.

Jinga's brother died in 1624, possibly at her hands. She is also credited with the death of a nephew, whose heart she is said to have devoured, in

This wildly fanciful French print shows Queen Jinga Mbandi as a 'noble savage' clad in her regal finery. From Pierrre Duclos's *Collection of Prints showing People of Various Ranks and Dignitaries in the National Dress of all known Countries* (1780).

the style of Hannibal Lecter. She was now ready to abandon her hastily acquired Christianity and take power. This prompted reprisals from the Portuguese, who appointed a puppet chief to supplant Jinga, and drove her into exile.

Jinga's response was twofold. First she struck an alliance with a neighbouring tribe, which closed the slave routes to the Portuguese. She then led her own people to the kingdom of Matamba. Here she overcame the cannibalistic Jaga tribe and adopted wholesale their grisly rituals, which included infanticide, as a means of promoting tribal strength.

Jinga's military prowess owed much to a Dutch mercenary, the commander of her bodyguard, who left a detailed account of her remarkable rule. He noted that she donned male attire for ritual sacrifice and was festooned fore and aft with animal skins. She carried a sword, an axe, and bows and arrows and, although well into middle age, remained extraordinarily agile. In addition to her ritual clothes and formidable personal armoury, she also repeatedly hammered at two iron bells: 'When she thinks she has made a show long enough, in a masculine manner, then she takes a broad feather and flicks it through the holes of her Bored Nose for a Sign of War.' Jinga was now ready for the first sacrifice. The victim was selected, his head cut off and the blood gathered in a cup, which she drained in a great gulp.

Engraving of Jinga Mbandi's notorious audience with the Portuguese governor of Angola, João Correia de Sousa, in 1622, during which she reputedly sat down on a crouching slave to assert her rights as a queen.

Jinga may have had a 'masculine manner', but she had a legendary
appetite for men. She kept a harem of male concubines who could take as
many wives as they pleased, provided they dressed as women at all times.
There was a sinister edge to this playful role reversal. If a young man failed
in his obligations, he would never be seen again.

By shutting down the slave routes at their source, Jinga forced the
Portuguese to mount ever-longer expeditions into the interior. Seizing the
advantage, the Dutch cut the Portuguese supply lines and in 1641 took
Loanda, after which they struck a treaty with Jinga, which in turn enabled
her to harry rival tribes and the Portuguese. She recorded a string of
successes, but in one engagement the Portuguese captured her sister
Mukumbu (Dona Bárbara). Her other sister, Kifunji (Dona Engrácia) had
long been a prisoner of the Portuguese, who drowned her in October 1647.

In August 1648 the Portuguese recaptured Loanda, forcing Jinga to fall
back on her stronghold in Matamba, where she negotiated peace terms
with them in 1656, principally to obtain the release of her sister. The price
of the deal was the provision by Jinga of 130 slaves and her agreement
not to interfere with the Portuguese slave trade. She also abandoned ritual
sacrifices, and allowed Christian missionaries into Matamba. In return the
Portuguese pledged military help whenever she needed it. The grizzled old
warrior was buried with a bow and arrow in her hand.

Catalina de Erauso was a real historical figure, a fact attested by many authenticated documents, including her own 1625 petition to the King Philip IV of Spain requesting that he grant her a pension in recognition of her military services, which was supported by the testimony of her superior officers. In addition, Erauso was, in all probability, the author of a memoir of her roller-coaster career in Spain and the New World, which was not published until nearly 200 years after her death.

Catalina de Erauso
1592–1650

In recent times her story has been revisited to produce another Erauso, an extraordinary individual who cuts a more contemporary figure, the subject of films, plays and transgender and lesbian studies of the late 20th and early 21st centuries. She is therefore both a phantom from the distant past, and a woman whose career throws a shaft of light on the sexual politics of our own time. The bare facts of Erauso's life, as recounted in her autobiography *A History of the Nun Ensign* (1829), are interesting enough. She was the child of high-born Basque parents who consigned her as a child to a convent in San Sebastián, northern Spain. Erauso escaped in 1607 at the age of 15 and exchanged her vows as a nun for a life of adventure dressed as a man.

An uncle, a sea captain, engaged her as a cabin boy on a voyage to the New World. In 1610 Catalina sailed to South America, retaining her male disguise and stealing money from the sea captain when they landed in Panama. She then embarked on a career of chaotic adventure. At the age of 19 she was living in Sana in Peru and working in a shop. In an incident that prefigures the trajectory of much of her later life, she got involved in an argument with a man while attending the theatre, claiming that he was blocking her view. The next day she discovered that the man was stalking her. Her response was swift and violent – she chased and cut down her antagonist with a saw-tooth dagger, inflicting 'a slash worth ten stitches'.

Erauso attempted to escape arrest by fleeing to the safe haven of a church, another recurrent theme in her life, but was arrested and imprisoned. On her release, she found the scarred theatregoer in hot pursuit and intent on revenge. A duel ensued in which she stabbed her opponent, and this time successfully claimed sanctuary. Thus she established a pattern of wounded vanity leading to violent aggression, which was repeated time after time: a duel with a man precipitated by some slight or insult, often over a misunderstanding about a young lady. In later years, Erauso was to enter into many highly ambiguous relationships with attractive young women.

In her twenties, Erauso joined the Chilean Army as Alonso Diaz Ramirez de Guzman. Posted to the Pacific port of Concepción, she was agreeably surprised to discover that the governor's secretary was her own brother Miguel, who failed to recognize her and despatched Erauso on an expedition to fight the Mpauche Indians in Paicabi.

Erauso was pitched into a bloody campaign in which she found herself 'trampling and killing and slaughtering more men than there are numbers'. In one engagement, she boldly recaptured her company's flag, winning a temporary captaincy after her commanding officer fell in battle: 'When I saw the flag being carried off, I rode after it with two horsemen at my side, through the midst of a great multitude of Indians, trampling and slashing away and taking some wounds in return. Before long, one of the three of us fell dead, and the two that remained pressed on until we overtook the flag. But then my other companion went down, spitted on a lance. I had taken a bad blow on the leg, but I killed the chief who was carrying the flag, pulled it from his body and spurred my horse on ... '

The brawls and stabbings continued unabated until, in an incident worthy of the most lurid soap opera, she unwittingly killed her own brother in a fight that erupted after a duel in which Erauso had acted as a second. The grief-stricken Erauso watched her brother's funeral from a distance and then deserted. Swordplay, skewerings, the narrowest of shaves and improbable escapes followed thick and fast, all narrated in deadpan fashion. After fatally stabbing a man in Piscombia, Catalina was sentenced to death by hanging, but

Portrait of the 'Nun Ensign' ('la Monja Alférez') by José Luis Villar. In 17th-century Spain, gender roles were less rigidly defined than in later ages, so the mere fact of her being a woman did not disbar Catalina from her chosen lifestyle.

escaped the gallows after a last-gasp pardon obtained by a sympathetic fellow Basque. In 1619 she was arrested again and revealed her true name and gender to Bishop Fray Augustin de Carvajal. Examined by midwives and found to be *virgo intacta*, she was sponsored by the bishop and found a place in a convent. The wheel had turned full circle, but in three years it was in motion again. Convent life was no substitute for Catalina's frantic existence as a swordsman and gambler, and in 1624 she took ship to Spain.

When she landed in Cadiz, she was greeted like a hero. She travelled on to Rome, where writer Pietro Della Valle was introduced to the Ensign Nun. He recalled that she was: 'tall and sturdy of stature, masculine in appearance, she has no more bosom than a little girl. She told me that she had applied I don't know what method to make it disappear. I believe it was a plaster administered by an Italian; the effect was painful but much to her liking. She is not bad looking, but well worn by the years. She has the look of a Spanish gentleman and wears her sword as big as life, tightly belted. Only by her hands can one tell that she is a woman as they are full and fleshy, although large and strong, and occasionally gesture effeminately.'

> **' ... tall and sturdy of stature, masculine in appearance, she has no more bosom than a little girl.'**
>
> Pietro Della Valle on meeting Catalina

Catalina's European trip was attended by the usual misadventures. She was arrested in both France and Italy, but still successfully petitioned King Philip for a pension in recognition of her military service in the New World. Sheer curiosity prompted Pope Urban VIII to grant her an audience and a dispensation allowing her to continue to wear male clothing.

In 1630 she returned to Mexico, where she collected the pension, and later founded a mule-train business plying between Mexico City and Veracruz. By now, she was styling herself Don Antonio Erauso. A Capuchin monk who saw her in Veracruz in 1645 noted: 'She went about in male clothing and carried a sword and dagger decorated in silver; she then seemed about fifty years of age, with a dusky olive complexion, with a few little hairs for a moustache.'

Catalina had not entirely mended her ways. She later became infatuated with a young woman whom she escorted to a convent in Mexico City. When the object of her affection married a *hidalgo*, Erauso continued calling, much to the displeasure of the new husband, who barred her from their house. Inevitably, Erauso responded by challenging him to a duel. The husband, doubtless mindful of his rival's reputation, had the good sense to decline.

They later became reconciled, and Erauso even came to his aid when he fell into a fight with three men. Her remarkable life has been the subject of many books, several films and, in 2010, a play performed in Los Angeles. The bringer of death and celebrant of a life fully if not always wisely lived, the Ensign Nun still has the power to excite the modern imagination.

A man who for nearly half a century fooled the world into thinking he was a woman, the Chevalier d'Eon is, not surprisingly, the patron saint of transvestites. He was born in Burgundy, the son of a noble family, and as a young man was described as: 'small and slight in build, with a high-pitched voice, delicately cut features and singularly smooth skin which emphasized the beardlessness of his face.'

In 1756 he joined the *Secret du Roi* ('The King's Secret'), an intelligence network that reported directly to Louis XV, and was despatched to the court of the Russian empress Elizabeth I. The envoy assumed the identity of Mademoiselle Lia de Beaumont and began to ingratiate himself with the St Petersburg court – the European upper classes at the time were fascinated by the notion of men and women assuming opposite roles for society events. By the time d'Eon returned to France, diplomatic ties with Russia had been restored.

He subsequently undertook a similar mission to the Empress Maria Theresa of Austria and was commissioned as a captain of dragoons. In 1762 d'Eon saw action in the closing exchanges of the Seven Years' War between France and Britain. In 1763 he was despatched to London as France's plenipotentiary minister, suing for peace with the British while simultaneously gathering intelligence for a French invasion plan that Louis was considering. D'Eon was then appointed Chevalier, which entitled him to wear the Cross of St Louis.

On his recall to France, d'Eon decided to remain in England and settled down to live in London, where he assembled a vast library. In 1770 rumours – possibly fanned by d'Eon himself – began to circulate that in spite of his dragoon's uniform and markedly masculine manner he was a woman. The question mark over his

CHARLES D'EON DE BEAUMONT
1728–1810

gender became the talk of London's coffee-house gossip, inspired a play, *The Female Chevalier*, and became the stuff of bawdy cartoons.

Louis XVI, who had ascended to the French throne in 1774, agreed to settle the Chevalier's debts on the condition that he returned to France and lived as a woman. The Chevalier agreed, but protested by sporting black dresses and stubble. When he rebelled and donned his dragoon's uniform for an audience at Versailles, he was sharply reminded of his undertaking and ordered to don female attire.

He returned to England in 1785 on the understanding that he would continue to wear women's clothes. To make ends meet, he undertook fencing bouts for money while wearing petticoats. The Chevalier attracted the admiration of the feminist Mary Wollstonecraft, who considered him a fellow pioneer with a unique perspective on the roles of the sexes. In 1792 he wrote in vain to the French National Assembly volunteering to raise and lead a regiment of women in the war against Austria.

After his death, a postmortem examination confirmed his masculinity, something of a shock to his last companion, a Mrs Cole, who had never doubted for a moment that her companion was a woman. D'Eon had once written: 'God created man and woman, the one for doing, the other for doing bad. So long as a man is a man, the Earth is his; so long as a woman is a woman, virtue is hers.'

A contemporary mezzotint of the diplomat Beaumont sporting women's clothes.

Around 1634, Sir John Bankes, Chief Justice of the Common Pleas and a privy councillor to Charles I, and husband of Lady Mary Bankes, acquired Corfe Castle, a strategic strongpoint near the Dorset coast in southwest England, which was considered one of 'the impregnable forts of England'. Situated on a commanding hill with a clear view of the surrounding countryside, the castle had been a royal residence for several centuries. Behind its massive walls, the castle boasted a rich interior. Its rooms were decorated with gilded green leather, damask hangings, crimson velvets and rugs from the Middle East.

Lady Mary Bankes
1598–1661

When the English Civil War broke out in 1642, Sir John rallied to the Royalist cause, joining Charles I in York and leaving his wife Lady Mary in charge of the castle, which was surrounded by a population sympathetic to the Parliamentarians. A contemporary portrait of Lady Mary shows a handsome, determined woman clutching the keys of Corfe Castle firmly in her hand. Characteristically, she laid in provisions, kept the gates of the castle locked, resisted demands by the local Parliamentary committee to surrender her home, and faced an uncertain future with firm resolve. The only armaments within the castle were four small cannon served by just five men.

In May 1643 commissioners arrived from Poole, now in Parliamentary hands, to demand the surrender of the castle's cannon. Lady Bankes was unfazed, calling on the five men left in the castle, and her maidservants, to mount the cannon on their carriages and open fire on the Parliamentary delegation, which fell back on Poole empty-handed. Lady Bankes then used the breathing space she had thus gained to secure a larger garrison of some 50 men detached from a force commanded by the Royalist Prince Maurice of Nassau.

However, many of Lady Bankes's neighbours lacked the stomach for a fight. Another delegation arrived at Corfe Castle, weeping and wringing their hands and begging: 'their husbands to come home and not by saving others to expose their own houses to spoil and ruin.' With great reluctance Lady Bankes said goodbye to her cannon. Nevertheless, their departure enabled her to revictual her stronghold while she prepared for a siege.

The redoubtable Lady Mary Bankes holding the keys of Corfe Castle, in a contemporary miniature portrait by Henry Bone.

The siege began on 23 June 1643 and climaxed with an all-out assault on the castle, in which the 600 attackers were reinforced by a rabble of sailors inflamed with drink, and criminals released from local prisons.

Commanding this egregious force was Sir Walter Erle, a notably eccentric soldier who wore a bulky bearskin coat to counter musket shot. Not without reason, Erle had little faith in the men under his command, and resorted to bribing them with hopes of: ' ... rich booty and the like; so during the siege they used all base unworthy means to corrupt the defendants to betray the castle unto their hands; the better sort they endeavour to corrupt with bribes, to the rest they offer double pay and the whole plunder of the castle.'

A more practical measure was Erle's employment of two siege engines, named the 'Sowe' and the 'Boare', to reduce the castle. The 'Sowe', some 10 metres (35 ft) long and 3 metres (10 ft) wide, was made of solid oak logs held together by iron hoops. Mounted on four huge wheels, it had in the spelling of the time 'cros beames within to worck with there levars, to forse har along thaie pleased to guide har'. The 'Sowe's' top timbers were covered with 'two rowes of hides and two rowes of sheep skinnes; so that noe musket bullet or steele arrow could pierce it, of which triell was often made'. The 'Boare' was of similar design, but smaller and marginally more manoeuvrable. These elaborate and unwieldy engines of war proved to be quite useless as the defenders on the walls peppered their crews' legs with shot, producing predictable results: ' ... nine ran away, as well as their broken and battered legs would give them leave, and of the two which knew neither how to run away nor well to stay, for feare one was slaine.'

Lady Bankes and her daughters took part in the defence of the upper ward of the castle, heaving stones and hot embers on the besiegers below. The defence held, and the siege was abandoned by Erle on hearing rumours of an approaching Royalist relief force. Sir John Bankes died in December 1644 and in 1645, after the Royalist defeat at the Battle of Naseby, Corfe Castle came under siege for the second time by a substantial Parliamentary force of two regiments of foot and one of horse.

After Corfe Castle finally fell to Parliamentary forces in 1646, it was destroyed by explosives and undermining to ensure it could never be used as a Royalist stronghold again.

Lyme (later Lyme Regis) on the Dorset coast is described in Camden's *Britannia* (1610) as 'a little town situated on a steep hill … which scarcely may challenge the name of a Port or Haven town, though it be frequented by fishermen' being 'sufficiently defended from the force of winds with rocks and high trees'.

In the early phases of the Civil War, in April 1643, the Royalists considered the capture of Lyme as no more than 'breakfast work … they would not dine until they had taken it'. In the event, they had a long wait. The little town was stoutly defended by about 1,000 men whose blood coloured their water supply a rusty brown. The town was bombarded from the sea by warships while the besiegers fired clouds of fire arrows on to Lyme's defences. A maid lost her hand while carrying a fire bucket to douse the conflagration and another woman was killed while hanging out clothes to dry.

The townswomen filled the soldiers' bandoliers as they fought, and acted as look-outs, particularly at night, as was recorded by a local clergyman, James Strong, who had been educated at Wadham College, Oxford. His long 1645 poem 'Joanereidos' was dedicated to the 'Feminine Valour Eminently Discovered in Westerrne Women':

Alas! Who now keeps Lime? Poor female cattell
Who wake all night, labour all day in Battle
And by their seasonable noise discover
Our foes, when the works are climbing over

After the siege was raised in June, the women of Lyme fell upon the abandoned Royalist earthworks and within a week had levelled them with spades and mattocks. In 1645 Parliament set aside £200 a week for the relief of the widows and children of Lyme, which gained its royal designation following the escape of Charles II after the Battle of Worcester (1651).

Corfe was now the only garrison between Exeter and London to hold out for the Royalist cause. The resourceful Lady Bankes remained defiant until February 1646, when she was betrayed by one of her officers, Lieutenant-Colonel Pitman, who had left Corfe Castle to gather more reinforcements, but returned instead with a band of Parliamentarians masquerading as Royalists. Once introduced to Corfe, this 'Trojan horse' quickly overcame its garrison.

The gallant Lady Bankes and her daughters were allowed to leave Corfe in safety, although the castle's handsome furnishings were ransacked by the Parliamentarians and its fortifications demolished. It is a measure of Lady Bankes's strength of character that she died on the day of the wedding of her son Sir Ralph Bankes, having successfully concealed from him the fact that she was grievously ill. In the Ruislip church where she is buried, a tablet records that she: 'had the honour to have borne with a constancy and courage above her sex a noble proportion of the late Calamities.'

In 1661 Lady Bankes's bumbling tormentor, Sir Walter Erle, wrote plaintively to Ralph Bankes about the pillaging of Corfe Castle: 'And when the spoil was made, and the materials were carried away, I never gave any direction by letter or otherwise for bringing any part of its to my house, nor knew any such thing done more than the child unborn, until a good while after, coming down into the country, I found some part thereof among other things remaining of the ruine of my own house, laid by for future use.'

The warrior women of Dahomey, an ancient kingdom in West Africa and present-day Benin, first came to the attention of European travellers in the late 16th century. A German book of 1598, Vera Descriptio Regni Africani, describes an African royal court whose palace guard consisted of women, and similar royal formations were found elsewhere in the world from ancient times, particularly in the East. The kings of ancient Persia had female bodyguards, as did a prince of Java. As late as the 19th century, the king of Siam was guarded by a battalion of 400 women. They were said to perform drills better than male soldiers and were crack spear-throwers.

Warrior Women
of Dahomey
1600–1900

Women were often regarded as more loyal and trustworthy than men, as they were less likely to be bribed or suborned, and many rulers preferred female bodyguards for this reason, just as the king of Jordan and the sultan of Oman chose women as their personal pilots in the 20th century.

The women of Dahomey outdid them all. Over 250 years after publication of *Descriptio Regni Africani*, we encounter them again in the high summer of the British empire when the British general Sir Garnet Wolsey, recounting his successful campaign against the Ashanti, compared his energetic and disciplined Fanti female porters to the king of Dahomey's 'corps of Amazons'.

Accounts of Dahomey by 18th-century European merchants and slave traders – slavery was the basis of the kingdom's wealth – paint a picture of a colourful feudal world whose kings were surrounded by hundreds of serving girls and guarded by armed women. Dahomey's nobility aped the royal retinue to the extent that the kingdom's lower-class males were faced with a shrunken marriage market and forced into the more accessible arms of prostitutes. One of Dahomey's kings, Bossa Ahadee, would march in ceremonial procession accompanied by several hundred wives, surrounded by female messengers and slaves, and escorted by a 120-strong male guard armed with blunderbusses and 90 women under arms.

The presence of the armed women was, at this stage in Dahomey's history, more of a symbol than a real threat to Dahomey's neighbours. The tables were turned, however, when one of them, the king of Oyo, took to

Armed women of Dahomey go to war, with the king at their head, in this print of 1793. One of the functions of the armed female element of the court, all of whom were recruited in their early teenage years, seems to have been the capture and execution of women from rival tribes.

the field against the Dahomeans with a raiding party of 800 women to enforce a claim of female tribute he had levelled against King Adahoonzou. It was left to the all-male Dahomean army to defeat the Oyan Amazons.

An account of King Adahoonzou's funeral in April 1798 claims that: 'five hundred and ninety-five women were murdered by their companions on this occasion and sent, according to the notion that prevails in this unhappy country, to attend Adanhoonzou in the other world.'

By the time of King Ghezo, Dahomey's royal court consisted of some 8,000 people, the majority of them women, many of whom existed in a minutely graded pyramid of concubinage, at the top of which were the so-called 'Wives of the Leopard', the women who bore the ruler's children. All the women warriors carried giant folding razors, with blades over 0.6 metres (2 ft) long, which were apparently used to decapitate female enemies and castrate male foes. Ghezo, a usurper who always had to watch his back, told a visiting Englishman, Captain William Winnier, that he could trust women better than men. Unlike men, they could be confined to the royal palace, thus becoming completely dependent on him.

'Let's march together like men.'

CHANT OF THE DAHOMEY 'AMAZONS'

From the late 1830s, Ghezo seems to have used members of his predominantly female court in battle against neighbouring tribes. It is possible that he deployed 4,000 female warriors, in an army totalling 16,000. When in 1851 he laid siege to the city of Abeokuta, the siege was repulsed with losses of some 3,000, of whom two-thirds were women. A French account of the engagement describes their officers standing in the front line 'recognisable by the riches of their dress' and carrying themselves with 'a proud and resolute air'. Nevertheless, these women warriors occupied an inferior and ambivalent position in the hierarchy of the Dahomean court and, significantly, referred to themselves as men in their war cries and battle chants. In one of the chants, they celebrated themselves as 'strong men, very strong with muscular busts'. Another urged: 'Let's march together like men.' In yet another they proclaimed: 'we are men not women.'

Far from discouraging Ghezo, the setback at Abeokuta spurred him on to include more women in his army. They seem to have been divided into a regular corps of well-trained and highly disciplined 'Amazons' armed with muskets and machete-like swords, who also formed an élite personal bodyguard, and a rather less satisfactory reserve, armed with cutlasses, clubs and bows and arrows, who were more interested in rum than rigorous military discipline. In peacetime the 'Amazon' corps was wholly segregated from men, and outside the confines of the royal palace, its approach was signalled by the ringing of bells, upon which civilians had to turn their backs, and males had to move away.

In spite of their fearsome reputation, the 'Amazons' were no match for small but well-armed and disciplined colonial armies. In 1892 the French

There were several practical reasons for Ghezo's use of women in battle. Dahomey was exceptionally warlike and lost many men on campaign, while simultaneously depending for its wealth on a slave trade that favoured the disposal to slavers of a large proportion of its able-bodied male population. At its peak strength in the early 1860s, the Dahomean army was approximately 50,000 strong – one fifth of the total population – of which the female element numbered 10,000, a quarter of their number consisting of the feared 'Amazons'.

It has been suggested that many of the women, as well as some of the men in the Dahomean army, went to war as camp followers, much in the manner of the *soldaderas* who marched with Mexican armies in the 19th and early 20th centuries. The Victorian explorer Sir Richard Burton, who saw them in 1863, likewise poured derision on the 'fighting Amazons'. 'Mostly elderly and all of them hideous', he ruminated with all the arrogance of the

KING GHEZO

European white male, 'the officers decidedly chosen for the size of their bottoms ... they manoeuvre with all the precision of a flock of sheep'. Nevertheless, Burton also noticed that the army, then some 2,500 strong, was well armed and effective in battle. Nor could all of them have been old and hideous, since all 2,500 were official wives of the king.

In a series of battles in 1892, the French beat the 'Amazons' of the Dahomean King Behanzin (below) and annexed the kingdom as a colony of France.

easily overran Dahomey. The French commander, a mulatto by the name of Alfred Dodds, praised the 'Amazons' for their speed and boldness. Their king, Behanzin, was driven into exile, first in Martinique and later Algeria. A puppet ruler, Agoli-agbo, was installed and allowed a few token women in his bodyguard. At the 1889 World's Fair in Paris, a troupe of Dahomean 'Amazons' danced and drilled under the newly erected Eiffel Tower.

One of the most celebrated of Britain's female soldiers who masqueraded as men, Snell ended her remarkable life in Bethlehem Hospital, London's notorious lunatic asylum, better known as Bedlam.

Hannah Snell
1723–92

Hannah was the daughter of a Worcester hosier and the grand-daughter of a regular soldier, Samuel Snell, a Welsh Fusilier who had fought under the duke of Marlborough at Blenheim and Malplaquet and had eventually died of his wounds. Orphaned at the age of 17, she went to London to live with her half-sister Susannah Gray in Wapping, London. In 1743 she married a Dutch sailor, James Summs, who deserted her the next year when she was heavily pregnant. After the death of her child, Snell decided to pursue the feckless Summs while posing as a man in clothes borrowed from her brother-in-law.

Snell's subterfuge proved all too convincing. She was 'pressed' (forcibly enlisted) into the British army in Coventry and, according to her own account, obliged to march with a foot regiment in pursuit of the retreating army of the failed pretender to the British throne, Charles Stuart, 'Bonnie Prince Charlie'. In Carlisle Snell fell foul of a sergeant who invited her to join him in the seduction of a young woman. She chose to warn the woman of the sergeant's intentions, and for this 'betrayal' found herself charged with gross neglect of duty and sentenced to 400 lashes.

This was an extremely severe punishment. In the Napoleonic Wars, some 50 years later, the maximum number of lashes that could be administered in the duke of Wellington's army was set at 1,200, sufficient to permanently disable a man. One soldier was sentenced to 400 lashes, but was let off after 175 before being hospitalized for three weeks. The historian Charles Oman observed: 'If anything was calculated to brutalize an army it was the wicked cruelty of the British military punishment code, which Wellington to the end of his life supported. There is plenty of authority for the fact that the man who had once received his 500 lashes for a fault which was small, or which involved no moral guilt, was often turned thereby from a good soldier into a bad soldier, by losing his self-respect and having his sense of justice seared out.'

If Snell is to be believed, she nevertheless survived the lashing without revealing her sex – a highly improbable feat – while displaying such stoicism that the officer supervising the punishment ordered it to be stopped after 300 strokes had been administered. Shortly afterwards, Snell deserted when a recruit, George Beck, who had known her in Wapping, joined her unit. She stole some clothes and made her way to Portsmouth, where she joined a regiment of Marines under the name of James Gray. This episode is more likely to have marked the start of her military career rather than her service in the regiment of foot in the campaign against the Young Pretender which, in all likelihood, was a fabrication.

Shortly afterwards Snell's unit embarked on the warship HMS *Swallow*, bound for the East Indies on an expedition commanded by Admiral Boscawen. Having rounded the Cape of Good Hope, the admiral declined to attack the French island of Mauritius, but pressed on to India. In August 1748 Snell went into action against French troops on the coast of Madras at Pondicherry. Nearly a year later she fought in the Battle of Devicotta, where she was badly wounded in the legs and groin. Surgeons removed the musket balls from her legs, but Snell did not reveal that another ball was lodged in her groin. To avoid discovery, she: 'communicated her design to a black woman who waited on her, and who could get at the surgeon's medicines and desired her assistance, and her pain being so very great that she was unable to endure it much longer, she intended to try and

Hannah Snell, who lived as James Gray, one of Britain's many distinguished female soldiers. This engraving of her in her prime was made by G. Scott in 1804.

experiment on herself, which was to endeavour to extract the ball out of that wound … !

Snell was taking an enormous risk. She probed the wound with her finger: ' … till she came to where the ball lay, and then upon feeling it thrust in her finger and thumb and pulled it out. This was a very rough way of proceeding with one's own flesh, but of the two evils as she thought, this was the least, so rather choosing to have her flesh tore and mangled rather than have her sex discovered … she made a perfect cure of the dangerous wound.'

After three months in hospital, Snell was discharged and enrolled as a deckhand on a man-of-war, HMS *Eltham*. She was soon in trouble and, once again, sentenced to lashes, although this time it was only 12. On the return

ANNE BAILEY
1742–1825

A frontier legend, 'Mad Anne' Bailey was a short, stout, whisky-loving woman who wielded a tomahawk and chewed tobacco. After a career as a scout in the American Revolutionary War, she spent the later years of her life roaming the frontier in Ohio and Virginia.

She was born in Liverpool, England, in 1742 and emigrated to America when she was 19, where it is thought she became an indentured servant. In 1765 she married a frontiersman, Richard Trotter, and settled in the Allegheny Mountains. Trotter joined the border militia, and in October 1774 was killed in a skirmish with Native Americans at Point Pleasant, West Virginia.

Vowing to avenge the death of her husband, Anne Trotter wore buckskins under her petticoats, taught herself how to shoot, and volunteered as a scout in the War of American Independence. She became a familiar figure between Fort Randolph at Point Pleasant and Fort Savannah (now Lewisburg), acting as a scout and messenger, and in 1785 married the frontier scout John Bailey.

In 1788 she accompanied him to Fort Clenendin, established on the site of present-day Charleston. It was from this outpost in 1791 that Anne Bailey volunteered to ride 100 miles (160 km) through wild country to Fort Savannah to warn its garrison of an impending Native American attack, and to request fresh supplies of gunpowder.

Spurning the offer of an escort for the return journey, she returned with the gunpowder, carried on an extra horse, and the Native American assault was repelled. In recognition of her bravery, the men at Fort Clenendin presented her with the horse on which she had made her daring ride and which she named 'Liverpool' in honour of her birthplace.

After the death of her second husband in 1794, Anne led a peripatetic frontier life in the wilderness for 20 years, delivering coffee, gunpowder and cooking utensils to remote settlements. In 1817, at the age of 75, she made her last trip to Charleston, walking all the way. Her restless wandering finally ceased when she was installed in a log cabin near her son's home in Ohio.

Anne's famous ride to Fort Savannah was commemorated in a poem of 1861:

She heeded not the danger rife,
But rode as one who rides for life;
Still onwards in her course she bore,
Along the dark Kanwha's shore,
Through the tangled wood and rocky way,
Nor paused to rest at close of day.

Contemporary sketch of the hardy frontierswoman Anne Bailey.

journey to England the *Eltham* docked at Lisbon, where Snell received the discouraging news that her errant husband was long dead, executed for murder in Genoa.

Once ashore again in England, Snell seized the opportunity to tell her shipmates that she was a woman. She announced to her dumbfounded comrades: 'Gentlemen, you will never see your friend and fellow soldier, James Gray any more. Why Gentlemen, James Gray will, before we part, cast his skin like a snake and become a new creature. I am as much a woman as ever my mother was, and my name is Hannah Snell.'

Snell was honourably discharged and briefly became the toast of London, appearing on the stage of the Royalty Theatre, clad in male attire in episodes recounting her colourful career. A contemporary newspaper noted that: 'in a most masterly and correct manner she went through the manual of platoon exercises etc and sang several songs of a lively and diverting character.' A verse from one of songs runs:

In the midst of blood and slaughter,
Bravely fighting for my King,
Facing death from every quarter
Fame and conquest home to bring.
Sure, you'll own 'tis more than common,
And the world proclaim it too,
Never yet did any woman
More for love and glory do!

Prudently, Snell also presented a petition to the duke of Cumberland, commander-in-chief of the British army, requesting financial compensation for her service in the armed forces. In 1750 the Royal Hospital in Chelsea granted Snell a pension of a shilling a day, which in 1785 was increased. After her triumphs on the London stage and the publication of her memoirs *The Female Soldier,* Snell opened a public house in Wapping, called 'The Widow in Masquerade' or 'The Female Warrior'. Over the door hung a sign showing Snell half-dressed as a Marine and half-dressed in regimentals. The bold landlady promised her customers that the Widow in Masquerade would sell 'strong liquors at the lowest prices' and often appeared in the bar sporting male attire.

Within a few years the pub venture had foundered, and by the mid-1750s she was living in Newbury, Berkshire. Here in 1759 she married one Richard Eyles, with whom she had two children. Another marriage, to Richard Habgood, followed in 1772, and the couple moved to the Midlands. By 1785 she was back in London, living in Stoke Newington with her son. But Snell eventually fell on hard times and in 1791 she was admitted to the Bethlehem Hospital for the insane, popularly known as Bedlam, where she died six months later. She was buried in the grounds of Chelsea Hospital, a fitting final resting place for an old soldier.

The quintessential enlightened despot, Catherine was the ultimate small-town girl made good, a royal version of Becky Sharp, the anti-heroine of William Thackeray's novel Vanity Fair. The wars she waged took up only six years of her 34-year reign, but nearly doubled the population of Russia. She once cannily observed: 'We need population, not devastation. Peace is necessary to this vast empire.'

Catherine II
1729–96

Catherine was born Princess Sophia Augusta Frederika of Anhalt-Zerbst, in Stettin, now Szczecin, in modern Poland. Aged 15, she visited Russia, where her marriage was arranged to the 16-year-old Grand Duke Peter, after her formal conversion from the Lutheran faith to Russian Orthodoxy in 1745. The marriage was unsuccessful, and was not consummated for nine years because of Peter's impotence and mental immaturity.

Peter succeeded to the throne as Tsar Peter III at the beginning of 1762, but his eccentricities and the huge unpopularity of his pro-German policies led to his overthrow six months later by his own guardsmen, who then proclaimed Catherine their empress. Peter was imprisoned and later killed – supposedly accidentally – by Alexei Orlov, younger brother of Grigori Orlov, one of Catherine's many lovers.

The short, stout Catherine was gallantly but inaccurately characterized by William Richardson, the tutor to the children of the British ambassador, as 'taller than middle-sized, gracefully formed, but inclined to corpulence'. Richardson went on to confess: 'With regard to her appearance altogether, it would be doing her injustice to say that she was masculine, yet it would not be doing her justice to say it was entirely feminine.' Certainly, Catherine had a masculine cast of mind, a quality she noted in her memoirs. To the deeply conservative Russian nobility, she was seen as a prime example of the monstrous regiment of women and a threat to the traditional morals of 'Mother Russia'.

Presenting herself as an enlightened ruler, a 'philosopher on the throne', Catherine corresponded with the French writers and thinkers known as the 'Encyclopedists' and the philosopher Voltaire, who dubbed her 'the Star of the North'. With great drive, she initiated an ambitious but uncompleted programme to reform the laws, education and administration of Russia. Yet by the end of her reign, the powerful nobility was even more entrenched than when she had taken power. And despite making her capital St Petersburg a vibrant cultural centre, all intellectual dissent was stifled.

Portrait of Catherine II of Russia by Dmitri Levitzky (1794). Shrewd and adaptable, she took pains to assimilate herself into her adopted country. Under her energetic reign, the boundaries of the Russian empire were greatly expanded.

The only female ruler in the long history of the Habsburg dynasty, the Empress Maria Theresa achieved a remarkable success in binding together the diverse elements of the Habsburg empire. However, she had the misfortune to take on Frederick II of Prussia ('Frederick the Great') when he was at the height of his military powers.

In 1736 Maria Theresa underwent a marriage arranged by her father, the Holy Roman Emperor Charles VI, to Francis Stephen, the son of the duke of Lorraine. Unexpectedly, this marriage of convenience blossomed into a love match and the couple had 16 children, ten of whom survived to adulthood, including Marie Antoinette, the ill-fated future queen of France.

On her father's death, the 23-year-old Maria Theresa, then pregnant with her fourth child, immediately took control. Where she had once been impetuous and frivolous, she was now stern and autocratic. Her husband took a back seat, performing an essentially secretarial role in their marriage. In 1745 Maria Theresa ensured that he was elected Holy Roman Emperor.

By then she had become engaged in a five-year struggle to save her inheritance from Frederick II of Prussia, who fielded a well-trained and superbly equipped army. In 1740 he invaded and overran Silesia, a Habsburg possession, thus instigating the War of the Austrian Succession (1740–48), a conflict that eventually drew in most of the great powers of Europe.

Maria Theresa was obliged to cede most of Silesia to Prussia in a treaty signed at Breslau on 11 June 1742. The war was concluded in 1748 by the Treaty of Aix-La-Chappelle, which, apart from the loss of Silesia, confirmed Maria Theresa in possession of all the Habsburg lands she had held in 1739.

In 1756 Maria Theresa felt that Austria was sufficiently strong to reopen hostilities with Frederick II. She prepared the ground by securing alliances with France and Russia, but was the victim of a pre-emptive strike when Frederick II moved first, invading one of Austria's allies, Saxony, in the first campaign of what became known as the Seven Years' War. The conflict was concluded with the Treaty of Hubertusberg (1763) in which Maria Theresa conceded possession of Silesia to Prussia. This signalled the end of her military career.

Engraving of Maria Theresa on horseback by Martin Engelbrecht (c.1745).

In foreign policy, Catherine was an ambitious expansionist. She extended the borders of the Russian empire westward and southward at the expense of two rival powers, the Polish-Lithuanian Commonwealth and the Ottoman empire. Voltaire was a keen supporter of her wars against the Turks, chiefly on the grounds that Catherine's adversaries did not speak French. In November 1768, a month after she had gone to war against the Ottoman empire, Voltaire wrote to Catherine: 'Clearly, people who neglect all the fine arts and who lock up women deserve to be exterminated.'

Victory in the first Russo-Turkish War (1768–74) gave Russia access to the Black Sea and to vast tracts of land in what is now southern Ukraine, where the new city of Odessa was founded. In 1783 Catherine annexed the Crimea, which nine years earlier had gained independence from the Ottoman empire. She attended the twice-weekly war councils at which the campaign was planned and in all probability was the originator of the daring indirect strategy in which the Russian Baltic Fleet sailed 5,000 miles (8,000 km) round the coasts of Europe to engage the Ottomans. In 1787 the Turks launched a catastrophic second war, which ended in 1792 with the Treaty of Jassy and the legitimization of the Russian claim to the Crimea. However, the ambition she nursed to seize Constantinople was unrealized.

Catherine also established herself as a formidable power broker with the nations of Western Europe and acted as a mediator in the War of the Bavarian Succession (1778–79) between Prussia and Austria. In 1780, mindful of her enlightened image, she refused to intervene in the American Revolution in support of the British. In the Russo-Swedish War of 1788–90, she thwarted Swedish designs on St Petersburg. The grounds of the imperial palace at Tsarskoe Selo were littered with columns and obelisks marking her military victories – all 78 of them.

> *'Clearly, people who neglect all the fine arts and who lock up women deserve to be exterminated.'*
>
> VOLTAIRE

During her long reign, Catherine greatly enjoyed recreational sex and took many lovers, the last of whom, Prince Zubov, was 40 years her junior. She was domineering but notably generous with her lovers, although she was a harsh mother to her son Paul, who was kept in a state of house arrest and denied any independent authority. To the end of her life, she remained supremely self-aware of her image. When she consolidated the *coup d'état* of 1762 in which her husband was overthrown, she borrowed the green and red uniform of a suitably small lieutenant in the Semeonovsky regiment to create an iconic symbol, and throughout her life remained extremely conscious of every nuance of her appearance as a public figure. Sometimes she was military and masculine; at other times she was noted as greeting a delegation of French diplomats like 'a charming lady on her country estate', an effect that was minutely choreographed to linger in her visitors' memories. Her own memoirs were written in different versions for different readers and allies.

Catherine suffered a stroke while taking a bath in November 1796 and died on the following day. She was buried at the Peter and Paul Cathedral in St Petersburg. Palace intrigue ensured that a scurrilous fiction about the details of her death quickly gained circulation and has survived to this day. She is supposed to have expired in the throes of being serviced by a stallion, a cautionary myth that clearly reveals the depths of fear, loathing and incomprehension that attend any powerful woman of abundant sexual appetite.

A water-bearer to the troops in one of the hardest-fought battles of the American War of Independence (1775–83) 'Molly Pitcher' became the stuff of legend when she took the place of a fallen artilleryman, her husband, and kept on fighting. Her story abounds in vivid detail, including a meeting with George Washington, but historians have questioned whether her popular image owes more to fiction than fact.

Molly Pitcher
1754–1832

The woman with whom Molly Pitcher is identified was born Mary Ludwig to German immigrants in New Jersey on 13 October 1754. The young Ludwig moved to the Pennsylvania town of Carlisle, where she became a servant to Dr William Irvine, later a brigadier-general in the Colonial army. Her first husband, John Hays, enlisted in the Pennsylvania Artillery in 1775 when the Revolutionary war broke out, and she was soon permitted to join him in the field, as many wives did at the time.

The Battle of Monmouth took place on 28 June 1778, one of the hottest days ever known on the east coast of the US. Mary earned her nickname by returning to the battle lines again and again with pitchers of water for her husband and his fellow soldiers: 'Molly' was a common form of 'Mary', and 'Pitcher' commemorated the welcome sight of the water arriving for the hard-pressed men. When Hays, now a sergeant of artillery, was knocked unconscious in the bombardment, Molly came forward and seized the rammer staff from his hands. She kept the cannon firing for the remainder of the battle, and continued to fight until the close of day.

Other legends grew up around 'Molly's' service. While tending the wounded, she is supposed to have carried a crippled soldier 'on her strong, young back' out of reach of a furious British charge. Another soldier, Joseph Plumb Martin of Connecticut, recounted this sexually-tinted story of her coolness under fire: 'While in the act of reaching for a cartridge, a cannon shot from the enemy passed directly between her legs without doing any other damage than carrying away all the lower part of her petticoat. Looking at it with apparent unconcern, she observed that it was lucky it did not pass a little higher, for in that case it might have carried away something else.'

Her bravery was rewarded by General George Washington himself, who issued a warrant making her a non-commissioned officer on the spot, resulting in

An engraving, dated 1859, showing 'Molly Pitcher' operating her fallen husband's artillery piece in the Battle of Monmouth. Like many episodes in America's rise to nationhood, the facts of this case have become obscured beneath a patina of much patriotic mythmaking.

another set of nicknames, 'Sergeant' or 'Major' Molly. In some versions of the story, Washington's cameo appearance also involved him presenting her either with a gold coin or a whole hatful of gold. Others provide a spirited dialogue between the lowly camp woman and the commander-in-chief, with Molly speaking in an Irish brogue, while in others she is represented as German, despite being American-born.

After the war Mary and John Hays returned to Carlisle, where he died in 1789. Mary remarried one of her late husband's comrades in arms, a John or George McCauley, but McCauley is said to have treated her like a servant, a fate Mary, now known as Molly, had escaped years before. Release from this unhappy union came when McCauley also died before too long.

But without a male provider, Mary/Molly struggled financially, and she petitioned the US government for relief. Her war service was officially recognized in 1822, when the state legislators of Pennsylvania awarded her a veteran's annuity of $40, which she claimed for the next ten years.

'Molley McKolley', as some sources call her, died in Carlisle on 22 January 1832. Her son by her first husband, John Ludwig Hays, became a soldier and was buried with full military honours when he died about 1853. At the age of 81, John's daughter, Polly McCleester of Papertown, Mt Holly Springs, unveiled a monument to her grandmother, which boldly asserts Mary/Molly's claim to fame: 'MOLLY McCauley, Renowned in history as MOLLY PITCHER, The Heroine of Monmouth, died Jan 1833 [in fact 1832], aged 79 years. Erected by the Citizens of Cumberland County, July 4, 1876.'

Since that date, 'Molly Pitcher' has been firmly identified with Mary Ludwig Hays McCauley. She remains a cherished character of the American Revolution, and an unmarked grave believed to be hers was opened during the centenary events of that year, 1876, and the remains were reburied with honours under a plaque declaring her to have been the embodiment of the famous Molly Pitcher. In reality, it is likely that 'Molly Pitcher' is not one woman, but a composite (see box feature right). A number of women are known to have fought in the War of Independence, and her story draws on many of them. But 'Molly Pitcher' embodies key themes of outstanding courage in time of her nation's greatest need: unswerving loyalty to the newly-emerging American republic, and fearless devotion to her husband. True or not, the legend refuses to die. Mary Ludwig Hays McCauley may not have been the real Molly Pitcher, but she was undoubtedly a rare fighter and exceptionally brave. The $40 a year she was awarded by the State of Pennsylvania was more than the usual war widow's pension granted to all soldiers' wives. The citation published in *The American Volunteer* on 21 February 1822, makes this plain: 'A bill has passed both Houses of the Assembly granting an annuity to Molly McCauley (of Carlisle) for services she rendered during the Revolutionary war.' It appeared satisfactorily that this heroine had braved the hardships of

In Carlisle, the town where Mary Ludwig Hays McCauley was born, where she returned after the war and where she now lies buried, there is no doubt that their Mary was the Molly of the story. But Molly died at least a year earlier than 1833, as her monument in the town records, since the last application for her pension was made in January 1832.

Other problems arise from Mary's extremely common first name, and the frequency of 'Molly' as a variant. The longstanding association of Mary Ludwig Hays McCauley with Molly Pitcher rested on the fact that she was born Mary Ludwig and married a John Hays in Carlisle. This identification with Mary Ludwig was later challenged in favour of another Mary, who married another Hays with another extremely common first name, William. Another woman known as 'Molly Pitcher', described as 'the heroine of Fort Washington' and buried along the Hudson, is a different individual, though frequently confused with the heroine of the Battle of Monmouth.

The confusion arose because Molly Pitcher was not unique. Mary

Ludwig Hays was not the first or only woman to take an artilleryman's place on an American battlefield and to man a field gun. A Margaret Corbin did so during the defence of Fort Washington in 1776, and was possibly the heroine of Fort Washington described here. Corbin was recorded as staying resolutely at her post in the face of heavy enemy fire, ably acting as a matross (gunner). Other women too fought in numerous engagements in the Revolutionary and American Civil Wars (see Deborah Sampson and Harriett Tubman, pages 144–147 and 176–179). Historical sources confirm that at least two women fought in the Battle of Monmouth, one at an artillery position and the other in the infantry line. There is no evidence linking either of them to Mary Ludwig Hays McCauley. And when she died, there was no mention of cannon or the Battle of Monmouth in her obituary.

Bronze statue marking the grave of Mary Hays McCauley in the town of Carlisle, Pennsylvania.

MOLLY
PITCHER

the camp and dangers of the field with her husband, who was a soldier of the revolution, and the bill in her favour passed without a dissenting voice. Note the date; in 1822 veterans of the Battle of Monmouth were still alive to dispute any false claims of heroism, yet her award was unanimously passed. The 'services rendered' by Mary/Molly Ludwig Hays McCauley undoubtedly amounted to something above and beyond the ordinary conditions of war, and her place in history is assured.

A soldier of the American Revolution, Sampson was wounded several times and in 1792 was recompensed by the Massachusetts General Court for service in the United States army, where she 'did actually perform the duty of a soldier ... and exhibited an extraordinary instance of female heroism, by discharging the duties of a faithful, gallant soldier, and at the same time preserving the virtue and chastity of her sex unsuspected and unblemished, and was discharged from the service with a fair and honourable character ... '

Deborah Sampson
1760–1827

Deborah Sampson was born in Plympton, Massachusetts, and was brought up in considerable hardship after her father abandoned his family and went to sea. On her mother's side, her ancestral line stretched back to William Bradford, governor of Plymouth Colony, and her spirited grandmother, Bathsheba Bradford, regaled the young Deborah with tales of Joan of Arc. One of her father's cousins, Captain Simeon Sampson, had been held hostage during the French and Indian Wars (1754–63) and had escaped by dressing as a woman. The captain, however, laughingly rejected the four-year-old Deborah's pleas to allow her to be his cabin boy. Between the ages of 10 and 18 Sampson worked as an indentured servant on the farm of the Thomas family of Middlesborough, and the hard labour this entailed toughened her physically. In her teens she became an expert shot, hunting with her employer's sons, and later worked as a teacher in a public school.

During the War of Independence, the American army found itself desperately short of volunteers, and resorted to offering cash bounties. Sampson was attracted by the appeal and in 1778, enlisted wearing men's clothing pilfered from friends with whom she was staying. She assumed the name of Thomas Thayer, received the bounty, spent most of it in a tavern and missed the regimental roll call the following morning. In

'I considered this as a death wound, or as being the equivalent of it, as it must, I thought, lead to the discovery of my sex.'

DEBORAH SAMPSON, ON BEING WOUNDED DURING A SKIRMISH IN 1782

addition she had been recognized when she enlisted by an old woman who was a neighbour of Benjamin Thomas. Confronted by the authorities, Sampson was relieved of the residue of her bounty and warned that if she attempted to enlist again she would be very severely punished.

In May 1782 Sampson tried again. She made her way on foot to Bellingham, bound her breasts, acquired a new male wardrobe and enlisted successfully. She signed up for three years in the 4th Massachusetts Regiment of the Continental Army as 'Robert Shurtliff', the name of her mother's son, Robert Shurtliff Sampson, who had died at the age of eight.

An unattributed 20th-century painting showing a woman, disguised as a man, at the forefront of a charge during the American Revolution.

Firm-jawed, physically robust and 170 cm (5 ft 7 in) tall, Sampson had no trouble in passing for a man. But the risk of detection remained, particularly while in action. She suffered the first of several wounds in an engagement in East Chester, when her camp was attacked by a detachment of Tories – settlers who remained loyal to the British. She recalled: 'I considered this as a death wound, or as being the equivalent of it, as it must, I thought, lead to the discovery of my sex.' Covered in blood from a head wound, she was carried to the French army hospital at Crompond on a comrade's horse. The doctor who tended her was suspicious, but failed to discover – or was not told by Sampson – that she had sustained other wounds in the thigh, where musket balls had lodged. Sampson subsequently removed one of the balls with a penknife and a sewing needle, but a second was too deep to extract.

Sampson's sex was discovered in 1783 when, joining the forces sent by George Washington to put down a mutiny in Philadelphia, she developed a fever. She was examined in a Philadelphia hospital by a physician, Barnabas Binney, who said nothing, but arranged for Sampson to stay in his house. He remained silent about her sex, nor did he tell his own family that she was a woman.

The War of Independence ended in September 1783 with the signing of the Treaty of Paris. 'Robert Shurtliff' was ordered to the fort at West Point where the 4th Massachussets was about to be disbanded. Sampson took with her a letter, written by Dr Binney to General Patterson, the commander at West Point, which told her story. At first Patterson refused to believe it, but changed his mind when confronted with Sampson in women's clothes. Patterson, too, was discreet enough to keep her secret, thus ensuring that in October 1783 Sampson received an honourable discharge and sufficient money for her journey home.

In April 1785 she married a farmer, Benjamin Gannett, with whom she had three children and adopted an orphan girl. In January 1792 she won the first round in a long legal battle, receiving from the Massachusetts state legislature back pay withheld by the army because she was a woman. The court awarded Sampson £34.

In 1802, dressed in military regalia, Sampson embarked on lecture tours of New England and New

Bronze statue of Deborah Sampson outside the public library in Sharon, Massachusetts.

ANNE SOPHIA DETZLIFFIN
1738–?

Detzliffin was born at Treptow, some 100 miles (160 km) north of Berlin. At the age of 19 she travelled to Colberg disguised as a man and enlisted in the local militia, a form of Home Guard that had been formed at the beginning of the Seven Years' War, when East Prussia was threatened with invasion by Russia.

Six months later she joined a regiment of cuirassiers (heavy cavalry) with whom she served for two years, fighting in several battles and being wounded near Bamberg by a sabre slash to her left arm. She was also in action at Kunersdorf (1759), an engagement in which the Prussians were defeated and suffered heavy casualties.

Detzliffin's regiment returned to Saxony, where she fell ill and was taken to the hospital in Neissen. She recovered and avoided discovery, but was unable to rejoin her regiment as it had been committed to battle elsewhere. Detzliffin then enlisted in a grenadier regiment, shock troops who were required 'not to have an effeminate aspect' and were obliged to sport moustaches. It is not clear how Detzliffin fulfilled the second requirement, but she nevertheless saw action at several engagements. At Torgau on 3 November 1760, she suffered severe head wounds and was captured and hospitalized by the Austrians. Not only did she avoid discovery a second time, but she also escaped from her captors after making a partial recovery, and reached safety.

In 1771 Detzliffin enlisted in a volunteer formation raised by an infamous mercenary, Colonel Colignon. Her ill-disciplined and gun-shy comrades represented a drastic step down from the élite grenadiers; within two months Detzliffin was falsely accused of stealing from another mercenary and placed under arrest. At this point she revealed herself as a woman to her lieutenant, adding for good measure that in all her previous years of service she had never been put on a charge. She was still only 33 at the time. Thereafter she disappeared from history, with not even the date of her death being recorded.

York State, talking about her experiences during the War of Independence. She described her military service before returning to the stage in uniform to demonstrate rifle drill and sing a few songs. Her theatrical career failed to solve her family's money worries, however, so in 1804 her friend Paul Revere, the American revolutionary hero, requested that Congress grant Sampson a military pension: 'I have been induced to enquire her situation, and character, since she quit the male habit and soldier's uniform, for the most decent apparel of her own sex; and obliges me to say, that every person with whom I have conversed about her, and it is not a few, speak of her as a woman with handsome talents, good morals, a dutiful wife, and an affectionate parent.' In March 1805 Congress placed Sampson on the Massachusetts Invalid Pension Roll, paying her four dollars a month.

Revere subsequently proved to be a loyal friend, loaning Sampson money while she petitioned Congress to backdate her pension to the time of her discharge in 1783. Congress held out against her request until 1816, when it approved an annual pension of $76.80. Sampson died at the age of 66 on 29 April 1827 and was buried in Rock Ridge cemetery in the town of Sharon, Massachusetts, where her statue now stands in front of the public library.

Anne-Josèphe Théroigne de Méricourt was the unlikeliest of revolutionaries. A courtesan in her youth, she subsequently became a fiery advocate for women's rights during the French Revolution, before descending into destitution and madness.

Anne-Josèphe Théroigne de Méricourt
1762–1817

Born Anne Terwagne, the child of Belgian peasants, de Méricourt went into domestic service before becoming the companion of an Englishwoman, Mrs Colbert, in 1799. In London she took singing lessons and a series of rich lovers before returning to Paris, where she amassed a fortune as a courtesan and moved in circles where she met influential figures like the comte de Mirabeau and the lawyer Georges Jacques Danton. She travelled to Italy, where she established her reputation as a singer, before returning to Paris in 1789 at the start of the French Revolution to launch herself on a new career as an agitator. She had now reinvented herself as Théroigne de Méricourt, having appropriated and modified the name of her birthplace, Marcourt, a small town in Luxembourg.

On 14 July 1789, the official date of the start of the Revolution, she is said to have played a prominent part in the storming of the Bastille, the medieval fortress in Paris that had become a state prison and was a hated symbol of France's *ancien régime*. However, the story owes much to the 19th-century writer Alphonse Lamartine's account of the Revolution, and in all probability de Méricourt was on the other side of Paris when the Bastille was stormed. Nonetheless, it is clear that the Revolution freed her from emotional dependence on men, and filled her with a passion for the freedom she had never known.

The following October, legend has it that de Méricourt led a march of 6,000 women, many of whom were armed, to the palace of Versailles, where the king and queen were in residence. At the head of the march, de Méricourt rode a horse and wore men's clothing, with pistols in her belt and a sword at her side. There is no doubt de Méricourt set off on the march, but it is unlikely that she was on horseback and leading the column of protesters. The next day Louis XVI and his queen, Marie Antoinette, were driven back to Paris as virtual prisoners. Their carriage was escorted by women carrying pikes upon which were impaled the

Contemporary portrait of Théroigne de Méricourt, whose beauty earned her the sobriquet *la belle Liégeoise* ('the beautiful woman from Liège'). She became a familiar sight on the floor of the Revolutionary Assembly, rousing the mob with her anti-aristocratic harangues.

The storming of the Bastille on 14 July 1789. The writer Alphonse Lamartine fostered the fiction that de Méricourt played a part in this historic event. He also popularized the myth that she took up the revolutionary cause after being jilted by an aristocrat during her days as a courtesan.

heads of royal guards killed in the skirmishing in the precincts of the palace.

A key element of the events of 1789 was the desperate attempt of women to claim legal equality, improved education and better working conditions. De Méricourt was in the vanguard, prowling the Revolutionary Assembly, in a figure-hugging riding habit and posing challenging questions to the women of France: 'Why should we not enter into rivalry with the men? Do they alone lay claim to have rights to glory? No, no ... And we too would wish to earn a civic crown and court the honour of dying for a liberty which is dearer perhaps to us than it is to them, since the effects of despotism weigh still more heavily upon our heads than upon theirs ... let us open a list of French Amazons; and let all who truly love their Fatherland write their names there.'

She also founded a women's club dedicated to the proposition that in the new republic women should have the vote, a point of view that found little favour both among male revolutionaries and royalists. De Méricourt then fled to Belgium, where she attempted to start a revolutionary journal, but was arrested by Austrian agents on suspicion of being involved in a plot on the life of Marie Antoinette, the daughter of an Austrian empress, Maria Theresa.

She eventually found herself imprisoned in Vienna, regaining her freedom in 1792 after an audience with the Emperor Leopold, and returned in triumph to Paris, where she immediately began to agitate for the prosecution by France of an offensive war against the European monarchies. In the summer of 1792 she took part in the storming of the palace of Les Tuileries, where Louis XVI and his family were held, and was personally responsible for the murder of a journalist who had lampooned her. When the scribbler was pointed out to her, de Méricourt propelled him into the clutches of the enraged Paris mob, who stabbed the hapless hack to death.

As the Revolution descended into bitter factional infighting, de Méricourt backed the wrong horse, the moderate republican Girondists, who in 1793 were ousted from power by the radical Jacobins. In May 1793 she was cornered in the Tuileries gardens by a mob of Jacobin women, who stripped her naked and whipped her. She was rescued by a member of the Revolutionary government, Jean-Paul Marat, but he was unable to save her from the slew of scurrilous cartoons that appeared immediately after the incident and showed de Méricourt receiving her whipping, her naked buttocks criss-crossed with savage stripes.

De Méricourt never recovered from this rough revolutionary justice, and within a year had lost her mind. In 1800 she was taken to an asylum in a state of mania and was confined naked, caked in her own excrement and chained to the wall. Historians have often used de Méricourt's life as a metaphor for the French Revolution, because it had flared so briefly and brightly before burning itself out. She was not always on the spot at many key points in the Revolution, but because she cut so striking and symbolic a figure, people subsequently wanted her to have been there.

RENÉE BORDEREAU
1766–1824

The most famous of the female soldiers who fought against the French Revolution of 1789–93 was Renée Bordereau, commonly known as *L'Angevin*, after her birthplace near the town of Angers.

When the Revolution swept through France, Paris and much of the country rejoiced at the overthrow of King Louis XVI and his queen, the hated Marie Antoinette. But the Vendée, a poor region in western France, remained deeply conservative and monarchist, and therefore intensely hostile to the Revolution and its aftermath. Facing war abroad, the revolutionary government introduced conscription in 1793, a measure deeply resented by the inhabitants of the Vendée, who rose in revolt.

While the revolutionary government was distracted by bouts of rioting from Marseilles to Normandy, the nobility of the Vendée joined forces with a 30,000-strong 'Catholic and Royal Army' of poorly armed peasants, later renamed the *Grande Armée*. After seizing a number of towns, including Saumur, the rebels planned to march on Paris, but the Republicans mounted a stubborn defence of the city of Nantes on the Atlantic coast deep in the counter-revolutionaries' rear, and the advance of the *Grande Armée* was checked.

The Republicans regrouped, and in October 1793 inflicted a heavy defeat on the *Grande Armée* at Cholet before slicing up the rebel remnants in a succession of smaller actions. They then embarked on a rampage through the whole region, killing and looting as they went. Among the victims were 42 members of Bordereau's family, including her father, whose murder she witnessed. Bordereau vowed revenge on the Republic, acquired a musket and became a crack shot.

She taught herself how to drill, and wearing male attire, joined the Royalist forces, marching under the flag of the comte de la Rochejaquelin, who later became the commander of a remnant of the *Grande Armée*.

During the subsequent years of sporadic skirmishing and guerrilla warfare, Bordereau took part in over 200 actions, usually on horseback. She volunteered for the most dangerous missions, was always in the thick of the fighting, and became a byword for courage. No-one suspected she was a woman. After Napoleon Bonaparte crushed resistance in the Vendée, his offer of amnesty excluded Bordereau, who had a price on her head. She was swiftly betrayed, exposed as a woman and spent three years in chains in a prison in Angers before being transferred to a dungeon in Mont St Michel, where she languished for two more years.

After the restoration of the Bourbon King Louis XVIII in 1814, Bordereau was released. She declared her devotion to the Bourbon cause, and citing the years of suffering she and her family had endured, petitioned the king for a pension. Louis's response was a pension of just 200 francs, but he had not reckoned with the extraordinary tenacity of *L'Angevin*. A welter of renewed pleas and protestations of hardship, backed up with doctors' certificates and statements from the widow of the comte de la Rochejacquelin, which described in graphic terms the many and various physical disabilities from which Bordereau now suffered as a result of her time as a guerrilla and a high-security prisoner, rained down on the hapless Louis XVIII. They fell on deaf ears and, like every old soldier, Renée Bordereau faded away.

Few of the women who disguised themselves to become soldiers have told their own stories of their lives as men. Perhaps the best known of those who have given an insight into this secret world is Nadezhda Durova, a minor member of the Russian aristocracy, who fought in the Napoleonic Wars.

Nadezhda Durova
1783–1866

Nadezhda Durova was the first Russian woman known to see active service. Later, in the Soviet era, many women served openly in frontline combat in Russia's 'Great Patriotic War' against Hitler's Germany. Before her death Durova published her memoirs and four novels advocating women's rights.

Nadezhda Durova suffered neglect and abuse at the hands of her mother, who even tried to get rid of her by throwing her out of a moving carriage when she was still very small. To protect her from further harm, her father, a captain in a Russian regiment of Hussars, took her under his wing and initiated her into a life of soldiering. From her early childhood, Nadezhda became familiar with drilling, marching and the world of military encampments. She declined to take up girlish pursuits, taught herself to ride and subjected imaginary formations to punishing drill exercises and blood-curdling battlefield manoeuvres.

At the age of 18 Nadezhda submitted to an unhappy marriage and bore her husband a child. But she chafed at her dependent status and yearned to become: 'a warrior and a son to my father and to part company forever from the sex whose sad lot … had begun to terrify me.' She ran away, cut her hair short, and assuming the name of Alexander Vasilevich Sokolov, enlisted in a Polish cavalry regiment. She enjoyed training and revelled in the new feeling of independence. Later she wrote: 'You, young woman, only you can comprehend my rapture, only you can value my happiness! You, who must account for every step, who cannot go 15 feet without supervision and correction … only you can comprehend the joyous sensations that filled my heart.'

For the next seven years, Durova saw active service in the long struggle against Emperor Napoleon I's *Grande Armée*. She underwent her baptism of fire near Guttstadt in Germany, where her conduct won her a silver

'[I yearn to become] a warrior and a son to my father and to part company forever from the sex whose sad lot … had begun to terrify me.'

NADEZHDA DUROVA, FROM HER MEMOIR *A CAVALRY MAIDEN* (1836)

Napoleon at the Battle of Borodino, an engagement at which Durova fought with distinction. One of the biggest and bloodiest battles of the era, Borodino saw casualties of 77,000 men; 44,000 Russian and 33,000 French.

St George's Cross for saving a wounded officer, and later fought at the battles of Friedland (1807) and Borodino (1812), two of the bloodiest engagements of the period. In her memoir, however, she claimed never to have killed anyone. Paradoxically she was happiest in battle; when the bullets were not flying, she was forced to remain aloof from her fellow-soldiers to avoid exposure. She seems to have been fearless in combat, but otherwise was timid, frightened of the dark, fretful about her inability to grow a moustache and, on one occasion, alarmed by the innocent advances of her colonel's amorous daughter. She even transferred to a Lithuanian Uhlan regiment to escape these unwanted attentions.

Eventually she made the mistake of writing a letter to her father in an attempt to reassure him. He immediately took the matter up with the Russian minister of war, whom he urged to find his daughter. In 1807 Durova was summoned to St Petersburg to be interviewed by Tsar Alexander I, who was so impressed by her that he ordered her promotion to lieutenant. But at the same time he also proposed to discharge her with honour, a prospect that horrified her.

She succeeded in being returned to her regiment with a commission, but thereafter was treated more like a military mascot than a serving soldier. In 1812 she was introduced to Marshal Kutuzov, the Russian commander-in-chief and hero of Borodino, who told her archly that he knew exactly who she was, and was delighted to meet her. She finally left the army as a captain in 1816 to tend her ailing father.

Most women who saw service in the armed forces did not seek promotion to the rank of officer, if only to avoid the risk of discovery which prominence would entail. An exception to this rule was the Cuban-born Loreta Janeta Velazquez, who like Durova took to military service for family reasons. The widow of a Confederate soldier in the American Civil War who had died of accidental gunshot wounds, Velazquez also lost her three children to a fever, and utterly bereft, left her home in New Orleans bent on becoming a 'second Joan of Arc'.

At her own expense, she raised and equipped an infantry unit in Arkansas, thus avoiding the risk of being recognized by any of her New Orleans acquaintances, and took the name Harry T. Buford. To hide her curves, she wore a complicated metal and wire corset, and completed the disguise by adopting a false moustache and a roguish swagger.

As Buford, she commanded her Arkansas Grays at the First Battle of Bull Run (1861) and later campaigned in Kentucky and Tennessee, where she was badly wounded and cited for gallantry. However, her extraordinary demeanour led to her being arrested in Richmond, Virginia, as a suspected Union spy.

According to her own account, Velazquez turned the situation to her advantage by convincing the Confederate authorities of her loyalty, and persuading them to employ her as a secret agent. While acting in this role in

LORETA VELAZQUEZ
1842–c.1897

Loreta Velasquez signed this steel engraving of herself in military uniform as 'Harry T. Buford, Lieutenant Independent Scouts, C.S.A. (Confederate States Army).'

Washington, DC, she claimed to have met both Abraham Lincoln and Union Secretary of War Simon Cameron. One of the exploits to which she laid claim was the theft of electrotype impressions of Union bond and note plates to enable the Confederates to make forgeries. In her memoir *A Woman in Battle: A Narrative of the Exploits, Adventures and Travels of Madame Loreta Janeta Velasquez*, published in 1876, she observed: 'Notwithstanding the fact that I was a woman, I was as good a soldier as any man around me, and as willing as any to fight valiantly and to the bitter end before yielding.'

During the Civil War, she married Captain Thomas de Caulp, a Scot serving in the Confederate Army, and lost her second husband when he was killed in action. Her third husband was a Major Wasson, an explorer who had the misfortune to die of 'the black vomit' at the start of an expedition the couple had launched into the jungles of Venezuela. Bereft again, Velazquez soon acquired a fourth husband, a gold prospector, in whose company she met the Mormon leader Brigham Young, finding him to be 'a pleasant, genial gentleman, with an excellent fund of humour and a captivating style of conversation'.

Velazquez's story has long been treated with scepticism by historians of the period and the facts behind many aspects of her colourful career remain unproven. But her war service, her courage, her misfortunes and her gallantry are beyond dispute.

A stirring reversal of the old adage that 'crime doesn't pay', Cheng I Sao was a ferocious privateer who profited mightily from her reign of terror in the South China Sea. Indeed, she is considered by many naval historians to have been the most successful pirate in history.

Cheng I Sao
1785–1844

A former prostitute, in 1801 she married Cheng I, the commander of a pirate fleet operating in the South China Sea. In the late 18th century, Chinese pirates had flourished in these waters with the support of the Tay-son rulers of Vietnam. After the overthrow of the Tay-son, the pirates

were driven from the seas off Vietnam by the navy of the Emperor Gia Long. They regrouped in China, and Cheng I and his wife emerged as their leaders, welding an ill-disciplined and fractious collection of gangs into a confederation of six separate fleets sailing under their own colours. By 1805, the year of the British Admiral Horatio Nelson's great victory over the French and Spanish fleets at Trafalgar, the pirate confederation mustered some 1,500 ships, large and small.

On her husband's death in 1807, Cheng I Sao secured her position at the top of the pirate hierarchy. She appointed as the commander of the powerful Red Flag fleet her 'adopted' son Chang Pao, a fisherman's son who had been captured and befriended by her husband. In time, Chang Pao became Cheng I Sao's lover and the father of her son.

With Chang Pao, Cheng I Sao codified the chaotic organization that had once characterized the pirates' armada into a formal structure of brutal simplicity. In battle, commands were to be issued only by the leader of the fleet. It was a capital offence to steal from villages that gave regular help to

A European merchant ship attacked by Chinese pirate junks, from a 19th-century illustration. At the height of its power, Cheng I Sao's formidable 'Red Flag Fleet' boasted ocean-going junks along with hundreds of coastal vessels and numerous small river boats.

the pirates. Raping female captives was also a capital offence. Even if intercourse had taken place with the female captive's consent, the sailor was beheaded and the woman tossed overboard with a heavy weight tied to one leg. Deserters, or those absent without leave, were punished by the removal of an ear, which was then displayed throughout the fleet 'to encourage the others'. You knew where you stood with Cheng I Sao. If they kept their ears and noses clean, her sailors could expect to receive two plundered pieces for every ten taken.

She also established an effective protection racket, whose principal features were the sale of 'safe passage' documents to all coastal fishing vessels and, for a price, ensured the protection of the salt fleets sailing to Canton. Posts were established along the coast to serve as fee-collection points. By 1810 the pirates had a stranglehold on the waters around Canton, killing a troublesome provincial commander-in-chief, nailing a captured officer to a ship's deck, destroying half of the government's fleet and threatening to seize Canton itself. The fleet's commander, Admiral Kwo Lang, committed suicide rather than face capture.

> '[Cheng I Sao spent the rest of her days in Canton] leading as blameless a life as can be consistent with keeping an infamous gambling house.'
>
> CONTEMPORARY ACCOUNT OF CHENG I SAO'S 'RETIREMENT'

Coastal villages raised militias to repel the raiders. In turn the pirates exacted bloody revenge on those who defied them. Such was the fate suffered by the village of Sanshan, where 80 of its menfolk were beheaded before all the women and children were abducted. They were ransomed or sold into slavery.

Officials in Canton turned to the European powers for help, leasing the British 20-gun warship HMS *Mercury*, which was crewed by American volunteers, and hiring another six men-of-war from the Portuguese. When these measures failed, the pirates were offered an amnesty, which Cheng I Sao personally negotiated in April 1810. Pirates who came forward voluntarily were allowed to retain their ill-gotten gains and were given preferment in the imperial bureaucracy. Chang Pao was appointed lieutenant, allowed to retain a private fleet of 20 junks and granted large sums of money to establish his followers ashore.

In the following November, the 'adopted son' and lover was precipitately promoted to lieutenant-colonel in the province of Fukien, where he lived with Cheng I Sao until his death in 1822. The next we hear of her is in 1840, when she filed charges against an imperial official, alleging that he had embezzled large quantities of silver entrusted to him by Chang Pao in 1810 to buy an estate. She must have been losing her grip, as this was one battle she lost and the case was subsequently dismissed. Cheng I Sao spent the rest of her days in Canton allegedly: 'leading as blameless a life as can be consistent with keeping an infamous gambling

The daughter of Lord William Talbot, son of the English lord chancellor and one of 16 of his natural children, Talbot was despatched to a dame school in Chester at the age of five. Her mother, the Honourable Miss Dyer, died young and Talbot passed into the guardianship of a Mr Duker, whom she heartily loathed. And not without reason, for Duker was after the fortune left her by her mother – of which she knew nothing.

Talbot passed into the charge of a Captain Essex Bowen of the 82nd Regiment of Foot and in 1792 sailed with him to the West Indies, disguised as a boy servant. When Bowen was ordered back to Europe, Talbot was enrolled in his regiment – he threatened to sell her into slavery if she resisted. As Bowen's servant and regimental drummer boy, Talbot saw action and was twice wounded. To avoid detection, she chose to treat herself.

When the disagreeable Bowen was killed, Talbot deserted and in Luxembourg signed on with a French lugger sailing down the Rhine. The lugger turned out to be a privateer, which several months later came off second best in an encounter in the

Channel with the British Royal Navy. Talbot was taken aboard Admiral Howe's flagship HMS *Queen Charlotte* for questioning, before being assigned to another warship, HMS *Brunswick*, as a powder monkey. The *Brunswick*'s captain made Talbot his principal cabin boy and she served under him in the Battle of the Glorious 1st of June 1794, where she received several wounds, including a musket ball through her thigh and grapeshot in her ankle.

The grapeshot partially crippled her, but within four months Talbot was serving on the *Vesuvius Bomb*, soon captured by French privateers in the Channel. She was held in Dunkirk for 18 months before being freed in an exchange of prisoners. She made her last voyage to America and back on the merchantman *Ariel*, before embarking on a brief stage career, spending time in the debtors' prison at Newgate and, in 1800, publishing a memoir of her adventures. She died in Shropshire on 4 February 1808.

During her time on board ships of the Royal Navy and merchant vessels, Mary Ann Talbot styled herself 'John Taylor'.

house.' A fictionalized account of Cheng I Sao's career appears in a short story by the Argentine writer Jorge Luis Borges, 'The Widow Ching, Lady Pirate', part of his *Universal History of Infamy* (1954). Borges claimed that his source was *The History of Piracy* by Philip Gosse (1932). A fictionalized movie account of her life, *Cantando dietro i paraventi* ('Singing behind Screens') was made in 2003 by the Italian director Ermanno Olmi. And the 2007 Hollywood movie *Pirates of the Caribbean: At World's End* features a 'Mistress Ching' as one of the nine pirate lords, a character seemingly inspired by the former mistress of the South China Sea.

An iconic figure in the defence of Saragossa against the troops of imperial France, 'La Saragossa' (Agustina Doménech) inspired a passage dedicated to her in Lord Byron's epic poem 'Childe Harold's Pilgimage' (1818).

'La Saragossa'
1786–1857

In 1795 Spain was reduced to the status of client state of France, and in 1808 Napoleon Bonaparte installed his brother Joseph on the Spanish throne. Saragossa, the capital of Aragón, was one of the first cities in which discontent with this humiliating arrangement erupted into open revolt.

In June the city, which had a civilian population of 60,000, was besieged by a strong force under General Charles Lefebvre-Desnouettes. Saragossa, which was only partially enclosed by a wall just under 4 metres (12 ft) high, was almost indefensible and garrisoned by 200 regular soldiers who were armed with ten antiquated cannon. Nevertheless, on 15 June the French were repelled by Saragossa's citizen militia who fought like wildcats.

The French advanced in three columns, each of which aimed for one of the principal gates into the city. A witness who was defending the Carmen Gate recalled the fighting there: 'It is impossible to give an idea of every detail of the scene; what is certain is that the Calle de la Puerta del Carmen was covered with people, the major part of them armed, that in the mass there were women, old men and boys, that now a platoon would detach itself to go towards the Plaza de Portillo, now towards Puerta de Santa Engracia, that some were carrying the wounded on their shoulders, that others, especially the womenfolk, were rushing towards the cannon to give drink to the gunners, that spirit reigned in every countenance, that they looked calmly or even enviously at the inanimate or dead citizens, that priests and monks came to give them their last comfort and that there were quarrels because the defenders would not let them go to the gate.'

Agustina Doménech ('La Saragossa'), heroine of the siege of Saragossa in 1808, pictured in an etching titled '*Que Valor*', one of a series of etchings by Francisco Goyer called *Los Desastres de la Guerra* ('the Disasters of War').

The French retired to lick their wounds and the city received a flood of military reinforcements from Madrid and Barcelona. At lunchtime on 30 June, the French began a 27-hour bombardment to soften up the city's defenders before a second assault. According to an eyewitness, the siege was taking on a nightmarish quality: 'The citizens were awed by the continuous crash of bombs and grenades. The horror of it all was increased by the tolling of the great bell and the quivering of the ground under each explosion. It seemed that there was not one single place in which one might hide from death.'

It was in the desperate hand-to-hand fighting which accompanied the second attack that an attractive young woman, Agustina Doménech, first made her presence felt, taking water to the city's hard-pressed defenders. The legend goes that, spotting a gap about to open up in the defences at the Portillo Gate, she seized a burning brand from the hand of a dying soldier and touched off, at point-blank range, a 26-pounder cannon. The advancing French infantry were shredded by the blast and the survivors fell back. While Doménech raced to the ramparts to exhort her fellow-citizens with the impassioned cry 'Death or Victory!', the threatened breach was plugged.

She became an instant legend, inspiring the artist Francisco Goya to include her in a series of etchings, *Los Desastres de la Guerra* ('The Disasters of War', 1810–20) as a slight figure dwarfed by a cannon under the title '*Que Valor*'.

The fighting continued for another 11 days before the French were once again beaten back and withdrew to Pamplona. In the ensuing lull, reinforcements were able to get through to the defenders of Saragossa, whose battered defences were shored up and approaches cleared by the cutting down of the olive groves outside the city walls that had provided the French with cover.

The French returned, but this time to starve out the defenders of Saragossa rather than storm the city. Heavy siege guns were brought up, and on 30 July, the new French commander, General Jean-Antoine Verdier, called on the citizens of Saragossa to surrender. When they rejected his demand, another heavy bombardment began. Doménech and other brave women sprang back into action, rescuing and nursing the wounded under constant fire and reinforcing the gun crews. After a French shell burst, Doménech found herself buried under a pile of dead and wounded.

As the French burst into the city, and house-to-house fighting raged, the citizens of Saragossa vowed to carry the fight 'even to the knife'. Leading a small group, Doménech succeeded in taking prisoner 15 French grenadiers, only to be taken prisoner herself when a larger French formation arrived on the scene. The French officer who captured her left a somewhat improbable account of her escape: 'All of a sudden she jumped

Plater was another fervent nationalist and patriot, a heroine of the 1829 Polish-Lithuanian revolution against the rule of Tsarist Russia. Born in Vilnius, the daughter of an aristocratic family, she was raised in an atmosphere of fervent patriotism and adopted Joan of Arc as a role model. Unusually for a woman of the period, she became an accomplished equestrian, and studied military history and the use of weapons.

In November 1829, after the outbreak of the November uprising in Poland, Plater formed a partisan formation with the aim of seizing the garrison town of Dyneburg (modern Daugavpils). She cut her hair, donned uniform and with the help of her cousin Cezaris recruited an insurgent formation consisting of 60 mounted gentry, 280 dragoons (mounted infantry) and several hundred peasants armed with scythes. After Plater's advance on Dyneburg was halted by the Russians, she joined forces with another insurgent unit, commanded by Karol Zauski, and took part in the capture of Ukmerge.

Emilija Plater, heroine of the Polish-Lithuanian struggle for independence, inspired many paintings and literary works.

Shortly afterwards a substantial force, commanded by General Dezydery Chlapowski, entered the theatre of operations and assumed command of all Lithuanian formations engaged there. According to legend, Chlapowski urged Plater to return home, but she refused and vowed not to take off her uniform until Lithuania was free. She was subsequently made a company commander in an infantry regiment, with the rank of captain, and fought in the Battle of Kaunus, a signal defeat for the Poles, following which Chlapowski went into internment in Prussia. Plater refused to accept defeat and, disguised as a peasant, attempted to make her way back to Lithuania to continue the struggle. However, she was taken ill, died and was buried in a village near Suwalki in northeast Poland. She later became a symbol of Lithuanian nationalism, the subject of paintings, poems and biographies and was commemorated in the street names of many Polish towns.

nimbly through the window and disappeared into the dusk … We rushed out … in pursuit of the fugitive but it was impossible for us to find any trace of her.'

The two sieges had claimed over 50,000 Spanish lives, and two-thirds of the city had been destroyed. Many years later, the British romantic poet Lord Byron met Doménech in Seville. She was wearing a raffish bemedalled military jacket, a token of her heroism, and her story prompted the poet to celebrate her in 'Childe Harold's Pilgrimage'.

Born a noblewoman in Benares, the daughter of a Brahmin father and a cultivated mother who died when her little girl was only four, Lakshmibai practised the arts of war from childhood. Brought up in a predominantly male household, she received an equestrian and martial training. Her birthplace on the holy River Ganges was later to give the rani an important religious significance when she turned on the heathen British, and prompted Sir Hugh Rose, the man who defeated her in battle, to dub her 'a sort of Indian Joan of Arc'.

Rani Lakshmibai
1835–58

In 1842 Lakshmibai married the raja of Jhansi, a small, prosperous and independent pro-British state. After the death of the raja in 1853, Lord Dalhousie, the governor-general of British India, annexed Jhansi, having refused to recognize the rajah's declared heir, his adopted son Damodar Rao. This decision based on the so-called 'Doctrine of Lapse' was contested in the British courts by the raja's widow, but her petitions were rejected. Insult was added to injury when the British authorities took punitive action against the rani by confiscating the state jewels, deducting her husband's debts from her annual pension and ordering her to quit the fort at Jhansi.

The rani remained in Jhansi and retired into private life. Jhansi was considered a backwater, and the British withdrew the greater part of the garrison there. This proved to be a grievous error of judgement when the Indian Mutiny broke out in May 1857. The Mutiny had many causes, but had been sparked by a rumour spread among native troops (sepoys) that the new cartridge casings for their Enfield rifles, which they tore off with their teeth, were coated with pork fat, taboo to Muslims, and beef fat, forbidden to Hindus, to whom cattle were sacred.

In Meerut on 9 May 1857, 85 sepoys who refused to use their rifles were tried and clapped in chains. The next day three regiments of sepoys stormed the jail, killed the officers and their families and marched on Delhi. Violent uprisings quickly spread throughout north and central India as local princes, whose wings had been clipped by the British, took charge and transformed the mutiny into organized resistance to the British.

At Jhansi native troops stormed the Star Fort, seizing the gunpowder stores and treasury. Sheltering in the fort were 66 Europeans, half of whom were women and children. They had an internal water supply, but little food. On 8 June they surrendered, having been given a promise of safe conduct that was betrayed. Emerging from their refuge, they were

Portrait of Lakshmibai, rani of Jhansi (c.1890) by an unknown artist of the Calcutta School. She is shown wearing a magnificent pearl necklace, which she looted from the treasury at Gwalior.

Dubbed the 'Bandit Queen', Devi was a notorious Indian dacoit (armed bandit) who later became a politician. Her career ended when she was shot by an assassin.

Born into a poor family in Uttar Pradesh, Devi displayed striking qualities of toughness and resolution from an early age. Forced into marriage at the age of 11, she was raped and mistreated by her husband before being reclaimed by her family, who then accused her of stealing from them. She was turned over to the police, who in turn subjected Devi to rape.

In 1979 she was abducted by a gang of dacoits. Devi narrowly avoided being raped by the gang's leader, and married his second-in-command after he had killed his boss. She then returned to raid the village where her first husband lived, leaving him dying by the road as a warning to older men who married and violated young girls.

Devi then enthusiastically embarked on a career of banditry, operating from a base in the Chambal ravine. She survived a period of internecine gang warfare and further rapes to emerge as the leader of her own gang, which embarked on a string of robberies in north and central India, targeting upper-caste Indians. In February 1981 she took revenge on her former comrades, walking in on a wedding dressed as a police officer and ordering her gang to execute the men who had raped her.

For several years she evaded the police before surrendering on her own terms in front of a crowd of some 10,000 people and 300 police officers. Her trial was delayed for 11 years while she languished in custody. In 1994 she was released on parole and immediately launched a self-defence programme for lower-caste Indians before marrying a New Delhi businessman.

Devi successfully sued the producers of *Bandit Queen*, a film about her life, and despite being illiterate, published her autobiography, co-written with two authors. In 1996 she won a seat in the Indian parliament, vowing to devote her life to India's poor, although her opponents frequently accused her of high-handed behaviour. On 25 July 2001 she was assassinated outside her New Delhi home.

The 'Bandit Queen' Phoolan Devi at her surrender to the Indian authorities in 1983.

massacred. Until now, the rani had sat out the mutiny. She was not responsible for the act of treachery, but the British believed otherwise. For the next few months they were content to allow her to act as the effective ruler of Jhansi. Meanwhile, she strengthened her position by forging alliances with two neighbouring rajas, both of whom were rebels.

Lakshmibai cut an impressive figure, dressing as a warrior and a queen in jodhpurs and silk blouse with a jewelled sword and two silver pistols in her belt. Her daily routine included riding and target practice. However, time was running out for the rani. The British had now quelled the mutiny and were mopping up the last pockets of resistance. She had been tarred with the blame for the massacre of the defenders of the Red Fort, and her days in Jhansi were clearly numbered. The rani decided that she had nothing to lose if she took up arms against the British.

She strengthened the defences of the fort and assembled a volunteer army, 14,000 strong, including women who had received military training. Some of the recruits had been responsible for the massacre at Jhansi's Red Fort. These moves only served to harden the growing British conviction that the rani had been a key player in the Mutiny.

A force under the command of General Sir Hugh Rose was despatched to Jhansi, which was besieged on 23 March 1858. The women who had been trained by the rani were seen by the British frantically working the batteries, hauling ammunition and bringing food and water to the soldiers. The rani was everywhere. Men of the 14th Light Dragoons laying siege to the fort recalled the rani as: 'a perfect Amazon in bravery ... just the sort of daredevil woman soldiers admire.'

By 30 March most of the rani's artillery had been put out of action and sections of wall had been breached. On 3 April the British burst into the city, took the palace and stormed the fort. They exacted a terrible revenge. Thomas Lowe, an army doctor, witnessed the scene and recorded that the enemy dead lay in their 'puffed-up thousands' in the blazing sun ' ... such was the retribution meted out this Jezebel Ranee and her people'.

> ## 'a perfect Amazon in bravery ... just the sort of daredevil woman soldiers admire.'
>
> A BRITISH SOLDIER APPROVES OF THE RANI'S PLUCK

The day before the fort fell, the rani escaped with four companions, one of whom was her father, and rode hard to Kalpi, some 90 miles (144 km) away, to join the rulers still holding out against the British. Their forces were routed in two battles on 6 and 22 May. The rebels were forced to flee to Gwalior, a town that controlled the Grand Trunk Road and the telegraph lines between Agra and Bombay, and was held by Indian allies of the British.

On 1 June her forces captured the fortress at Gwalior. Her success was shortlived. On 16 June the British counter-attacked and in the fierce fighting, the rani was killed while leading her troops from the front, clubbed and shot by two British soldiers. Her dying words were to beg that the British should not touch her body. This was respected – her own men bore her corpse to a nearby haystack and set it alight. Her father was captured and shot a few days later. Her adopted son was granted a pension by the British, but never recovered his inheritance.

British newspapers trumpeted the death of the 'Jezebel of India', but General Rose compared her to Joan of Arc, and in the report he submitted to his commander-in-chief William Augustus, the duke of Cumberland, he observed that: 'the rani is remarkable for her bravery, cleverness and perseverance; her generosity to her subordinates was unbounding. These qualities, combined with her rank, rendered her the most dangerous of the rebel leadership. Although she was lady, she was the bravest and best military leader of the rebels. A man among the mutineers.'

The dowager empress of China was one of the most formidable women in modern history. Famously beautiful, she was a good friend and a fearsome enemy who never shrank from war, and sought ways to profit from it. She was greedy, ruthless and an immensely skilled manipulator of the tortuous court politics of the moribund Manchu empire.

Tz'u-Hsi
1835–1908

Tz'u-Hsi's father was a minor bureaucrat, a clerk in government service and later a provincial administrator. In 1852 she was selected as a low-ranking concubine of the young but degenerate Emperor Hsien-feng. She rapidly rose in status, working as his secretary, gaining insights into the administration of the state, and bearing him his only son, T'ung-chih, in 1856.

When Hsieng-feng died in 1861, Tz'u-hsi was still in her twenties and the mother of the new six-year-old emperor. The young ruler was advised by a council of eight elders, but none of his decrees could be passed without the seal being approved by his grandmother, the dowager empress. She thus became the effective ruler of China together with the late emperor's chief wife Tz'uan, her co-regent. Together with Hsieng-feng's brother, Prince Kung, they rode out a succession of crises, including the Taiping rebellion (1850–64), which was triggered by famine and only finally put down with the help of Western military commanders, foremost among them the British general Charles George Gordon.

The precarious maintenance of order was accompanied by the cautious Westernization of China, with the establishment of a school of foreign languages, the creation of modern customs services and the reform of the army and navy. Simultaneously, Tz'u-hsi gathered more power into her own hands; as the official wife Tz'uan was not interested in affairs of state. In 1873, when her son came of age, Tz'u-hsi refused to give up the regency. She declined a second time when he died in 1875 (he had begun to resent her, and there was a strong suspicion that his mother arranged his death). Instead, she flouted all precedents for the succession, adopted her three-year-old nephew as her son and made him the new Emperor Kuang-hsu. In 1881 Tz'uan died, possibly from poisoning, and the late emperor's brother Prince Kung was deposed in 1884.

In her fifties Tz'u-hsi ostensibly retired to her sumptuous summer palace outside Beijing, the rebuilding of which was funded by siphoning off revenue intended for the Chinese navy. The palace boasted a huge room filled with ingenious mechanical toys and dolls, an entire wing stocked with fabulous dresses, and another stuffed with jewels – she was obsessed with pearls and jade. She officially handed over power in 1889, but kept herself exceptionally well-informed while making a fortune peddling influence.

In the 1890s China was faced with a new regional military power in the form of Japan, which in 1894–95 expelled the Chinese from Korea. The blow to Chinese morale led the Emperor Kuang-hsu to implement a new series of reforms designed to sweep away the stifling corruption of China's bureaucracy. He also decided to confine Tz'u-hsi to the summer palace. His adoptive mother reacted swiftly. She rallied the support of conservative mandarins by moving reliable army units to Beijing to replace guards loyal to Kuang-hsu. She then descended on the Forbidden City, with a train of eunuchs scurrying in her wake, to confront the quaking Son of Heaven and strike him full in the face with her fan, the only physical blow delivered in this remarkable coup. After

The formidable Tz'u-Hsi (sometimes transliterated as Cixi) held sway in China for almost half a century. She was highly adept at balancing the various factions at court. This painting of the dowager empress, by a Chinese artist of the naïve school, is dated 1908.

compelling the emperor to issue an edict proclaiming her his regent, she confined him to a palace where he could do no harm. The most dangerous reformers were either beheaded or strangled, and Tzu-hsi once again gathered in the reins of power.

That power, and the remnants of China's integrity, were now increasingly compromised by the encroachment of European powers seeking to divide the spoils of the decaying Manchu dynasty. Tz'u-hsi sent an imperial message to all the Chinese provinces: 'The present situation is becoming daily more difficult. The various Powers cast upon us looks of tiger-like voracity, jostling each other to be first to seize our innermost territories ... Let us not think about making peace.' The result was the Boxer Uprising of 1898–1901 in which Chinese nationalists, encouraged by the empress, rose up against the foreigners. When the Boxers marched on Beijing, the empress assured foreign diplomats that the Chinese army would crush the 'rebels'. When they entered the capital she did nothing. While the foreigners were besieged in their compounds outside the walls of Beijing, the empress quietly slipped away, disguised as a peasant.

> ‘The various Powers cast upon us looks of tiger-like voracity, jostling each other to be first to seize our innermost territories ... Let us not think about making peace.’
>
> TZ'U-HSI CHALLENGES FOREIGN DESIGNS ON IMPERIAL CHINA

By the time she returned in 1901, the power of the Manchu dynasty had been destroyed. The empress came back on terms dictated by the foreign powers, whose punitive expeditionary force had relieved a two-month siege and crushed the Boxers. Measures reluctantly introduced by the empress included the ending of foot-binding and the opening of state schools to girls. Railways were constructed, opium growing was suppressed, the centuries-old civil service exams ended, and work began on writing a constitution. The modern world, which she had kept at bay for so long, had finally broken in.

Nevertheless, she retained her ruthlessness to the end. When she was dying, she ensured that her adoptive son, the Emperor Kuang-hsu, was poisoned. Tz'u-hsi had wielded greater power than Queen Victoria, whom she greatly admired, but in so doing had destroyed any lingering hope for a modernized imperial China.

In a life largely spent shut away in Beijing's Forbidden City, where the emperors of China lived isolated from the real world among a colossal retinue of officials, eunuchs, concubines and servants, she was unable to gain any insight into the workings of the modern world. But combined with her steely will and force of character, these factors enabled the 'Dragon Lady', as she became known, to rule a vast and chaotic empire for almost 50 years.

Born Li Shumeng in Sandong Province in 1914, she escaped an unhappy early marriage to pursue a movie career in Shanghai. When the Japanese occupied Shanghai in 1937, she joined the Chinese Communist Party, taking the revolutionary pseudonym Jiang Qing, and at its headquarters in Yan'an met Mao Zedong, whom she married. However, as Mao had not divorced his third wife, He Zizhen, Jiang Qing was made to sign a marital contract that she would not appear in public with Mao.

In the 1950s and 1960s Jiang Qing exercised an increasingly baleful effect on Chinese culture and politics. In 1966 Mao appointed her to the post of deputy director of the Central Cultural Revolution Group. In 1969 she became a member of the Politburo and forged close links with the other members of what became known as the Gang of Four – Zhang Chunqiao, Yao Wenyuan and Wang Hongwen.

By the late summer of 1976 Mao was on his deathbed while his wife bickered with the doctors over the dying man's treatment. Mao died on 9 September, and a power struggle ensued in which Jiang Qing assumed that as Mao's widow, she would continue to exercise a pre-eminent role in Chinese politics.

She was wrong. In October 1976 all member of the Gang of Four were arrested. Their role in the Cultural Revolution was seen as wholly negative and they provided convenient scapegoats for the ten years of turmoil that characterized that traumatic upheaval. The Gang of Four stood trial in 1980; the 20,000-word indictment listed a host of heinous crimes. The major charges specifically levelled against Jiang Qing concerned her systematic persecution of artists during the Cultural Revolution.

She remained defiant and unrepentant, declaring: 'I was Chairman Mao's dog. Whoever he told me to bite, I bit.' Jiang Qing was sentenced to death, later commuted to life imprisonment. Diagnosed with throat cancer, she committed suicide by hanging herself in a prison hospital bathroom. She is supposed to have left a suicide note, vowing: 'Chairman [Mao]! I love you! Your loyal student and comrade is coming to see you!'

Jiang Qing pictured in Yanan during the winter of 1940–41.

In a cemetery in Asunción, the capital of Paraguay, a monument marks the final resting place of one of the most extraordinary adventuresses of the 19th century. Its inscription reads simply: 'Homage of the people, government and armed forces to Elisa Lynch.'

Elisa Lynch
1835–86

Now neglected and little visited, the monument in Asunción stands as a reminder of the remarkable career of one of the great anti-heroines of Latin America, a woman both reviled and respected, hailed as the faithful companion of Paraguay's General President López and damned as a malign enchantress, hell-bent on the single-minded acquisition of colossal personal wealth.

After an upbringing in Cork in southern Ireland that remains obscure, Elisa was taken by her mother to Paris, where in 1850 she met a soldier, Lieutenant Xavier de Quatrefages, on leave from the French colony of Algeria. She married him in Folkestone, Kent, in June of that year. The new wife accompanied her husband to Algeria, but within three years had left him and returned to Paris, where she became a courtesan. There she met Francisco Solano López, the son of the dictator of Paraguay, Carlos Antonio López. When López returned to his native country in 1854, Eliza followed him.

The Paraguay of the 1850s was an exotic, impoverished backwater, but the tall, red-haired self-styled 'Madame' Lynch, now installed as López's principal mistress, was determined to transform Asunción, its flyblown capital, into an imperial city and herself into its empress. She launched a vainglorious building programme of opera houses and palaces, all of which were unfinished or remained uninhabited. She controlled access to López, who succeeded his father in 1862, and used the influence she gained to amass a considerable fortune.

López, a psychopathic, lecherous and ugly dwarf who modelled himself on France's Napoleon III, to whom he had been presented in 1854, began his rule by declaring a suicidal war on Argentina, Brazil and Uruguay over access to the sea. The six-year War of the Triple Alliance (1864–70) heaped misery on the wretched population of Paraguay and provided Lynch with greater opportunities to enrich herself. She acquired at scandalously low prices over 124,000 square miles (320,000 sq. km) of land in Paraguay, looted jewels from its wealthy womenfolk, ostensibly to fund the war effort, and stashed many thousand pounds' worth of Paraguayan gold in

A sketch of Elisa Lynch, made in 1855 when she was 20 years old. The unofficial First Lady of Paraguay is seen by some as foreshadowing the Argentinian Eva Perón in the role of the manipulative, self-serving consort of a ruinous South American dictator.

European bank accounts. While tens of thousands of her lover's soldiers – many of whom were women and children – suffered and died in the meaningless conflict, Lynch toured their ramshackle camps, grand piano in tow and resplendent in silk and velvet. While she dined off gold plate, the soldiers starved.

In spite of Lynch's depredations, women played an important part in Paraguay's survival against the odds. Initially they were conscripted for all types of agricultural work, and also to labour in Paraguay's primitive native industries and maintain its ramshackle bureaucracy. By the end of the war, women joined pre-pubescent boys in the desperate fight for survival. At the Battle of Pirebebuy (1868), after their ammunition had been exhausted, some 600 Paraguayan women made their final stand, hurling sand, stones and bottles at the enemy before being mown down by a hail of gunfire and a bayonet charge by the Brazilian infantry.

> ' … *surpassed by none in her courage her selflessness and her loyalty.'*
>
> LAUDATORY INSCRIPTION ON ELISA LYNCH'S TOMBSTONE

López's futile war had wrecked his country's economy and devastated its people. It is estimated that up to 90 percent of Paraguay's male population died, and it would take three generations for numbers to recover. Incredibly, the dictator now embarked upon a reign of terror. Convinced of a conspiracy to overthrow him, he ordered the torture and murder of those who had the questionable fortune to be left standing. He was at least egalitarian in his cruelty and included among his victims his brothers, sisters and brothers-in-law, even ordering the assassination of his own mother. He met his own death at the Battle of Cerro Cora (1870), the last battle in the war and little more than a glorified skirmish in which, having refused to surrender to the Brazilians, he was cut down and his body mutilated. Lynch was allowed to bury López and their eldest son Panchito, who was also killed at Cerro Cora, with her own hands. But López's corpse was dug up during the night and subjected to more abuse. Lynch buried López for the second time the following morning.

With her assets frozen and a trial for war profiteering in preparation, Lynch left Paraguay in the summer of 1870 to live in London and Paris. But with her own fortune dwindling, she returned to Paraguay in 1875 in a bold but fruitless attempt to recover some of her ill-gotten gains. She was sent packing, and lived out her days in Jerusalem and Paris as a respectable widow of modest means. She died of stomach cancer and was buried in Père Lachaise cemetery.

Her life was subsequently mythologized and Lynch transformed from tyrant to martyr. A century after fleeing the ruined Paraguay, she was proclaimed a national heroine – 'surpassed by none in her courage, her selflessness and her loyalty' – and her remains returned to Asunción in a bronze urn wrapped in the Paraguayan tricolour.

BELLE BOYD
1844–1900

One of the most celebrated Confederate spies of the American Civil War was Belle Boyd of Martinsburg, Virginia. Her father's hotel provided the forceful and flirtatious Belle with a ready-made listening post, where she gathered overheard fragments of conversation from amorous and indiscreet Union officers, and then conveyed the information she gleaned to the Confederacy.

During the Shenandoah Valley campaign in the spring of 1862, Boyd provided valuable intelligence about the Union forces' intentions to General T.J. 'Stonewall' Jackson. The grateful Jackson appointed her a captain and honorary aide-de-camp on his staff, enabling Boyd to attend troop reviews. In July 1862 she was arrested by the Union and detained for a month in Washington before being released in an exchange of prisoners.

Belle proved to be a lively prisoner, gaily waving Confederate flags from her window and warbling 'Dixie' to admirers below. She communicated with them by means of a rubber ball, which was tossed in and out of her cell and onto which she sewed messages. She was arrested for a second time in June 1863, but contracted typhus and was released. In May 1864 she sailed for England, but her ship was intercepted and she was arrested as a courier for the Confederacy. She escaped to Canada with the help of a Union officer, Samuel Hardinge, who accompanied her to England and married her in August 1864.

In England she composed a colourful memoir, *Belle Boyd in Camp and Prison*, and appeared on stage. She returned to the United States in 1866, after the death of her husband. Here she prolonged her stage career, billed as the 'Cleopatra of the Secession' and appearing in Confederate uniform. Two more husbands followed before she died, broke but unbowed, while touring in Wisconsin.

Belle Boyd was awarded the US Southern Cross of Honor for her services as a spy.

Tubman's unique life and exploits as an abolitionist, Union spy in the American Civil War and supporter of the struggle for women's suffrage will ensure that she remains an enduring and inspirational figure in the history of human liberation. A tiny woman, barely 1.5 metres (5 ft) tall, she had the heart of a lion. Once she set her course, there was no turning back. As the first female 'conductor' on the 'underground railway', escorting slaves north from the American South to freedom in the North and Canada, she had a blunt but effective way with faint-hearted passengers who wanted to retrace their steps. Brandishing a revolver, she told them 'You go on or die'. In her own words, she 'never lost a passenger'.

Harriet Ross Tubman
1820–1913

Harriet Tubman was born into slavery in Maryland on a large plantation near the Blackwater River in Madison County, and christened Araminta. Her mother was a cook and her woodsman father managed the estate's timber. Early in her life, the cruel norms of slavery conspired to split her family. Three of her sisters were sold by the plantation owner and she never saw them again. When a would-be purchaser from Georgia came to the slave quarters for Tubman's youngest brother Moses, he was successfully warned off by her mother who told him: 'You are after my son; but the first man that comes into my house, I will split his head open.' The man from Georgia backed away and called off the sale, convincing the young Tubman to follow a simple principle – never give in.

Tubman was often loaned out to other slave-owners. She was worked hard and beaten frequently, bearing the scars for the rest of her life. As she grew older and stronger, she graduated to gruelling field work – ploughing, hauling timber and driving cattle. In her adolescent years she was badly injured in an incident in a store when an overseer threw a heavy weight from the scales at an absconding slave. It missed its target and struck Tubman on the head, knocking her out. She received no treatment and was put back to work within 48 hours, her hair matted with blood. Thereafter she suffered from seizures in which she appeared to slip into unconsciousness, but remained conscious of her surroundings, possibly the result of a temporal lobe epilepsy caused by the injury. After suffering this trauma, Tubman experienced frequent visions and dreams, mainly of a religious nature. They reinforced her growing faith and confirmed the comfort she found in Old Testament tales of deliverance, particularly those to be found in Exodus. The parallels with her own life were clear.

Around 1844 she married a free black man, John Tubman, simultaneously adopting her mother's first name, Harriet. In 1849, with her brothers Ben and Henry, she made a first and unsuccessful attempt to escape from slavery. Her brothers had second thoughts and turned back, taking their sister with them. Shortly afterwards Tubman tried again, as a 'passenger' on the 'underground railroad', the secret route to freedom in the North and Canada managed by free and enslaved blacks and abolitionists, among whom the Quaker community played a significant part.

The 'underground railroad' consisted of a system of meeting points, secret routes, and different methods of transportation, mostly on foot or by wagon, but occasionally on real trains. The individuals who ran the railroad knew little or nothing about its overall structure, just the minimum they needed to operate the small section for which they were responsible. In this the railroad closely resembled the escape lines of Nazi-occupied Europe in the Second World War (see Andrée de Jongh, pages 252–255). Maintaining security in an environment in which 'slave catchers' flourished and were actively encouraged by legislation, was the paramount concern of those who rode the freedom railroad.

In December 1850 Tubman slipped back to Baltimore to help her sister and two children to get away. In ten years she made approximately 19 trips to the South to lead slaves along the railroad, eluding slave catchers and their bloodhounds, displaying matchless stamina and ingenuity and earning the nickname 'Moses'. She chose to work in the depths of winter, when the nights are long and dark and people tend to stay inside. Once she had gathered a group of slaves, she ensured that they set off on Saturday evenings, since newspapers would not run stories on the runaways until the following Monday morning.

Photograph, dated between 1860 and 1875, of the 'underground railroad' organizer Harriet Tubman. A fellow abolitionist wrote of her: ' ... in point of courage, shrewdness, and disinterested exertions to rescue her fellow-man, she was without equal.'

DOROTHY HEIGHT
1912–2010

Height was born a year before the death of Harriet Tubman, at a time when American women did not have the vote and the nation's blacks had very few rights. Her life nevertheless marked a significant step on the road of civil rights signposted by her great predecessor.

Born in Richmond, Virginia, a city where the siren songs of secession and segregation still linger in the 21st century, Height later moved with her family to Rankin, Pennsylvania, a tough steel town in the suburbs of Pittsburgh. In 1929 she gained a place at Barnard College, but could not attend because of the institution's unwritten policy of admitting only two black students a year. In 1933 she left New York University with a master's degree in educational psychology. Four years later she travelled to England as one of a delegation of ten young Americans who attended a church youth conference. This proved a decisive formative experience and on her return to the United States, Height joined the Young Women's Christian Association (YWCA) in Harlem, eventually

becoming director of its office for racial justice.

She launched her career as a civil rights activist when she joined the National Council of Negro Women, founded in 1935 to encourage mainly middle-class black women to support humanitarian causes and programmes of interracial action. In 1938 she gave evidence to the New York City Council about the daily 'slave market' at street corners in the Bronx and Brooklyn, where young black girls would bargain with passing motorists – often white middle-class women from the suburbs – for a day's housework at subsistence wages.

In 1957, when the National Council of Negro Women was becoming more militant, she became its fourth president. She initially resisted the rallying cries of Black Power, but by the 1960s supported calls for a more radical approach to racial injustice. In 1963 she was with Dr Martin Luther King when he delivered his 'I have a dream' speech in Washington. Tirelessly active into her 90s, she was one of the most honoured women in America when she died.

Tubman eventually helped some 300 fugitives, including her parents, to reach the northern states and Canada. She also acted as an adviser to the abolitionist John Brown, prompting her ally Frederick Douglass to declare of Tubman: 'Excepting John Brown – of sacred memory – I know of no one who has willingly encountered more perils and hardships to serve our enslaved people than you follow.' It was Brown who, in recognition of Tubman's extraordinary flair for leadership by example, dubbed her 'General'.

When the American Civil War broke out in April 1861, Tubman saw a Union victory as a vital step on the road to the abolition of slavery. Initially she was highly critical of US President Abraham Lincoln, whose attitude towards emancipation she considered pusillanimous, observing that: 'God won't let master Lincoln beat the South till he does the right thing.'

Lincoln eventually did the right thing with the implementation, in January 1863, of the Emancipation Proclamation. At the beginning of the Civil War Tubman had served as a nurse, fearlessly treating men with dysentery and smallpox. The fact that she did not fall ill herself prompted rumours that she was blessed by God. In 1863 the Union Army asked Tubman to organize a network of scouts (and spies) among the black population of South Carolina, where she had been working with slaves abandoned by owners who had fled the advancing Union Army. Tubman established a sophisticated system to gather information and recruit men for the Union's black regiments, a task for which her work on the 'underground railroad' had provided an ideal training.

In the spring of 1863 Tubman led troops commanded by Colonel James Montgomery on a mission to disrupt the South's interior lines by blowing bridges and cutting rail links. The mission also freed some 800 slaves from plantations along the River Combahee. On 2 June 1863 she guided three steamboats through heavily mined water to embark the slaves, who stampeded towards the vessels when their whistles shrilled liberation. Tubman watched the scenes of chaos that ensued as the slaves cascaded towards the boats – babies hanging from their necks, pigs slung in bags across their shoulders, steaming pots of rice swinging from poles – while the slave owners and their overseers vainly attempted to impede their progress with pistols and whips. Tubman remained calm throughout the tumult. Her commanding general reported to the US Secretary for War: 'This is the only military command in American history wherein a woman, black or white, led the raid and under whose inspiration it was originated and conducted.'

In three years of service with the Union Army, Tubman received only intermittent pay amounting to $200, and supported herself by selling beer and food that she prepared in such spare time as she had. After the war she applied unsuccessfully for a pension in her own right, but received one only as the widow of her soldier husband. She devoted her later years to founding schools for freed slaves, teaching and preaching, and also became a supporter of the women's suffrage movement. A white woman had once asked Tubman if she believed that women should have the vote. Tubman replied: 'I suffered enough to believe it.' She also founded a home for elderly, indigent black people in Auburn. She was dismayed when its trustees demanded a $100 dollar fee from residents. She tried and failed to introduce a rule that 'nobody should come in unless they don't have no money at all'.

A photograph from around 1885, showing Harriet Tubman (far left) with former slaves whom she helped to freedom in the North during the US Civil War of 1862–65.

In 1890 Tubman underwent brain surgery, the legacy of the dreadful blow to her head. Characteristically, she declined anaesthesia, choosing instead to chew hard on a bullet, as she had seen soldiers do for amputations during the Civil War. She died on 10 March 1913 in the home for the elderly that bore her name. Tubman was buried with full military honours at Auburn's Fort Hill Cemetery. In 2002 she was named by Molefi Kete Asante as one of the 100 greatest African Americans. In truth she deserves a far higher place among the very greatest of all Americans.

In Women of the War, published in 1866, 'Gentle Anna's' service in the American Civil War was commended in the following words: 'Few soldiers were in the war longer, or served with so slight intermission, or had so little need of rest.'

Anna Etheridge
1839–1915

Born Anna Lorinda Blair to prosperous parents in Wayne County, Michigan, she married unsuccessfully at the age of 16. In the summer of 1861, while in Detroit, Etheridge enlisted in the 2nd Michigan Volunteers. She was one of 20 young women who offered their services as 'vivandières' to the regiment, supplying food, drink and medical attention to the troops. Within a few months only Etheridge remained.

She first saw action at Blackburn's Ford, Virginia, nursing the wounded on the battlefield and bringing water to the dying. After the second Battle of Bull Run (1862), and at the urging of General Phillip Kearney, the regiment provided her with a horse, which she rode side-saddle into the front line, frequently dismounting to come to the aid of wounded men while fighting continued around her. Having bound up their wounds and given them water or some other 'stimulating drink', Etheridge would then gallop off on her mission of mercy undeterred by the musket balls that often passed through her clothes. She was armed at all times with two pistols. Her brigade commander, General Berry, declared that Etheridge remained cool and self-possessed under fire as fierce as any he had experienced himself. The gallant General Kearney suggested that Etheridge should be made a regimental sergeant, but he was killed shortly afterwards and Etheridge never received a sergeant's rank or pay. She was, however, awarded a medal, the Kearney Cross.

When not in the field or working in military hospitals, Etheridge oversaw the cooking at brigade headquarters. On the march, she accompanied the ambulances and the surgeons. At the nightly bivouacs, she wrapped herself in a blanket and slept on the ground 'with the hardihood of a true soldier'. Bronzed, youthful and handsome, she was a great favourite with the troops. Nevertheless, her unconventional behaviour and consequent popularity earned the disapproval of the formidable Dorothea Dix, the social reformer who was in charge of all the nurses in the Union's military hospitals.

Etheridge was present at Antietam (1862), after which her regiment was sent to Tennessee. She decided to remain with the Army of the

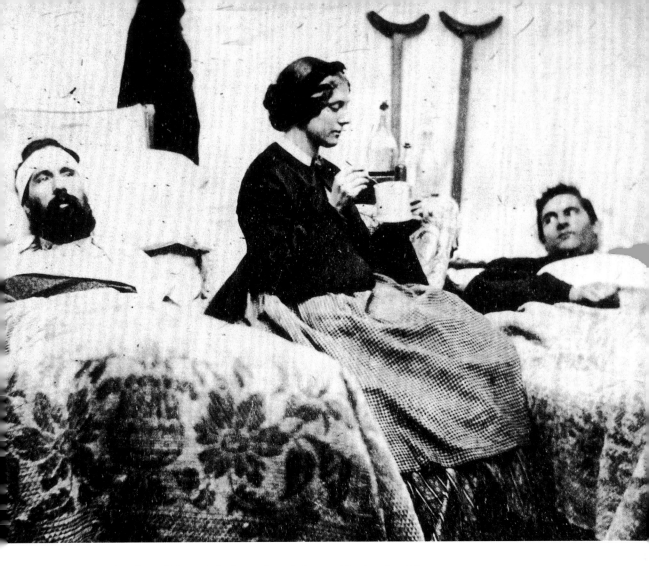

Potomac and enlisted first with the 3rd and then with the the 5th Regiments, serving at Fredericksburg (1862) and Chancellorsville (1863), where she was wounded when a Union officer hid behind her in a vain attempt to save his life.

A contemporary account again noted her coolness under fire. 3rd Michigan were: 'In such extreme peril, in consequence of the panic by which the 11th Corps were broken up, one company of the 3rd Michigan, and one of the sharp-shooters, were detailed as skirmishers. Annie, although advised to remain in the rear, accompanied them, taking the lead. Meeting her colonel, however, she was told to go back, as the enemy was very near, and he was at that very moment expecting an attack. Very loath to turn back, she turned and rode along the front of a line of shallow trenches filled with our men. She called to them, "Boys, do your duty and whip the rebels". The men rose and cheered her, shouting, "Hurrah for Annie! Bully for you!" This revealed the position to the rebels, who immediately fired a volley in the direction of the cheering. Annie rode to

A nurse prepares to spoon-feed soldiers in this photograph taken by Jim Enos in the Union hospital at Carlisle Barracks, Pennsylvania, USA, around 1861. The suffering that Anna Etheridge and other nurses encountered in this conflict – in the days before anaesthetics, effective sterilization of wounds and modern painkillers – was truly appalling.

the rear of the line, then turned to see the result. As she did so, an officer pushed his horse between her and a large tree by which she was waiting, thus sheltering himself behind her. She looked round at him with surprise, when a second volley was fired and a ball, whizzing by her, entered the officer's body and he fell, a corpse, against her and then to the ground. At the same moment another ball grazed her hand (the only wound she received during the war), pierced her dress, the skirt of which she was holding, and slightly wounded her horse. Frightened by the pain, he set off on a run through a dense wood ... so rapidly that Annie feared being torn from her saddle, and crouching on her knees clung to the pommel. The frightened animal as he emerged from the wood, plunged into the midst of the 11th Corps, where his course was soon checked.'

In the same engagement, Etheridge appeared from nowhere beside a shattered Union battery, which had lost all its horses and many of its men. She talked the survivors out of abandoning their position with the words: 'That's right, boys – you've got the range, keep it up and you'll soon silence those guns.' The men raised a cheer, went to work with their guns and sent her to the rear. One artilleryman observed that all the officers in the Union Army could not have had such an effect on them as 'that brave sergeant [sic] in petticoats'.

On numerous occasions Etheridge rallied demoralized troops and, seizing the colours, led them in a charge. She faltered only once, at the Battle of the Wilderness (1864), when a teenage orderly to whom she was talking fell into her arms, killed instantly by a bullet to the heart. Etheridge was so disoriented that she ran into the advancing Confederate line, through which she passed unharmed.

In July 1864 General Ulysses S. Grant ordered that all women be removed from military camps in his theatre of operations, and thereafter Etheridge worked in the hospital at City Point, Virginia, although it seems she was with 5th Michigan when it mustered out a year later in July 1865.

After the Civil War, Etheridge married a disabled veteran of the conflict and found temporary employment at the Treasury Department. In 1886 she formally requested a pension of $50 a month. A year later Congress granted her a pension of half that amount. She was buried in Arlington National Cemetery. A poem of 1866 celebrates Etheridge's exploits during the Civil War:

Hail, dauntless maid! whose shadowy form,
Borne like a sunbeam on the air,
Swept by amid the battle-storm,
Cheering the helpless sufferers there,
Amid the cannon's smoke and flame,
The earthquake roar of shot and shell,
Winning, by deeds of love, a name
Immortal as the brave who fell.

Jennie Hodgers, one of approximately 400 women who fought in the American Civil War, was fortunate to survive without a scratch and, unusually, lived her life thereafter as a man. It was only many years later that an automobile accident and the inevitable arrival of a doctor revealed her true identity as a woman.

Born in Northern Ireland, she stowed away on a ship bound for the United States. In September 1862, describing herself as a farmer, she joined the newly formed 95th Illinois Regiment under the name 'Albert Cashier', a poignant *nom de guerre*, which must represent a desire for increased prosperity or financial security after the grinding poverty of rural Ireland. Serving with the 95th Illinois under General Grant, 'Cashier' gained a reputation for courage and robust health, fighting in some 40 engagements, including the siege of Vicksburg. 'Cashier' was never wounded and the name is recorded in the Vicksburg monument to Illinois soldiers who fought there.

After the Civil War, Hodgers retained the male identity of 'Cashier', working as a farmhand and labourer in Illinois. Sadly, her alias failed her in 1890, when 'Cashier' failed to win a pension for 'his' Civil War service after Hodgers declined a medical examination. Her true identity was revealed in 1911, when she was hit by a car owned by her employer and suffered a broken leg. A doctor in a veteran's hospital examined her and discovered that 'Cashier' was a woman, but the understanding physician kept Hodgers's secret, and found her a place in an Illinois old soldiers' home.

Among the other women who served during the Civil War, Sarah Edmonds enlisted in the Union Army. Not only did she successfully conceal her identity, but she was also able to carve out an effective career as a

CIVIL WAR HEROINES

Photograph of the Civil War nurse and spy Sarah Edmonds, a.k.a. Franklin Thompson. On covert missions 'disguised' as a woman, she called herself 'Bridget O'Shea'.

spy. Edmonds grew up in New Brunswick, Canada, and was greatly impressed in her youth by a book published in 1844, *Fanny Campbell or the Female Pirate Captain*. She had a difficult childhood – her father had wanted a boy and, to prove herself, Edmonds behaved in all respects like a boy. In her teens she ran away, disguised as a boy, to escape an unwelcome marriage. In the United States she worked as a Bible salesman, and in the early summer of 1861, using the name Franklin Thompson, enlisted as a male nurse in a Michigan volunteer regiment of the Union Army. On a number of occasions she undertook spying missions, sometimes 'disguised' as a woman.

For two years, Edmonds maintained her male identity, but was faced with a dilemma when she fell ill with malaria. She chose to desert, and worked for the rest of the Civil War as a female nurse in Washington. In 1865 she published her memoirs, *Nurse and Spy in the Union Army*, a racy but largely fictional page-turner that became a bestseller. In 1867 Edmonds married Linnus Seelye, a carpenter from her native New Brunswick. After the deaths of their three children, the couple adopted two boys.

In July 1884 Edmonds was granted a government pension of $12 a month, and a letter of that year, dated 30 June and from the secretary of war, recognized Edmonds as a 'female soldier ... who served as a private ... rendering faithful service in the ranks'. Edmonds lived out her days in Texas and was buried in the military section of the Washington Cemetery in Houston. Of her Civil War adventures, she wrote: 'I am naturally fond of adventure, a little ambitious, and a good deal romantic – but patriotism was the true secret of my success.'

One of the most tempestuous and celebrated female 'Communards' – supporters of the shortlived 1871 Paris Commune founded after France's defeat in the Franco-Prussian War – Michel was dubbed 'The Red Virgin' for her fiery temperament rather than any aversion to men. Her funeral in Paris brought traffic to a standstill and produced crowds to rival the tribute paid to the writer Victor Hugo when he was laid to rest in 1885.

Louise Michel
1830–1905

Louise Michel was born in a castle in the region of Haute-Marne, the illegitimate daughter of the son of the house and a housemaid, and was brought up by her grandfather. She became a teacher, but in 1852 was dismissed for her outspoken criticism of the royalist government of the day. In 1866 she moved to Paris where she studied science and natural history at night. She rapidly acquired a reputation as a radical opponent of the Emperor Napoleon III and as a fanatical member of republican clubs. She published several novels, all with the theme of strident social protest.

In the summer of 1870 France stumbled into a war with Prussia in which the French army suffered a rapid succession of humiliating defeats. In March 1871 the French capital fell to the Prussians after a long siege. During the siege, Michel had become a member of the Committee of Vigilance for Montmartre, her region of Paris, and, under the influence of her lover, Théophile Ferré, had grown increasingly militant. With fellow committee members , she frequented the club *La Patrie en Danger*, which had been founded by the radical thinker Louis Auguste Blanqui. Here she spent many happy hours during the siege, as she recalled: ' ... one was a little more fully alive there, with the joy of feeling oneself in one's element in the midst of the intense struggle for liberty.'

At the end of March 1871, with the Prussian army encamped outside Paris, President Adolphe Thiers negotiated a humiliating peace treaty, agreeing to the cession of Alsace and most of Lorraine and the payment of a massive indemnity. The Paris mob went on the rampage, Paris burned and Michel was everywhere, a baleful sight lit by flames, stalking the streets in a man's uniform armed with a rifle and fixed bayonet.

The Paris Commune, which was declared on 28 March amid the ruins of defeat, was inspired by France's revolutionary past, but its leaders lacked any coherent political programme. With the loyalty of the National Guard militia in Paris wavering, regular troops were despatched to Paris from

Versailles, where the government had taken refuge. A bombardment of the capital began on 1 May and at the end of the month the city was stormed with the loss of some 25,000 lives. Louise wrote of the street fighting of this chaotic period: 'I could not take my eyes off the pale, savage figures who were firing on us, emotionlessly, mechanically, as they would have fired on a pack of wolves. I thought – we will have you one day, you scoundrels … .'

During the Commune, Michel had been in charge of its social and educational policies, had worked as an ambulance woman and had fought on the barricades alongside the brigade of women that she had raised. She had been one of the last defenders of the cemetery in Montmartre, the Communards' final redoubt, but escaped the débâcle in Paris only to give herself up when she learned that her mother was being held as a hostage. The government, reluctant to confer instant martyrdom on her as they had on many Communards, including her lover Ferré, imprisoned Michel in Versailles and put her on trial.

She appeared in court in black, a token of mourning for the thousands of Communards who had been summarily executed. Justifying her part in the burning of Paris, she declared: 'I wanted to oppose the Versailles invaders with a barrier of flames … Since it appears that every heart that beats for freedom has no right to anything but a slug of lead, I demand my share. If you let me live, I shall never cease to cry for vengeance. If you are not cowards, kill me.' The judiciary of the Third Republic refused to oblige and despatched Michel to a penal colony in New Caledonia in the South Pacific, where she insisted that she receive the same treatment as male prisoners and worked selflessly among native tribespeople.

Imprisonment did not dull Michel's ardour, and on her return to France after an amnesty in 1880 she resumed her career as a radical agitator, with the police in constant attendance. In 1881 she attended the anarchist congress in London. In

Undated photograph of Louise Michel, heroine of the Paris Commune. The long novel *La Misère* ('Misery', 1882), which she co-authored, has become a favoured text for feminists.

In an allusion to the artist Eugène Delacroix's famous painting of the French Revolution, *Liberty Leading the People*, in 1901 the illustrator Théophile Steinlen produced his print *La Libératrice* for the magazine *Le Petit Journal*. He reputedly based the female revolutionary figure on Louise Michel.

1883 a six-year jail sentence, for inciting a mob to loot bakeries during a food riot, failed to silence her. She was released in 1886, but was in no mood to moderate her behaviour. In 1890 she led strikes in the district of Vienne, and survived an assassination attempt in which she was shot in the head.

Plans were now being laid to certify Michel as insane, and she fled to London where she befriended the young painter Augustus John, wrote about the Paris Commune, raised funds for revolutionary groups in Europe and met the American revolutionary and anarchist Emma Goldman ('Red Emma'). In 1896 she returned to France, her revolutionary fervour undimmed, and engaged in the furious debate provoked by the Dreyfus affair. She was forever in and out of prison; at one point statesman Georges Clemenceau secured her release so that she could see her dying mother.

She was still firing on all cylinders when she died on a trip to Marseilles in January 1905. Her fierce reputation belied her intelligence, generosity and the affection in which she was held by many of her contemporaries. After her death many French primary and secondary schools took her name, in recognition of her early days as a teacher. A Paris Métro station was also named after her and in 1975 a courtyard in front of Sacré Coeur was dedicated to her as 'Heroine of the Commune'. In 2005, the centenary of her death, there were many celebrations to honour 'la bonne Louise'.

WOMEN OF THE PARIS COMMUNE

The Paris Commune was the provisional national government of France formed in March 1871 when Paris was besieged by German troops during the Franco-Prussian War. Consisting of socialists and left-wing republicans, it is considered by many to have been the first socialist administration in history.

Women played an important part in the Commune. In April 1871 Nathalie Lemel, a socialist bookbinder, and Elisabeth Dmitrieff, a Russian exile and a member of the Russian section of the First International, created the Union of Women for the Defence of Paris and Care of the Injured. They believed that victory over a dominant patriarchy could only be achieved by a struggle against global capitalism. They demanded gender and wage equality, the right of divorce for women and of professional education for young girls.

The Women's Union was involved in a number of co-operative ventures. Lemel founded the restaurant *la Marmite*, which served food to indigents. In May 1871 the Commune was overwhelmed by 20,000 troops despatched from Versailles by the French government. Lemel fought on the barricades thrown up in the Commune's last-ditch defence of central Paris during the so-called 'Bloody Week' while simultaneously tending the wounded. After the crushing of the Commune, she was sent into exile with Louise Michel.

Another Russian, Anne Jaclard, who had declined a proposal of marriage from the Russian novelist Dostoevsky and eventually married a follower of Blanqui, founded the newspaper *La Sociale* with André Léo. Jaclard was also a member of Montmartre's Committee of Vigilance alongside Louise Michel as well as of the Russian section of the First International.

Victorine Brocher-Rouchy was a Parisian who came from a long revolutionary tradition. Her husband had fought as a *franc-tireur* (irregular) in the Franco-Prussian War and she had served as the driver of an ambulance. On 20 March 1871 she had accompanied her husband in the toppling of a statue of the Emperor Louis Napoleon before joining him in the Battalion for the Defence of the Republic. She was initially in charge of an officers' mess, but when the fighting broke out in earnest she returned to ambulance driving and later fought on the barricades during 'Bloody Week'. After the fall of the Commune she was arrested and sentenced to death, but escaped to Switzerland and then London, where her husband died. She returned to Paris in 1878, where she continued to flourish as an anarchist. In 1881, at a conference of international anarchists in London, she met fellow revolutionary Gustave Brocher, whom she later married and with whom she adopted five orphans of the Commune.

The *soldaderas* reflected several significant aspects of warfare in Mexico from the days of the Spanish conquest to the 20th century. Ostensibly at war to provide food and female services, they frequently proved to be soldiers as valiant as their men. The term '*soldada*', which is of Aragonese origin, means a salary and was applied both to female camp followers and combatants in Mexico's many wars.

Soldaderas
19th and 20th Centuries

Traditionally armies in Mexico did not feed their soldiers, but provided meagre pay that could be used to forage. This function was performed by the so-called *soldaderas*, female camp followers who accompanied an army on the march in large numbers and who were often referred to disparagingly as a *chusma* (mob). Mexican generals of the 19th century were often hostile to the *chusmas* and petitioned for their abolition. However, it was pointed out that without their presence, many Mexican soldiers would desert rather than face starvation.

A vivid picture of the *chusma* that followed the army of General Santa Anna in 1841 was painted by the writer Frances Calderón de la Barca. She observed: 'various masculine women with ... large straw hats tied down with coloured handkerchiefs, mounted on mules or horses ... Various Indian women trotted on foot in the rear, carrying their husbands' boots or clothes. There was certainly no beauty amongst these feminine followers of the camp, especially among the mounted Amazons, who looked like very ugly men in a semi-female disguise.'

At the start of the 1841 march, Santa Anna's army numbered some 6,000 men while its accompanying *chusma*, consisting of 'numerous children, women, herb healers and speculative merchants', was over 1,500 strong. However it was rapidly reduced by disease and starvation to no more than 300. Despite this, the populations who lived in the path of the *chusma* feared its depredations more than those of the soldiery, likening it to a swarm of locusts.

In the 19th century, forces of the nascent Mexican state defeated the Spanish, clashed with the Americans, thwarted French colonial ambitions and endured perpetual internal conflict between their own warring factions. All the armies involved in these conflicts, including those of the French and the Americans, made use of the *soldaderas*, who were by no means exclusively women of low status confined to menial tasks. One of the many who fought alongside their menfolk was Ignacia Reachy. Born in

Soldiers and *soldaderas* of the Mexican Revolution, pictured in 1910. The Federal army opposing the revolutionaries also relied heavily on its female camp followers. The duties of the *soldaderas* not only included nursing and providing food, but also spying on the enemy and smuggling arms from the United States.

Guadalajara in around 1816, she recruited a woman's battalion to defend the city against the French in the War of Intervention (1862–67). Colonel Antonio Rojas presented her with a pair of riding boots and another officer, Colonel Gonzalez, provided her with a lieutenant's uniform. Her friend General Ignacio Zaragoza found her a place in the ranks of the Second Division of the Army of the East. In April 1862 Reachy distinguished herself in the Battle of Acultzingo, but was captured by the French while covering the retreat of her commander, General Arteaga. She spent a year as a prisoner of war before escaping and reporting to Arteaga for more combat duty. She was appointed commander of a cavalry formation in Jalisco and was killed in action in 1866.

Other *soldaderas*, like Augustina Ramirez, worked on the battlefield as nurses. Ramirez, who served in the Three Years' War of 1857–60 between the liberal and conservative elements in Mexico, cared for the wounded. She lost her husband and several of her 13 sons in this conflict. In recognition of her courage she received a small pension, which, however, lasted only a few years. Augustina Ramirez died in poverty on 14 February 1879, days before she was about to be honoured as a shining example of Mexican motherhood.

' … the smell of gunpowder and the crying of the wounded. I saw no romance in it. We were just poor people fighting for our stomachs; the talk of brotherhood and the flag-waving came later, from our suffering.'

SOLDADERA MANUELA QUINN (MOTHER OF US MOVIE STAR ANTHONY QUINN) ON HER WAR SERVICE FOLLOWING THE MEXICAN FLAG

During the Mexican Revolution of 1910–20, the Mexican bandit and revolutionary Pancho Villa had an ambivalent attitude towards the *soldaderas*. While respecting bravery in battle whether shown by men or women, he regarded the camp followers as a bar to mobility. On occasions he exacted harsh summary punishment on those *soldaderas* whose loyalty he considered questionable. His fellow revolutionary Emiliano Zapata was more flexible. Rosa Bobadilla became a colonel in Zapata's army and participated in over 150 engagements. Another *soldadera*, Carmen Amelia Robles, was at pains to disguise her femininity under a buttoned-up shirt and heavily knotted tie. Contemporary accounts remark on her sullen face, glowering from under a black felt hat. Even when asleep her fingers would caress the pistol she carried on her right thigh. She shot with her right hand while cradling a cigar in her left. Petra Ruiz, a follower of Venustiano Carranza, Zapata's former ally and a future Mexican president, was another tough customer. Dubbed 'the shooter' because of her pugnacious character, she was an expert sniper with 'an aim better than a torpedo'.

In 1914 Petra Herrera donned male disguise to fight in the army of Pancho Villa, displaying impressive qualities of leadership. Having established her credentials, she wore her hair in braids, and commanding a force of 200 men, rose to the rank of captain.

In the Battle of Torreón she rode in Villa's vanguard, and was the first to break into the city. Possibly frustrated by her failure to gain further promotion, Herrera then formed a female brigade, forbidding men to enter its camp after nightfall.

In 1917 she petitioned to be promoted to the rank of general. Herrera's commanding officer initially refused, but later made her a colonel. At the same time, though, he disbanded her brigade, which then numbered some 400 women. Herrera subsequently worked as a spy for the faction supporting President Venustiano Carranza and was killed in a bar-room brawl, possibly the victim of a vendetta.

PETRA HERRERA
early 20th century

Two armed 'soldaderas', one of whom is believed to be Petra Herrera.

By the 1920s Mexico's regular soldiers and military administrators regarded *soldaderas* with deep suspicion. In 1925 they were banned from federal barracks by the Minister for War, General Joaquín Amaro, who observed that they were 'the chief cause of vice, illness and disorder'. This did not prevent women from following federal and rebel armies, or the formation in 1926 of the Feminine Brigades of Saint Joan of Arc. The Feminine Brigades, who played an important role in the Cristero rebellion, were organized into squadrons whose principal tasks were the manufacture and distribution of ammunition.

In the 1930s *soldaderas* who had fought in the liberation struggle became eligible for small pensions, although these benefits were not awarded to the camp followers. By the end of the 1930s the term *soldaderas* had come to signify little more than the female relatives of a male soldier. Behind them lay a history of hardship and great courage, often borne with characteristic Mexican stoicism. Manuela Quinn, the mother of the movie actor Anthony Quinn, who had followed her lover into the army of Pancho Villa, recalled that while her menfolk believed that the revolution would usher in an earthly paradise, the only thing that service as a *soldadera* meant for her was: 'the smell of gunpowder and the crying of the wounded. I saw no romance in it. We were just poor people fighting for our stomachs; the talk of brotherhood and the flag-waving came later, from our suffering.'

The daughter of a clergyman, Sandes enjoyed shooting and riding as a girl and regretted being female. Her autobiography begins with the words: 'When a very small child, I used to pray every night that I might wake up in the morning and find myself a boy.' She worked as a secretary in London before 1914 and received elementary medical training in the First Aid Nursing Yeomanry and the St John's Ambulance Brigade. In August 1914 she joined a small party of nurses sailing from London bound for Serbia, which by then had found itself at war with Austria-Hungary.

Flora Sandes
1876–1956

Initially attached to the Serbian Red Cross, Sandes had a contract for only three months, after which she returned to England to raise money for more medical supplies. She returned to Serbia in February 1915 with 120 tons of supplies and found herself in the middle of a typhus epidemic. Illness forced her to return to England a second time, but she was soon back in the Balkans, where she joined the ambulance unit of the 2nd Infantry Regiment, the 'Iron Regiment', one of the best formations in the Serbian army, which was fighting in the Baboona Pass near Monastir.

Sandes quickly exchanged her nurse's uniform for the khaki and puttees of a front-line private soldier in the war that the Serbs were now waging against Austro-German forces and their Bulgarian ally. In November 1915 Sandes, now enlisted in the Serbian army, joined the 'Great Retreat' across the mountains of Albania to the island of Corfu in the Adriatic.

Buxom, open-faced and immensely tough, Sandes relished the military life and was idolized by her Serbian comrades. She quickly adapted to trench warfare, explaining that she derived particular satisfaction from the passages of fighting in which the explosion of her grenades was followed by 'a few groans, then silence' since a 'tremendous hullabaloo' indicated that she had inflicted 'only a few scratches, or the top of someone's finger .. . taken off'. In later life she insisted that her wartime experience – with its mixture of discomfort and boredom, interspersed with moments of terrible savagery – bestowed upon her a freedom that would otherwise have been unimaginable.

In 1916 she was promoted to the rank of sergeant before being badly wounded and temporarily blinded by a grenade. One of her comrades saw her lying in no man's land and crawled back to snatch her: 'from under the very noses of the Bulgars.' He was later joined by two of Sandes's comrades,

Flora Sandes, the only official British female combatant in the First World War, pictured in her full Serbian military regalia. Always an adventurous woman, before the war she cycled through Central America to visit her brother, who was helping to build the Panama Canal.

On the home front in Britain during the First World War, the massive exodus of men from the factories and mines in 1914–15 to join Kitchener's New Army left industry gravely short of skilled labour. In the factories their places were, in large part, filled by women, an important step on the road to female emancipation.

In 1914–18 there was no conscription of women, but in both voluntary and government-sponsored schemes, they were required to go through a form of 'enlistment' in which they signed a contract agreeing to either six or 12 months' service. In a conscious echo of the word 'suffragette', the women in war factories were often called 'munitionettes'.

Women war workers earned less than men, although in some munitions plants they outnumbered them by three to one. Trade unionists argued

Exposure to sulphur earned women munitions workers (here seen filling shells) the nickname 'canaries'.

that the employment of so many women would force down the men's wages. Long hours and tough conditions were the lot of many women in the factories. Women working with the highly toxic explosive TNT suffered serious side effects, including nausea, vomiting, giddiness, diarrhoea, loss of memory and impaired vision. There were a number of serious explosions at munitions factories, in which over 200 women lost their lives.

By July 1914 some 200,000 women were employed in Britain's metal and engineering plants. During the course of the war this sector of industry became the one most closely associated with the war effort. The impact of universal male conscription (between January and May 1916) ensured that in this area by 1918 the figure for female workers had risen to nearly one million.

both of them very small men, who had to drag her slowly to safety. The next day they found ten of their wounded with their throats slashed, lying in a neat row near the spot where Sandes had fallen.

In driving snow Sandes was taken to a dressing station – a journey of two hours – where she underwent surgery without anaesthetic. While the doctors probed for grenade fragments, Sandes's self-control deserted her and she 'frankly yowled for the first time'. One of the medics thrust a cigarette in her mouth and told her to remember that she was soldier, a stricture that instantly stiffened her resolve.

After another nightmarish journey, this time lasting three days, Sandes arrived in a British field hospital for Serbian soldiers. Here she had the greatest difficulty in persuading the staff that she was a serving Serbian soldier and not an injured nurse. The day was saved by the matron who, on seeing Sandes, exclaimed: 'Not another one!' Among the regiment's wounded at the hospital was a second female NCO.

During her stay in the hospital, Sandes was decorated by the Prince Regent Alexander with the Kara George Medal, the highest Serbian award for bravery, which carried with it automatic promotion to sergeant-major. She was discharged from hospital in January 1917 and, most reluctantly, returned to convalesce in England. She noted that it was like 'losing everything at one fell swoop and trying to find bearings again in another life and in an entirely different world'. For the rest of the war she devoted her formidable energies to running a hospital and administering a fund, founded with the Honourable Evelina Haverfield, for the Promotion of Comforts for the Serbian Soldiers and Prisoners.

In her memoir *An English Woman-Sergeant in the Serbian Army*, published in 1916, Sandes revealed the humour and cool powers of observation that had marked her early days in the front line. In one attack: 'The companies were quickly posted in their various positions ... we did not need any trenches as there were heaps of rocks for cover and we laid behind them firing by volley. I had only a revolver and no rifle of my own at that time, but one of my comrades was quite satisfied to lend me his and curl himself up and smoke. We all talked in whispers, as if we were stalking rabbits, though I could not see that it mattered much if the Bulgarians did hear us, as they knew exactly where we were, as the bullets that came singing around one's head directly one stood up proved, but they did not seem terribly good shots.'

At the end of the Great War, Sandes decided to throw in her lot with the military of her adopted country. In June 1919 the Serbian parliament passed legislation enabling her to become the first woman to be commissioned in the Serbian army. Sandes rose to the rank of captain, retired in 1922 and was placed on the reserve list. In 1927 she published a second memoir of her life in the military, *The Autobiography of a Woman Soldier: A Brief Record of Adventures with the Serbian Army, 1916-1919*.

In the same year she married a Russian emigré, Yurie Yudenich, a former general of the White Army, and lived in France and Belgrade, where she endured much hardship in the Second World War. She recalled: 'I would sooner have spent this war at the front than in Belgrade.' Sandes's husband had died in 1941, and at the end of the war she returned to Suffolk, where her remarkable journey had begun. In her retirement Sandes donned her military uniform to lecture in the New World and the Old on her wartime experiences. But the old warrior remained: 'Sometimes now, when playing family bridge for threepence a hundred in an English drawing room, the memory of those wild, jolly nights comes over me and I am lost in another world.'

> **' ... the Bulgarians did hear us, as they knew exactly where we were, as the bullets that came singing around one's head directly one stood up proved, but they did not seem terribly good shots.'**
>
> FLORA SANDES TAKES A SANGUINE VIEW OF WAR

The women of most modern revolutions are left to ponder the observation of the 18th-century British politician Edmund Burke that: 'Every revolution contains in it something of evil.' A self-styled 'tigress' of the First World War, Bochkareva's appetite for combat was not satisfied by fighting in the ranks of men. As Russia's soldiers faltered in the face of the German onslaught, Bochkareva created an all-female formation of women volunteers, initially some 2,000 strong, under her command.

Mariya Bochkareva
1889–1920

The 28-year-old Bochkareva had previously led a directionless, disordered life. Born near Novgorod, she was the daughter of a serf and in her teens became a child prostitute and the mistress of a succession of men. Both her first and second husbands were abusive men, and in 1913 the second, a criminal, tried to kill her. This traumatic experience seems to have transformed Bochkareva into a fanatical patriot. On the outbreak of the First World War she returned to Tomsk, where she had lived with her first husband. Here she sought and gained permission from Tsar Nicholas II to enlist as a soldier in the 25th Reserve Battalion of the Imperial Russian Army.

At first she was subjected to ridicule and sexual harassment, but Bochkareva rapidly showed her steadiness under fire, winning a chestful of medals and rising to the rank of sergeant. Her bravery was extraordinary, and she was famous for rescuing wounded comrades in the face of enemy machine gun fire. In May 1917, a low point for Russia in the war, Bochkareva persuaded Alexander Kerensky, the head of Russia's newly installed provisional government, to agree to the formation of a women's battalion – the so-called 'Battalion of Death' – a shock force with shaven heads that would challenge the prevailing mood of defeatism. In an emotional speech at St Isaac's Cathedral in St Petersburg in June 1917, where the battalion's banners were blessed, Bochkareva declared: 'Come with us in the name of your fallen heroes! Come with us to dry the tears and heal the wounds of Russia. Protect her with your lives. We women are turning into tigresses to protect our children from a shameful yoke – to protect the freedom of our country.'

Despite her own chequered past, Bochkareva set the bar high for her recruits. 'Our mother [Russia] is perishing!', she declared. 'I want help to save her. I want women whose hearts are pure crystal, whose souls are pure, whose impulses are lofty.' Some 1,500 women enlisted that night, and another 500 the following day. Adopting a male *nom de guerre*, 'Yashka', she welcomed them all. Bochkareva's vision and enthusiasm proved contagious, and similar units were organized all over Russia. The formation of the Battalion of Death was much applauded by the visiting English feminist and suffragette leader Emmeline Pankhurst, who took the salute at a march-past. Bochkareva's unit was the first, albeit the most famous, of some 15 all-female formations raised by the Russians before the end of the war.

Of the initial intake, several hundred members of the Battalion of Death – mostly peasants – were sent to Belarus under the overall command of General Denikin, where they went into action at Smorgon supported by a battalion of male troops. Some accounts claim that in their baptism of fire the battalion took three trenches, in the process uncovering a huge stash of vodka that

Mariya Bochkareva pictured near the end of the First World War. Her formation of a 'Women's Battalion of Death' was sanctioned by the Russian government as a final, desperate gamble to drum up support for a deeply unpopular war.

rendered the supporting male formation hopelessly drunk. Bochkareva, newly promoted to lieutenant, immediately ordered that any further caches of alcohol should be destroyed.

After three weeks of fighting, the Battalion of Death had suffered losses of 350 killed and 70 wounded, among the latter Bochkareva herself. In his memoirs, Denikin attested to the women's bravery, but observed that they were 'quite unfit to be soldiers', and claimed that they had to be locked up at night to prevent them from being raped by the men under his command. Nevertheless, some 200 members of the Battalion of Death continued to serve at the front, though their position was increasingly undermined by Bochkareva's autocratic style of command, so unpredictable and tyrannical that she drove her remaining supporters away.

> '*We women are turning into tigresses to protect our children from a shameful yoke – to protect the freedom of our country.*'
>
> MARIYA BOCHKAREVA ON HER MISSION

The battalion also incurred the hostility of the Bolsheviks, who in October 1917 had swept away Kerensky's government. On 21 November 1917 the Bolshevik Revolutionary Committee disbanded Bochkareva's formation and subsequently sentenced her to death. In 1918 she escaped to the United States via Vladivostok, disguised as a nurse, and dictated a colourful but unreliable book about her wartime experiences to the émigré journalist Isaac Don Levine.

In the United States she was sponsored by a wealthy socialite, suffragist and social reformer, Florence Harriman. She met President Woodrow Wilson and tried to persuade him to step up aid to the Russian White counter-revolutionaries, among whom her former commander Denikin was a leading figure. Apparently, the president was moved to tears by her appeal. Wiser counsels prevailed, however, and presidential support was not forthcoming.

She then turned up in England, where she petitioned George V in vain. By now Bochkareva was something of a hot potato and the British War Office paid for her passage back to Russia. Undaunted, she returned to the port of Archangel on Russia's White Sea in the autumn of 1918, and attempted to raise another Battalion of Death to fight the Bolsheviks. She was sent packing on the spot by the commander of the British Expeditionary Force, General Edmund Ironside, who gave her 500 roubles and a ticket back to Tomsk, where she was arrested by the Bolsheviks and executed, after four months of interrogations on 16 May 1920.

A photograph of Bochkareva at the height of her fame (see previous page), shows a plump, double-chinned figure, with a steady gaze and a faint smile. She is proudly wearing her medals on her chest, and her face bears a striking resemblance to that of Georgi Malenkov, the Bolshevik who was briefly Josef Stalin's successor and premier of the Soviet Union from 1953 to 1955.

One of the terrorists who plotted the assassination of Tsar Alexander II in 1881, Figner lived to a great age and died a heroine of the Soviet Union. The eldest of six children in a prosperous Kazan family, she had a happy childhood and was educated at home. After attending the Rodionovsky Institute for Women in Kazan, she studied medicine in Switzerland, where she lived with her lawyer husband Alexei Filippov and her sister Lidiya.

VERA FIGNER
1852–1942

In 1873 Figner and her sister joined a student discussion club, members of which would later form the nucleus of the All-Russian Social Revolutionary Organization. In December 1875 she returned to Russia and a year later joined the revolutionary group *Zemlya I Volya* ('Land and Liberty'). She obtained a licence as a paramedic, divorced her husband and went to work in the countryside, where she combined her medical duties with the distribution of revolutionary pamphlets. In 1879, after a split in 'Land and Liberty', Figner joined the terrorist branch of the movement *Narodnaya Volya* ('The People's Will'). She became the group's agent in Odessa, writing articles, establishing links with dissident members of the Russian military and planning the assassination of Tsar Alexander II with, among others, Sofya Perovskaya and her lover Alexei Zhelyabov.

In February 1881 Perovskaya directed the successful assassination of Alexander II in St Petersburg. She was arrested in March, tried, sentenced to death and hanged in April. Figner became the acting head of the remnants of The People's Will, based in Kharkov, but was betrayed and arrested in February 1883 and sentenced to death in the following year. The sentence was commuted to life imprisonment, initially in the Peter and Paul prison in St Petersburg and then, for 20 years, in the dreaded Schlusselburg Island fortress in the River Neva where, as she later wrote 'the clock of life stopped'. These bleak words later became the title of her 1921 memoirs. In 1904 she was released into exile in Archangel, on the White Sea. Two years later she made her way abroad, living in Switzerland until her return to Russia in 1915.

A bomb explodes beneath the carriage of Alexander II in St Petersburg in 1881, killing the Russian tsar.

A self-invented woman, Richard went to her grave honoured as an aviator, veteran of the French secret service and moral crusader. Shreds of truth cling to some aspects of her extraordinary life but the precise facts about this self-centred opportunist remain elusive. For many who tried to pin them down, it was easier to print the fiction peddled by Richard herself.

Marthe Richard
1889–1982

Marthe Richard was born Marthe Betenfeld in Alsace, at a time when the territory had reverted to Germany in the settlement that followed the Franco-Prussian War of 1870–71. At an early age she became a prostitute in the garrison town of Nancy and in 1905, at the age of 15, was given the card issued by the police to streetwalkers known to have contracted venereal disease.

Supremely ambitious but more than a little rough around the edges, she moved to Paris. Here she found her own personal Henry Higgins (the worldly mentor of Eliza Doolittle in *My Fair Lady*) in the form of Henri Richer, a prosperous fish merchant, who polished her manners and grammar and in 1913, encouraged her to qualify as a pilot. In 1915 Richer married her before going to the front where, perhaps conveniently for his new wife, he was killed in the Battle of Verdun (1916).

The resourceful Marthe moved on with the help of a shadowy Russian lover, 'Zozo', with whom she had taken up shortly after her husband's death. It was 'Zozo' who introduced her to the monumentally incompetent French spymaster, Captain Georges Ladoux, who also controlled the legendary courtesan and would-be mistress of espionage Mata Hari (see page 203). Ladoux had a similar mission in mind for Madame Richer, the popular euphemism for which was 'horizontal patriotism'. She was despatched to Spain to seduce Baron von Krohn, an elderly military attaché and submarine specialist with a glass eye.

Glass eye or not, the baron was so impressed with Marthe that he recruited her to the German secret service. As in the case of Mata Hari, the exact nature of her activities as a double agent remains tantalizingly vague. Her own account in one of her autobiographies must be treated with great scepticism. Apparently, in 1917 von Krohn despatched her to Argentina armed with eight thermos flasks of poisoned weevils, with which she was to contaminate consignments of wheat bound for the Allies. The patriotic Marthe thought better of this and flushed the weevils down the toilet.

Marthe Richer (or Marthe Richard or Marthe Crompton) led an adventurous life in which truth became inextricably bound up with fiction. After the Second World War, her talent as a fabulist and self-publicist helped her gloss over her activities as a passive collaborator with the Vichy régime and reinvent herself as a heroine of the Resistance.

Whatever the truth of her wartime career in espionage, by 1918 she was back in Paris, where her flying expertise gave her an entrée to the society of wealthy British expatriates residing in the French capital. She met Thomas Crompton, a director of the Rockefeller Foundation in France, and married him in 1926, happily acquiring British citizenship. Having gained respectability, Mrs Crompton now earned something akin to immortality. Ladoux had a contract with a French publisher to write a book about celebrated French spies he had recruited. Mata Hari loomed large in the deal, but the recently anglicized Marthe Crompton also fitted the bill, giving rise to a book (*My Life as a Spy in the French Service*) in which she acquired a new surname, Richard, and which was entirely fictitious from beginning to end.

Marthe did nothing to disown the ingenious inventions of Ladoux. She went into print with her first volume of mendacious memoirs and embarked on a series of lecture tours. Two years earlier, she had accepted on behalf of her English husband, now deceased, the posthumous award of the *Légion d'honneur*. Economical with the truth as ever, she was thereafter to claim it as her own.

In 1937 the tissue of lies was woven even tighter with the release of a movie, *Marthe Richard in the Service of France*, starring Edwige Feuillère as a nobly suffering Marthe and Erich von Stroheim, typecast as the 'beastly Hun' von Krohn. However, when the Second World War brought the German occupation of France, Marthe's conduct was less noble. She spent the years from 1940 to 1943 very comfortably sojourning in unoccupied Vichy France before returning to Paris, where she procured girls for soirées with German officers and dabbled in the black market. In 1944 she discerned which way the winds of war were blowing and, somewhat belatedly, joined the French Resistance. After the liberation she was elected as a city councillor, although as a British citizen she had no right to hold public office.

Her remarkable career had one further twist in store. The liberation of France had brought with it a savage backlash against women who had consorted and collaborated with the German occupiers, and the brothels – the so-called *maisons de tolérance* – catering for their needs. Immediately after the war, the former prostitute-turned-respectable-councillor launched a major campaign against legalized prostitution, a system she claimed exploited women as sexual slaves. The brothels of Paris were closed and legislation – the 'Loi Marthe Richard' – was later passed, covering all of France.

Marthe lived to a great age, and as a shameless mythomaniac to the last, she was only too happy to regale lazy journalists with invented versions of much, if not all, of her colourful life and times. The urn in which her ashes are buried at the Père-Lachaise cemetery bears the legend 'Marthe Crompton'.

In Mata Hari's heyday, her name was a byword for intrigue and exotic glamour. At the end of her life she was stigmatized as a spy and executed by a French firing squad. Separated from the myths that surround her, she emerges as a lost and desperate woman who, finally and fatally, swam out of her depth.

After a bourgeois upbringing in the Dutch city of Leiden, the young Margaretha Geertruida Zelle married Rudolph MacLeod, a Dutch army officer of Scottish descent and followed him to the East Indies. As Mrs MacLeod, she returned to Europe, divorced her husband in 1906 and reinvented herself as 'Mata Hari' ('Eye of the Dawn'), a Middle Eastern erotic dancer descended from the British aristocracy. Wearing a metal brassière of her own design and a fetching array of diaphanous veils, she became an overnight sensation, an early example of the modern cult of female celebrity, selling sex to survive.

By the outbreak of war in 1914, her popularity was waning as fast as her waistline was thickening. In 1915, while she was performing in Spain, British intelligence obtained information that Mata Hari was a German agent. Her return journey to Paris via neutral Holland was interrupted at the British port of Falmouth, where she was detained and sent to London for questioning. She claimed that she was working for Britain's allies the French, who had suggested that she seduce Crown Prince Wilhelm, the kaiser's son.

The British returned Mata Hari to Spain, where she had an affair with the German military attaché in Madrid. The attaché, Major Kalle, sent a coded message to Germany that an unnamed agent, H-21, had proved very useful. The French, whose intelligence service was notably incompetent, intercepted the message and assumed that H-21 was Mata Hari. In February 1917 Mata Hari was arrested in Paris and tried in a closed court. The evidence she gave in her defence was confused and unclear, as was the existence of H-21, who might well have been a figment of the fertile imagination of the French secret service.

However, the war was going badly for France, and the execution of a notorious courtesan like Mata Hari was deemed a tonic for national morale. Mata Hari was found guilty and faced the firing squad on 15 October 1917, refusing a blindfold and gallantly blowing kisses to her executioners. The 'Eye of the Dawn' was a victim of her own fragile grip on reality and the machinations of the French secret service. In death she became the eternal incarnation of the mysterious and suspect *femme fatale*.

Postcard of Mata Hari during her heyday as an exotic dancer before the First World War. Her stage name has now become synonymous with female spies using the 'honey trap'.

The abiding image of the Western Front in the First World War is that of the trenches, the long seemingly static strip of despoiled landscape that ran for nearly 500 miles (800 km) from the North Sea to the Swiss border. Living conditions in this frozen front line were often grim. During the wet season, dugouts became morasses. Men and mules could drown in the mud. Sanitary conditions were appalling. Rats gorged themselves on corpses lying in 'no man's land' or embedded in the walls of the trenches themselves. In four years of war, trench foot and frostbite disabled about 75,000 British soldiers. Even in 'quiet sectors', snipers and mortar fire claimed a steady stream of casualties. The trenches were a kind of hell on earth. They left their mark on every man who served in them.

Dorothy Lawrence
1896–1964

The trenches of the Western Front were surely the last place to find a woman. And yet in 1915 Dorothy Lawrence made her way into this nightmare environment and endured it for nearly two weeks. When she revealed her identity, exhausted and ill, she caused a ripple of panic in the upper echelons of the British Expeditionary Force.

Lawrence was the daughter of a Warwickshire drainage contractor and was living in Paris when the war broke out in 1914. She tried without success to travel to the front as a war correspondent, an almost impossible challenge for a male journalist at the time, let alone a woman. In the summer of 1915, when Allied casualties were beginning to mount alarmingly in the British sector of the Western Front, Lawrence decided to go it alone, cycling from Paris towards the front line. In her own words she: 'rode on a ramshackle bicycle, priced originally "a £2 bargain" in a London shop and costing another £3 for its conveyance over the water. From that wonderful home of fashion, Paris, I rode rigged out in an untrimmed felt hat – though sunshine broiled the very pavements – and the shabbiest of clothes, together with the largest brown-paper parcel that ever dangled behind the saddle of any lady's cycle.'

Lawrence cycled through what was a war zone to Creil, in Picardy, recently the scene of heavy fighting, where she stayed in a café and acquired a safe-conduct pass to the Senlis Forest, which still bore the scars of battle. Her presence there excited interest from the local gendarmerie, so she moved on and spent an uncomfortable night hiding in the woods.

An illustration, dated 1916, depicting German and Allied forces confronting each other across the trenches at Verdun. Such dangerous and squalid conditions were typical of what Dorothy Lawrence encountered when she made her impromptu sortie to the Western Front in 1915.

In August 1914 a Scottish doctor, Hector Munro, organized a flying ambulance unit to work with the Belgian army. Two of its members. Mairi Chisholm and Elsie Knocker, subsequently achieved celebrity as the 'heroines of Pervyse'.

THE HEROINES OF PERVYSE
1914–18

In November 1914 Chisholm and Knocker struck out on their own and set up a first-aid post immediately behind the front line. They found the perfect spot in a cellar in the town of Pervyse, which had been levelled by German shelling. Such proximity to the front line was in contravention of British army regulations, and until 1918 the two women worked with Belgian drivers and orderlies. Within a few months the British press had highlighted their efforts and King Albert of Belgium had personally decorated them with the Order of Leopold.

The women worked in conditions of extreme discomfort and danger, as Mairi Chisholm confided to her diary: 'taking wounded to hospital 15 miles back at night was a very real strain – no lights, shell-pocked, mud-covered, often under fire, men and guns coming up to relieve the trenches, total darkness, yells to mind one's self and get out of the way, meaning a sickening slide off the pavé [road] into deep mud – screams from the stretchers behind one and thumps in the back through the canvas – then an appeal to passing soldiers to shoulder the ambulance back on the pavé. Two or three of these journeys

by night and one's eyes were on stalks, bloodshot and strained. No windscreen, no protection, no self-starters or electric lights to switch on when out of reach of the lines – climb out to light with a match, if possible, the carbide lamps.'

After heavy shelling destroyed their first post, the two women moved into the ruins of a house and after a fund-raising tour in Britain, found a new home in a concrete structure swathed in sandbags and buried in the ruins of another dwelling. In this desolate landscape of flooded shell craters and rotting corpses, Elsie Knocker was married to an aristocratic Belgian airman who had been brought down in no man's land near the post; in the process she became the Baroness T'Serclaes.

In 1917 the heroines of Pervyse were awarded the Military Medal, but in 1918 they were both badly injured in a German gas attack. The baroness never returned to the trenches, and after suffering more wounds in a second gas bombardment the gallant Knocker was forced to call it a day, and the Belgians closed down the post.

The heroines of Pervyse driving their ambulance through the ruins of the Belgian town where they set up their field dressing station.

Artillery fire kept her awake, and she returned to Paris the next day to devise a fresh plan.

In Paris she befriended two English soldiers in a café, and persuaded them to provide her with a uniform. She bound her chest and padded her figure to add extra 'muscle'. The soldiers, who clearly thought that she would never get near the front line, taught her how to drill. She acquired an identity disc, had her hair cropped and darkened her skin with furniture polish. In this disguise, and carrying forged papers, she bicycled to the front.

At the front she fell in with a friendly former coalminer, Tom Dunn, a sapper in 179th Tunnelling Company, 51st Division. In the stalemate of trench warfare, engineers on both sides ran tunnels from their lines into no man's land, burrowing deep under the enemy's positions, where they would set massive charges to be detonated at the start of a big attack. This subterranean war was punishing and dangerous work. Dunn offered to help Lawrence.

According to her own account, Dunn found Lawrence a cap badge and accommodation in an abandoned cottage in the Senlis Forest close to the sappers' positions: 'In front lay the trenches, approached by a small cabbage plot; at the rear was a statue of the Virgin balanced in mid-air, brooding over the place; and immediately below these cottages cellar-dug-outs offered ready shelter. Into one of those dug-outs I plunged, pulling in that precious cycle ... '.

> 'Into one of those dug-outs I plunged, pulling in that precious cycle ... '
>
> LAWRENCE ON HER ARRIVAL AT THE FRONT

Each night she infiltrated herself into Dunn's platoon and marched off to war. She returned to her refuge after laying surface mines in no man's land and often coming under fire. Lawrence persisted with the deception for ten days before, chilled and exhausted, she revealed her identity to a non-commissioned officer who promptly placed her under arrest.

Lawrence was taken to the rear of the lines and then the headquarters of the British Expeditionary Force, where she underwent a succession of interrogations attended by three generals and at which her own ignorance of military terminology, and her interrogators' bafflement at her enterprise, raised the suspicion that she was a spy at worst, or at best a prostitute of remarkable perspicacity. It was a tragi-comic dialogue of mutual misunderstanding. This was soon overtaken by the army's dawning fear of embarrassment if it became known that a woman had tricked her way to the front. She was sent back to London after she had given an undertaking not to speak or write about her experiences. In 1919 she broke her promise and published an account of her time in the trenches, *Sapper Lawrence: the Only English Woman Soldier, Late Royal Engineers 51st Division 179th Tunnelling Company BEF*. In 1925, still not yet 30 years of age, she was committed to an insane asylum after claiming that she had been raped by an Islington churchwarden. Here, in this *oubliette* to which so many 'awkward' women were consigned, Lawrence languished until her death.

A great beauty, suffragette, artist, actress, freedom fighter and politician, Constance Markiewicz was the heroic female face of Irish nationalism. The bust of Markiewicz in St Stephen's Green, Dublin, which commemorates her role in the Easter Rising of 1916, bears the legend 'Constance Markiewicz, Major, Irish Citizen Army, 1916'.

Constance Markiewicz
1868–1927

Constance was born in London, the daughter of a wealthy family the Gore-Booths, who owned a substantial estate in Lissadell, County Sligo. Her sister Eva was later to become a trade unionist and advocate of women's suffrage. In contrast, Constance was presented at court in 1887, became a society beauty and in 1893 attended the Slade School in London to study art. In 1898 she went to Paris to continue her studies, where she met the Polish aristocrat Count Casimir Dunin Markiewicz, and married him in 1903.

In the same year the couple moved to Dublin, where Constance became closely involved with the cultural and national renaissance in Ireland, joining the Gaelic League and the Abbey Theatre and helping to found the United Arts Club. Before this, her life had never intersected with the politics of Irish nationalism, but in 1906 a random occurrence radicalized her. She rented a country cottage near Dublin, where the previous tenant had been the poet Padraic Colum, who left behind a collection of revolutionary publications urging Irish independence from British rule. Markiewicz became a convert overnight.

In 1908 Markiewicz joined both Sinn Féin and The Daughters of Ireland, a nationalist women's group founded in 1900 by Maud Gonne, a passionate Republican beloved by the poet W.B. Yeats. In 1909 Markiewicz founded *Na Fianna Éireann*, a youth movement resembling the Boy Scouts with a markedly militaristic flavour. In 1911 she was jailed for her part in the demonstrations against King George V when he visited Ireland, and in 1913 she played an active role in the Dublin General Strike.

At the outbreak of war in 1914, while thousands of Irishmen enlisted in the British army, Markiewicz and other nationalists decided to exploit the opportunity offered by the European conflict. Their chance came at Easter 1916 when some 3,000 radical nationalists staged an uprising against British rule and proclaimed an independent Irish republic. On 24 April they seized key buildings in Dublin, the prelude to a six-day battle in which the city centre was extensively damaged before the uprising was crushed

From socialite to socialist: a photograph of Constance Gore-Booth in 1890, later Constance Markiewicz. In Kilmainham Jail, when she was informed that her death sentence for her part in the 1916 Easter Rising was being commuted, she remarked: 'I do wish you lot had the decency to shoot me.'

The 'Irish question' had long been a thorn in the side of British politics. Since the occupation of Catholic Ireland in the 17th century, first by Presbyterian settlers from Scotland and then by the English armies of Oliver Cromwell, a successful merger of the political cultures of Britain and Ireland had never been achieved.

In 1900 a renewed surge of Irish nationalism was tapped by the formation of Sinn Féin ('Ourselves Alone'), but in 1914 the introduction of a Home Rule Act passed by the British parliament had been effectively blocked by the Protestant majority in Ireland's six northern counties of Ulster. Both Protestant and Catholic militias squared up, but a full-blown clash was prevented by the outbreak of the First World War. Over 200,000 Irishmen, both Catholic and Protestant, volunteered to fight.

Two years into the war, as deadlock gripped the Western Front, a group of nationalists staged an uprising in Dublin and declared an independent Irish republic. Some 2,000 men and women took over the Central Post Office and other key buildings in the city. A six-day battle with a force of 8,000 British troops followed, in which the centre of the city was badly damaged. The nationalists did not enjoy universal public support, but sympathy for their cause increased following the execution of 15 of their leaders after they surrendered. The chief among them, Éamon de Valera, later premier and president of the Republic of Ireland, escaped execution as an American citizen. After the executions, one Irish soldier serving in France with the British army observed bitterly: 'These men will go down in history as heroes and martyrs and I will go down – if I go down at all – as a bloody British officer.'

The 'martyrdom' of the nationalists inspired the Irish Republican Army in its guerrilla war against British troops and their Irish 'collaborators', which was partially resolved by the creation in 1921 of the Irish Free State, without the six counties of Ulster.

IRELAND IN THE FIRST WORLD WAR

Birth of the Irish Republic, 1916, a lithograph relating to the Easter Rising of 1916 and subsequent declaration of an Irish Republic.

by a force of 8,000 British troops. Markiewicz led 120 Republicans holding the Royal College of Surgeons. She emerged on their surrender wearing the green uniform of the Irish Citizens' Army and kissed her revolver before handing it over. The revolver can be seen today in Dublin's National Museum.

Markiewicz was one of 70 women arrested in the immediate aftermath of the uprising, but was the only one to be held in solitary confinement at Kilmainham prison. From her cell she could hear the firing squads – 15 of the Republican leaders were executed – and she was condemned to death. But her sentence was commuted to life imprisonment and she was released from Aylesbury prison in 1917, following the amnesty granted to all those who had taken part in the Easter Rising.

In 1918 she was jailed again for her part in anti-conscription activities. In prison she stood in the 1918 general election as a Sinn Féin candidate in a Dublin constituency and became the first woman to be elected to the British parliament in its 1,000-year history. However, she declined to take her seat in the House of Commons, as this would have entailed swearing an oath of allegiance to the British crown. In 1919 she became Minister for Labour in the outlawed Irish parliament, the *Dáil Éireann*, another first for a woman.

After the Irish War of Independence of 1919–21 she opposed the Anglo-Irish Treaty of December 1921, which partitioned Ireland, but kept the most prosperous sector, the 'Six Counties' of the North, under British rule. Outraged by this betrayal of the dream of a united Ireland, Markiewicz denounced its Irish signatories and supporters as 'traitors'. Michael Collins, one of the signatories, declared that Markiewicz could never understand the rationale behind signing the treaty because she was English. It is fair to say that a number of Irish similarly failed to get the point, and continued the struggle through the political party, Sinn Féin and its armed and dangerous wing, the IRA.

Undeterred, Markiewicz fought on, playing her part in the struggle for power behind rival factions of Irish nationalists which followed the signing of the treaty, and which erupted into the Irish Civil War. Markiewicz supported the anti-treaty faction and in 1922 joined 200 anti-treaty militants who stormed the Four Courts in Dublin to defend the Republic first declared in 1916.

In 1923 she was elected to the Dáil (Irish Parliament) as the member for Dublin South, but her staunch republican views ensured a further spell behind bars. Feisty as ever, despite her age (56), she went on hunger strike with 92 other female prisoners before being released. In 1926 she joined the Fianna Fail party led by Éamon de Valera, an opponent of the Anglo-Irish Treaty, and in 1927 was re-elected for Dublin South. She died in the same year and over a quarter of a million people lined the streets of Dublin for her funeral.

The first Turkish woman aviator and one of the first female combat pilots in the world, Gökcen came to prominence in the uneasy years after the First World War. Adopted as a child by the founder of modern Turkey, Kemal Atatürk, she learned to fly at his insistence, as part of his nationwide campaign to liberate the women of his country from the Islamic veil and bring them into the modern world. Trained as a military pilot, she accepted Atatürk's mission for her without hesitation, and her gender proved no bar to her deployment on bombing raids.

Sabiha Gökçen
1913–2001

Orphaned as a young girl, Sabiha gave an early indication of her character as a 12-year old in 1925, when she seized the opportunity of Atatürk's visit to her home town of Bursa to approach the charismatic revolutionary leader and ask for his help. Describing her miserable poverty and wretched life since the death of her parents, Mustafa Izzet Bey and Hayriye Hanim, she begged him to get her into boarding school, to give her the chance to study and make something of herself.

Impressed, the 45-year-old Atatürk investigated Sabiha's background and agreed. Contacting her nearest male relative, her brother, he asked permission to adopt her and take her to the Presidential Palace in Ankara, to live with his other adoptive daughters, Zehra, Afet and Rukiye. Adoptions like these were common in the Turkish culture of the time, and served a political purpose as well as a humanitarian impulse for Atatürk. He adopted eight children in all, intent on demonstrating that he was a father to his people in every way.

Sabiha received her primary education in Ankara and later attended a girls' college in Istanbul. Her formal schooling was interrupted by illness, but Atatürk attached great importance to aviation, and planned that she should find her vocation in the sky ('Gök' in Turkish). To that end, when the Surname Law was passed in 1934, he gave her the surname of 'Gökçen', meaning 'belonging to the sky'.

The next year, Atatürk took Gökçen with him to the opening ceremony of the newly-inaugurated Turkish Flight School on 5 May 1935. As they watched the air show with its spectacular display of gliders and parachutists from different foreign countries, Atatürk asked Gökçen if she would like to become a skydiver, and she agreed. Atatürk then gave orders that she should be admitted as the first female trainee.

But when Gökçen began her training, she was much more interested in flying than parachuting, and soon received her pilot's licence. Atatürk then sent her to Russia for an advanced training course, and when she returned, he decided to test her nerve. Handing her a gun, he ordered her to put it to her head and pull the trigger. Only when she had passed the test did she discover that the gun was unloaded.

Satisfied, Gökçen's adopted father now enrolled her in the country's Air Force Academy at the beginning of 1936, to train as Turkey's first female

Sabiha Gökçen was not the only woman to train as a military pilot in Turkey in the 1930s. A female contemporary (above) at the Turkish Flight School was Sahavet Yslamazturk.

military pilot. There she improved her skills by flying bomber and fighter planes, and Atatürk saw to it that she was deployed on bombing raids against Kurdish rebels in the Tunceli Mountains in 1937. Her active service during this military operation made one of her the world's first female air force combat pilots, and she was awarded the Turkish Aeronautical Association's first 'Jewelled Medal' for her outstanding performance during the anti-insurgency campaign.

On Atatürk's direct orders, Gökçen flew all her raids with a loaded gun on her lap, primed to kill herself if she crash-landed rather than fall into rebel hands. She was honoured for her bravery on her return, when Atatürk himself set aside the cares of state to meet her with an official welcome at Ankara military airfield.

In 1938 Gökçen made a five-day flight around the Balkan countries, to great acclaim. Like so many other women in traditional societies who stepped outside their prescribed role in the tumultuous years after the First World War, she found herself involved in the wider 20th century conflict over how much freedom women should be allowed. Despite herself, she became a living advert for her mentor's ideals. Deployed on high-profile exhibition flights to the Balkans, Yugoslavia and Romania, Gökçen, Atatürk's 'creature of the air', took to the skies as his trophy pilot, living proof that the women of Turkey were soaring into freedom under his regime.

Fine ideals: but Gökçen was also used by Atatürk in other ways. On one occasion he ordered her to put on her uniform, charge into a restaurant and fire her gun in the air over the head of the French ambassador who was dining there. She was arrested by the police and thrown into jail. The next day she defended herself on the grounds of an excess of patriotic fervour, as Turkey was currently involved in a territorial dispute with the French. She was sentenced to one night in jail, which she had already served, and released.

When Atatürk died not long after Gökçen's celebrated flight in 1938, he left a house to his 'Adopted Daughter and Airwoman Sabiha Gökçen' in his will. Gökçen's active flying career spanned 28 years until 1964, during which she flew all round the world. In later years she became the chief instructor at the Turkish Flight School, where she served until 1955, eventually being appointed to the association's executive board. She never married, but devoted her life to aviation, training four female aviators to follow in her footsteps. Her life and career amply vindicated Atatürk's faith in her and his staunch and unwavering championing of women's rights.

During her time in the Turkish Air Force, Gökçen flew 22 different types of aircraft and logged more than 8,000 flying hours. Thirty-two of these were on active combat and missions of enemy bombardment. In 1996, the USAF nominated her for a poster depicting the 'Twenty Greatest

Like Sabiha Gökçen, the First World War pilot Eugenie Shakovskaya was one of a handful of women who took to the skies in the early years of the 20th century, refusing to allow her sex to hold her back. While Gökçen is thought to be the first female combat pilot in the world, Shakovskaya can fairly lay claim to being the first woman to fly a military aircraft in war.

A Russian princess and a royal Romanov, cousin of the last tsar, Nicholas II, she learned to fly before the First World War, training in Germany with the Wright Company of the United States. At the outbreak of war, Shakovskaya petitioned the tsar for permission to serve her country, and in November 1914 he awarded her the honorary rank of ensign in the 1st Russian Aerial Squadron. She joined the Russian Army of the Northwest, where she flew as a reconnaissance pilot, executing audacious flights above German lines.

In the course of one perilous sortie, she was wounded by ground fire, and the tsar decorated her with the Military Order of Saint George. But her career with the air squadron was clouded when rumours began to circulate that she was promiscuous, pursuing affairs with high-ranking officers. Suspicions about her virtue later hardened into doubts about her loyalty. Accused of being a German spy at a time of national crisis when Russia was losing the war, she

EUGENIE SHAKOVSKAYA
1889–1918

was charged with treason and sentenced to death.

But the tsar could not permit a royal Romanov to die by firing squad. Using his power as an autocrat, he saved Shakovskaya from the death penalty and commuted her sentence to life imprisonment. When the tsar was overthrown in the Russian Revolution of 1917, all his political prisoners were automatically deemed to be friends of the new regime. Shakovskaya was released from prison by the Bolsheviks, and as one who knew the tsarist regime well, was soon employed by the new government's secret police in Kiev.

There she is said to have been the chief executioner for the organization that later became the most feared tool of the communist regime, the KGB. Much of her work must have consisted of tracking down and informing against her extended royal family and network of former tsarist friends. Small wonder, then, that she became a confirmed drug addict. In an unexplained hallucinatory and drug-fuelled shooting bout of 1918, described as 'a narcotic delirium', she shot one of her assistants before being shot dead herself.

Eugenie Shakovskaya at Johannisthal aerodrome near Berlin, where she received her pilot's licence on 16 August 1912 flying a Farman biplane.

Aviators in History', the only female pilot to be granted such an accolade. Her memoir, *A Life Along the Path of Atatürk*, was published by the Turkish Aeronautical Association in 1981 to celebrate the centenary of Atatürk's birth, and she is commemorated today in the Sabiha Gökçen airport at Istanbul, fittingly a companion airport to the main airport, Atatürk.

In the 'Long March', the Chinese Communist Party (CCP) and its armed forces made an 8,000-mile (13,000-km) trek from their bases in southeast China, which had been encircled by the Nationalist forces of the Guomindang, to a new stronghold in the northwest. As comrades in arms, lovers and porters, large numbers of women sustained the troops in the ordeal of this strategic retreat, during which Mao Zedong emerged as the supreme leader of the Chinese Communist Party.

Women of the Long March
1934–35

Mao's First Front Army, which set off from Jiangsi province in October 1934, consisted of 86,000 men and some 30 women. The Fourth Front Army, which struck out from Sichuan in March 1935, had about 2,000 women in its ranks. The Second Front Army, formed by a merger of 2nd and 6th Army Groups and containing about 25 women, began its own march from a mountain base near the border of Hunan almost a year after the First Front Army set out.

Before the First Front Army began its march, the decision was taken to leave all the children behind. Mothers had to find local families willing to

adopt their children. Children born on the march would also have to be placed in new homes with local populations. Few of these women ever saw their children again.

Most of the leaders of the CCP were with the First Front Army, and the women travelled with them. Women who had been peasants before the march and accustomed to heavy work in the fields, carried supply and medicine boxes and undertook stretcher work. Educated women performed propaganda and recruitment roles, seeking out short-term transport workers who travelled with the army for several days before returning home. These workers were of crucial importance because the First Front Army had no motor vehicles and a crucial shortage of pack animals. Kang Keqing, the wife of the Communist commander-in-chief Chu Teh, marched with the military headquarters as a political instructor. She was also armed and carried out the same tasks as the other women on the march. Liu Ying worked with the First Front Army's logistics department, dealing with everything from money and guns to uniforms and printing presses.

Also travelling with the First Front Army was Mao's second wife He Zizhen, who was pregnant when the march began and gave birth in the spring of 1935. She had to give her baby away, the third time she had been forced to abandon a child. Her first little girl with Mao was given to a peasant woman, when she and Mao had to flee their guerrilla base. A second, a two-year-old boy, had been left in the care of her sister before the march began. He Zizhen later suffered a mental breakdown and spent many years in a sanatorium in the Soviet Union, an exile engineered by Mao's third wife, Jiang Qing (see page 171), a former bit-part film actress who had not been on the Long March. He Zizhen died in Shanghai in 1984.

In June 1935 the First Front joined hands with the Fourth Front Army, whose 2,000 female soldiers had been able to travel with their children and

Women are depicted prominently in this heroic socialist realist portrayal of the Communist Long March, entitled *Revolutionary Ideal is Supreme.*

husbands. The older children were taken on as orderlies, messengers and buglers. The Fourth Front fielded a women's factory battalion responsible for clothing and an independent battalion, later a regiment. The principal factor in the larger role played by women in the Fourth Front Army was opium, a staple crop in Sichuan. The high rate of male dependency on the drug meant that the Fourth Front had no choice but to recruit women.

In the Fourth Front Army, there were strict rules prohibiting male soldiers from mixing with the female units. On the whole discipline was maintained, but the Army's female troops suffered badly if they fell into the hands of hostile forces. Many were captured and raped by the private armies of the Muslim warlords of northwest China.

The armies on the Long March also incorporated teenage recruits who were dubbed the 'Little Red Devils'. It is estimated that there were about 5,000 in the 100,000-strong Fourth Front Army, many of them young girls. One of them recalled how she 'grew up' in the tough environment endured by the marchers: 'When I saw a soldier with a bandage covering his head not long after I joined the Army, I was so frightened that I ran away from him. Now, sometimes, my own comrades were killed right beside me. I had to deal with the wounded and dead every day, so I stopped being afraid.'

Conditions on the Long March were gruelling in the extreme. Moving at a punishing pace and often under both ground and air attack by the Nationalists, the columns crossed and re-crossed freezing rivers, mountain ranges and treacherous swampy grasslands. Battle casualties, disease, desertion and political purges took a heavy toll. In October 1935 the First Front Army arrived in Yenan, its final destination, with its strength reduced to some 8,000.

Of the 30 women who began the march with the Army, 19 survived. The enormous privations suffered by the women of the First and Fourth Front Armies rendered many of the survivors infertile. One survivor observed of her sacrifice: 'It was a small price to pay for the revolution.' The observation reflects how Mao alchemized a seemingly wretched defeat into the founding myth of modern China. One survivor, recalling the trek across the grasslands and the ascent into the mountains, observed: 'I never had the feeling that we wouldn't make it and I wasn't scared.'

Many of the women on the Long March had exchanged their husbands and families for the Red Army and the Communist Party. This relationship was, if anything, more demanding, but the strain was eased by the revolutionary comradeship they experienced. But this was achieved only by the subordination of the needs of the individual to those of the collective.

However, revolutionary fervour exacted its own price. For many of these women the Long March was an episode in a much longer and more demanding journey from which Communist China emerged in 1949 when the Nationalist resistance finally crumbled.

'It was a small price to pay for the revolution.'

FEMALE SURVIVOR OF THE LONG MARCH

'When war comes, even women have to fight.' This ancient saying of the Vietnamese dates back to the Tru'ung sisters (see pages 40–43), who drove the Chinese from Vietnam in the year 40, but it could also apply to the 30 years after the end of the Second World War, during which the Vietnamese rid themselves of two more foreign interlopers, the French and the Americans.

By 1941, the French colony of Indochina had fallen to the Japanese, who established their headquarters in Saigon. In 1945 Vietnamese women seized Japanese food depots to stave off starvation, and joined Ho Chi Minh, leader of the Communist Viet Minh, in seizing power in Hanoi, in northern Vietnam. However, the French returned after the Japanese surrender and in 1946 reoccupied Hanoi.

At first, the Viet Minh suffered many defeats, before the French established a strategic base at Dien Bien Phu in Vietnam's northern highlands, provoking a siege that ended in the surrender of 10,000 French troops in May 1954. Minority tribeswomen played a vital role in the Viet Minh victory, hauling supplies from Chinese outposts to supply the North Vietnamese forces. They carried bicycles, artillery components and ammunition, as well as food and weapons, and evacuated the Viet Minh wounded.

In July 1954 the Geneva Agreements were signed, partitioning Vietnam into the Communist North and

VIETNAM'S WOMEN FIGHTERS
1945–75

Nguyen Thi Kim Lai, a 17-year-old NLF militiawoman, escorts downed US airman William Robinson into captivity in December 1972.

US-backed South. The struggle against the French had been fought principally in North Vietnam. Now the focus shifted to the South, where there was no front line. In the new campaign, women of the Women's Liberation Organization, an arm of the North Vietnamese military (NLF), played a vital role. This involved liaising between villages in the south and NLF units in the jungle; intelligence work; feeding, clothing and concealing NLF fighters; and nursing the sick and wounded. They also harassed US and South Vietnamese troops at every turn. Fitter women worked in support formations, carrying huge quantities of rice into the jungle to supply NLF units and returning with wounded fighters. Their routes took them up and down the so-called Ho Chi Minh Trail, the infiltration route running through Laos to South Vietnam. They often had to negotiate the trail carrying burdens greater than their slight body weight while suffering from malaria. Women were a vital force in the struggle, a factor badly underestimated by the US commander General William Westmoreland and his staff. Even so, many women were imprisoned, tortured and killed in Operation 'Phoenix', the CIA-sponsored attempt to eliminate the NLF.

In the 1980s Kang Keqing became chairperson of the Chinese Communist Party. The vengeful Jiang Qing, who had seized power during Mao's dotage, was overthrown in 1976, imprisoned and sentenced to death. 'I was Chairman Mao's dog', she protested. 'Whoever he told me to bite, I bit.' Her sentence was later commuted to life imprisonment and in 1991, diagnosed with throat cancer, she hanged herself in hospital aged 77.

During the Spanish Civil War of 1936 to 1939, Dolores Ibárruri won a legendary reputation as a fiery orator who coined the Republican slogan *No passaran!* ('They shall not pass!') and told European audiences that 'the Spanish people would rather die on its feet than live on its knees'. Universally known as *'La Pasionaria'* (passion flower) she was one of the greatest orators of the 20th century.

Dolores Ibárruri Gomes

1895–1989

Dolores was born to poverty in Gallarta, in the Spanish Basque country, the eighth of 11 children of a Basque miner and a Castilian mother. Strong-willed and mischievous, she left school at the age of 15 and educated herself while working as a seamstress and later as a cook. In 1915 she married Julian Ruiz Gabina, a trade union activist and socialist. In 1918 she published her first article for for a miners' newspaper, *El Mineiro Vizcaino*, under the pseudonym *'La Pasionaria'*. Two years later she played a part in the formation of the Spanish Communist Party (CPE) and in 1932 became a member of its Central Committee.

During this period she wrote for the left-wing newspaper *El Mundo Obrero* and in 1934 founded an anti-fascist women's group, Agrupacion de Mujeres Antifacistas. Of the early years of her own marriage to fellow-Communist Julian Ruiz Gabina, she wrote: 'I had lived in less than a year an experience so bitter that only the love of my little one [her infant daughter] kept me hanging on to life. And I was terrified not only by the present, hateful and unbearable as it was, but by the future which I could foresee as appallingly painful and inhuman.' These were hard years; she bore Gabina six children of whom four died very young. Ibárruri and her husband fashioned their coffins out of orange boxes. Only one of her daughters – one of triplets – outlived her.

In the early 1930s Ibárruri was twice imprisoned for her political activities, and in November 1933 was a member of the Spanish delegation to the Communist International, which met in the Soviet Union. Ibárruri was intoxicated by Moscow: 'the most wonderful city on earth. The construction of socialism was being managed from it. In it were taking shape the earthly dreams of freedom of generations of slaves, outcasts, serfs, proletarians. From it one could take in and perceive the march of humanity towards Communism.' In the spring of 1935 she despatched her own children to this New Jerusalem.

In the general election of February 1936, Ibárruri was elected to the Spanish *Cortes* (parliament) and played a part in the installation of the left-wing Popular Front government, one of whose policies was the release of political prisoners. Ignoring legal niceties, Ibárruri immediately confronted the prison governor in Oviedo demanding that he hand over the key to set the prisoners free: 'He handed them over and I assure you that it was the most thrilling day of my activist life, opening the cells and shouting, "Comrades, everyone get out!" Truly thrilling. I did not wait for parliament to sit or for the release orders to be given. I thought, "We have run on the promise of freedom for the prisoners of the revolution of 1934 [the failed October revolution] – we won – today the prisoners go free." '

After the outbreak of the Spanish Civil War in 1936, Ibárruri was tireless in her support of the Republic on the radio and at mass rallies. The journalist Vincent Sheean, who saw her in full flow in 1938, gave this arresting thumbnail sketch of her inimitable style: 'The voice was not what is usually called "musical" – that is, it had no melodious tones and little sweetness ... Where it became quite unlike any other voice I have ever heard was in the effect of passionate sincerity. This expressive gift abides in Dolores' voice throughout, in her slightest remark as in

'*La Pasionaria*' addressing a crowd in 1937. An electrifying platform performer, invariably dressed in black, Ibárruri made an indelible impression on her audiences.

the great sweeping statements, with the result that it is impossible to disbelieve anything she says while she is actually saying it.'

In October 1938 the International Brigades (the volunteers who had fought on the Republican side) said farewell to Spain after a dramatic parade in Barcelona watched by a crowd of 300,000, while fighters flew overhead to deter Nationalist bombers. Ibárruri sent them off in style: 'Comrades of the International Brigades! Political reasons, reasons of state, the welfare of that same cause for which you offered your blood with boundless generosity, are sending you back, some of you to your own countries and others to forced exile. You can go proudly. You are history. You are legend. You are the heroic example of democracy's solidarity and universality. We shall not forget you and, when the olive tree of peace puts forth its leaves again, mingled with the laurels of the Spanish Republic's victory – come back!'

By the time the victor in the Spanish Civil War, the Nationalist General Francisco Franco, took the salute on his victory parade in May 1939, 'La Pasionaria' had gone into exile in the Soviet Union. With the signing of the Nazi–Soviet pact in August 1939, she became an isolated figure in Moscow. A potential embarrassment to Stalin, she was discreetly placed under the watchful eyes of Red Army guards, although her faith in communism never wavered. After the German invasion of the Soviet Union in June 1941, she ran a radio station broadcasting propaganda to Franco's Spain.

There was a price to be paid. Her son Ruben was killed during the Battle of Stalingrad in September 1942, the year that Ibárruri became the secretary-general of the Spanish Communist Party. In 1960 she made way for Santiago Carrillo and became the party's president. In the 1960s the Soviet Union awarded her the Lenin Peace Prize and the Order of Lenin, but she was highly critical of the Soviet invasion of Czechoslovakia in 1968.

In May 1977, following the death of Franco, Ibárruri returned to Spain where she received an ecstatic welcome. Shortly afterwards, she changed her first name from Isidora to Dolores. No sooner had she returned to Spain than she embarked on the campaign trail for the first democratic elections to the *Cortes* for 40 years. She had lost none of her spellbinding

'*Where it became quite unlike any other voice I have ever heard was in the effect of passionate sincerity. This expressive gift abides in Dolores' voice throughout, … with the result that it is impossible to disbelieve anything she says … '*

JOURNALIST VINCENT SHEEAN ON HEARING '*LA PASIONARIA*' SPEAK IN PUBLIC IN 1938

The *Mujeres Libres* were a group of female radicals who campaigned for women's liberation and an anarchist revolution during the Spanish Civil War (1936–39). The movement was founded in 1936 by Lucia Sanchez Saornil, Mercedes Comaposada and Amparo Poch y Gascon, and at its peak had some 30,000 members. Anarchism in Spain had deep roots and a long history.

As anarchists, they rejected the relegation of women to a secondary position within the liberation movement and opposed the philosophy of feminism, arguing that it merely strove to establish the 'equality of women within an existing system of privileges'. Rather, they strove to struggle for themselves by establishing their own organization.

Beginning with consciousness-raising and active preparation, they moved on to the creation of a network of like-minded women anarchists. Peripatetic day-care facilities were established to enable working-class women to participate in trade union activities. A journal was established, which focused on the achievements of exceptional women, popular culture, sport and education. The movement's propaganda was further spread by radio broadcasts, travelling libraries and lecture tours. A literacy programme went hand-in-hand with classes in social studies.

At a more practical level, the *Mujeres Libres* established community dining rooms for the Republican militias, trained nurses and set up emergency clinics to tend those wounded in the fighting and to advise on birth control and provide post-natal care. A clinic in Barcelona was named after Louise Michel (see pages 184–187). Looking to the future, the *Mujeres Libres* founded rural collectives with the help of anarchist trade unions, although it insisted on remaining free of the influence of their male-dominated leaderships.

During the Spanish Civil War, the anarchist movement was crushed by the Republican movement. The triumph of General Franco and the Falange in 1939 was followed by the redoubling of the persecution of dissidents and the anarchist movement was driven underground.

Many women fought for the Republican cause in the Spanish Civil War to protect the freedoms they had won in an ultra-Catholic and patriarchal society.

powers, dazzling packed halls and winning one of the seats for Oviedo. When the *Cortes* was opened by King Juan Carlos on 22 July, Ibárruri joined in the general ovation that followed the royal address, but pointedly remained seated. There was much that she could neither forgive nor forget.

Her last years were spent in a round of feminist rallies and political meetings at which the ageing heroine of the Republic invariably received the respect due to a modern icon. She died in hospital on 12 November 1989, at the age of 93. Thousands filed past her catafalque and two days later, thousands more attended her funeral, raising the defiant cry: 'They shall not pass!' For '*La Pasionaria*', perhaps, it was a blessing that she did not live to see the passing of the Soviet Union and communism, causes to which she had devoted her life and for which she had given her all.

Litvak was not only a seasoned Second World War fighter ace, but also a gift to Soviet propaganda during a key passage of the war on the Eastern Front. Such was the respect in which she was held by her opposite numbers in the Luftwaffe that, according to legend, it required no fewer than eight of them to put an end to her life.

Lilya Litvak
1921–43

From her teenage years, Litvak was 'air-minded', and at the age of 14 joined her local *Aeroklub*, making her solo debut a year later and subsequently joining the Soviet paramilitary air formation, the *Osoviakim*, as a flight instructor. In the opening phase of the German invasion of the Soviet Union in June 1941, Operation Barbarossa, the Red Army Air Force (VVS) suffered grievous losses at the hands of the Luftwaffe. On the first day of Barbarossa, *Luftflotte 2* ('Second Air Fleet'), supporting Army Group Centre, destroyed 528 Soviet aircraft on the ground and 210 in the air. Between June and October 1941 the VVS lost 5,316 aircraft, many of them on the ground. Yet in the depths of disaster lay the seeds of recovery. The large numbers of obsolete aircraft destroyed on the ground did not entail the loss of aircrew, who were retrained on the potent new types which the VVS was able to bring into service.

The disastrous performance of the VVS in the first two months of Barbarossa encouraged the formation of all-female aviation groups. The driving force behind this innovation was Marina Raskova (see page 226), a celebrated record-breaking aviatrix of the 1930s, who secured the formation of three complete women's air regiments, the 586th Fighter, 587th Bomber and 588th Night Bomber Regiments. Litvak joined the 586th Fighter Regiment, which had originally been intended as a reserve formation flying support missions. However, in the spring of 1942 the attrition of the air war on the Eastern Front thrust 586th Fighter Regiment into the front line.

Litvak and a number of other women, including Katya Budanova, earned transfers in September 1942 to the all-male 437th Fighter Regiment flying over Stalingrad. On 13 September, piloting a Lavochkin La-5 fighter, Litvak scored her first victory, shooting down a Junkers Ju88 fighter-bomber. She scored two more victories with the La-5 before switching to the durable Yakovlev Yak-1, with which she scored all her subsequent kills. In late 1942 Litvak was transferred to the 9th Guards Fighter Regiment and then, in January 1943, to the crack 296th Fighter Regiment (subsequently

redesignated 73rd Guards Fighter Regiment) flying 'free hunt' missions against targets of opportunity. Shortly afterwards she received the Order of the Red Star to add to the Order of the Red Banner and the Order of the Patriotic War. Twice she had to make forced landings due to battle damage, and twice she was wounded.

In February 1943 Litvak married Aleksei Solomatin, a fellow pilot from 73rd Guards Fighter Regiment, who was killed in June 1943. A month later, she lost her comrade Budanova, who had also died in air combat. Litvak was by now a national heroine, albeit a reluctant one as she was physically and emotionally drained by the strain of combat flying. Photographs of the time show a slim fair-haired woman with a steady but anxious gaze. She became expert at giving Red Army photographers the slip.

Lilya Litvak (left) and two fellow women pilots – Katya Budanova (centre) and Mariya Kuznetsova – study their flight plans on the tailplane of a Yak-1 fighter in mid-1942.

In the Second World War, an influential pre-war Soviet airwoman, Marina Raskova, played a key role in promoting the use of female combat aircrew in the Red Air Force. A record-breaking pilot of the interwar years, Raskova used her personal influence with Stalin, and her position on the People's Defence Committee, to secure the establishment of Aviation Group 122, a training formation in which both the air and ground crews were female.

Raskova oversaw the recruitment and training of the intake and their eventual assignment to three air regiments – the 586th IAP (Fighter), the 587th BAP (Bomber) and, perhaps the most celebrated, the 588th NBAP (Night Bomber). The 588th's aircrew flew obsolete wood and fabric Polikarpov Po-2 biplanes on night operations against targets in the enemy's rear areas. The strategic importance of these missions was negligible, but the psychological effect was often considerable on exhausted German formations recovering from heavy fighting.

With its 110hp engine, the highly manoeuvrable Po-2 had a maximum speed of only 94 mph (150 kph), lower than the stall speeds of the high-performance German Me109 or FW190 fighters, which made it very hard to shoot down as it flew along the deck to launch its bombing run. Near the target, the Po-2's pilots would cut their engines and glide into the attack, the eerie whistling sound of the wind against the planes' bracing wires prompting the Germans to coin the phrase *Nachthexen* ('Night Witches'). In a practice that recalled the early bombing raids of the First World War, the bomb load was sometimes stored inside the cockpit of the Po-2 and tossed overboard by the aircrew. Most of the women declined to wear parachutes, preferring death to becoming prisoners of war.

The 588th Night Bomber Regiment, commanded by Yevdokia Bershanskaya, was in action from 1942 to the fall of Berlin in 1945. In February 1943, in recognition of its outstanding service, it was re-designated the 46th Guards Night Bomber Regiment, and by the end of the war had flown 24,000 combat missions, dropping 23,000 tons of bombs. No fewer than 23 of its aircrew became Heroes of the Soviet Union (the title 'Mother Heroine of the Soviet Union' was reserved for women who patriotically produced large numbers of children).

On 4 January 1943 while leading a flight of Pe-2 bombers to reinforce the Stalingrad front, Marina Raskova crashed in a heavy snowstorm and was killed. She received the Soviet Union's first state funeral of the war and was buried in Red Square. In September 1943 the formation she had commanded was re-designated 125th M.M. Raskova Guards Bomber Aviation Regiment.

Mariya Dolina, a later commander of the Marina M. Raskova Bomber Regiment, was decorated for her bravery on the Baltic Front in 1945.

On 1 August 1943, while escorting ground-attack aircraft on her third sortie of the day, Litvak's Yakovlev Yak-1b was intercepted and shot down by a gaggle of German fighters. Litvak had flown 168 combat missions, scoring 12 individual kills and three shared victories. Her aircraft was never found, prompting the Soviet high command to surmise that she might have been captured, and thus to deny her the award of Hero of the Soviet Union.

In 1979, after an extensive search which uncovered some 30 aircraft, it appeared that the crash site had been found near the village of Dmitrievka, in the district of Shakhterski, where a woman pilot's body had been buried. A forensic examination indicated that she had succumbed to a head wound. Ten years later Litvak was given an official burial, and in May 1990 President Mikhail Gorbachev posthumously made her a Hero of the Soviet Union.

Nevertheless, Litvak has not been allowed to rest in peace. The official line that the body at Dmitrievka was that of Litvak has been challenged by some of her old comrades, notably Ekaterina Polunina, chief mechanic and archivist of the 586th Regiment, and also by Kazimiera Janina Cottam, an author specializing in Soviet women in the military. Cottam maintains that Litvak survived a forced landing and was captured by the Germans and held. The truth will probably never be known, nor will it undermine Litvak's outstanding achievement in an arena dominated by men. In this context it is interesting to note that the highest-scoring fighter ace of the Second World War, and indeed of all time, was the German Erich Hartmann with 352 victories, all of them gained on the Eastern Front. In second place, with 301 kills (again all on the Eastern Front) was Gerhard Barkhorn. The highest-scoring Soviet fighter ace was Ivan Kozhedub with 62 victories. Litvak could not match these scores, but her courage was matchless.

On 1 September 1939 Article 13 of the universal military law was ratified by the Fourth Session of the Supreme Soviet, enabling the Red Army to accept women trained in critical medical and technical areas. During the 'Great Patriotic War' (the Russian term for the Second World War), some 40 percent of the front-line medical personnel would be women, fighting against Hitler's invasion of their homeland.

Red Army Women Soldiers
1941–45

In May 1941, on the eve of Operation Barbarossa, the German invasion of the Soviet Union, the Red Army's strength stood at some five million men. By the end of December, when Barbarossa had blown itself out, the Russians had lost over three million men taken prisoner in a series of massive 'cauldron' battles (battles of encirclement). The exact number of men killed and wounded has never been quantified. Continuing losses in 1942 nearly decimated the Red Army and changed the reluctance of the Soviet high command (*Stavka*) to recruit women to take a fighting role.

In the summer of 1942 a recruiting drive aimed at women began; in part its aim was to shame the men of the Red Army into greater efforts, and also to accelerate the integration of Soviet women into war industry. During the war some 800,000 Soviet women served in combat formations, some 8 percent of the Red Army's total strength.

Due to *Stavka* inefficiency and lack of foresight, women faced formidable problems of integration. Female recruits struggled with male uniforms and boots, which in many cases were several sizes too big. There was no female underwear in store and there were no segregated latrines. In a surreal move, when one considers the savagery that characterized the fighting on the Eastern Front, the Soviet high command introduced 43 mobile tea rooms for female troops, plus cosmetic counters and hairdressers. Women who did not smoke were given chocolate rations. However, they had to wait until the end of the war for uniforms specially designed for the female physique.

Some 70 percent of the women serving in the Red Army were posted to the front, but were often kept away from the sharp end of the fighting and assigned to anti-aircraft (AA) batteries or engineer battalions, where they performed their duties on an equal footing with men. Approximately 300,000 served in AA units and, in contrast to their British counterparts, performed every function, including the firing of the guns. For instance, Klavdia Konovaluva from the Georgian Republic, who served with 784th AA Regiment, had been a blacksmith in civilian life and joined her unit as a gunlayer. This Red Army Amazon quickly became a gunloader, which involved shifting 16-kilogram (36-lb) shells at high speed, often under heavy fire.

There were some all-woman AA units in which a female military subculture flourished, encouraging a warmer approach to the generally ferocious military discipline of the Red Army. Yet throughout the war male officers were reluctant to commit women to action, partly out of male shame and also from an apprehension that women 'were not up to the job'. 'Why are you bringing these girls here?' – the response of one disgruntled Red Army officer – was a common reaction.

Many clearly were up to the job. Some women trained tank crews, while others drove tanks in the field. Mariya Oktyabrskaya bought a tank from her personal

This section of the monument to the Red Army in Sofia, Bulgaria, shows a mother bidding farewell to her daughter as she leaves for the front. Women played a major part in the defence of the Soviet Union during the Great Patriotic War.

savings and fought as its commander, with the rank of guards sergeant, until she was mortally wounded in action in January 1944. Marina Lagunova graduated from a tank-training brigade as a driver-mechanic and later fought in the Battle of Kursk (1943) and the advance to the River Dnieper. In September 1943 her tank 'brewed up' after receiving a direct hit, and she was so badly burned that both her legs were amputated. Undaunted, no sooner had she left hospital than she learned to drive again and returned to duty as a tank instructor.

One tank family went to a shared wartime grave. On the death of Colonel Koponets his daughter Yelizaveta volunteered for the armoured corps, serving as a gunner/wireless operator only to be killed in 1945 in the Battle of Berlin. With one exception, all the women who fought in tanks rode in the medium T-34. The exception was Alexandra Boiko who, with her husband, pulled a great many strings to gain a place at the Tank Technical School at Chelyabinsk. They eventually rode into battle in the heavy IS-2 tank, which weighed 45 tons. Alexandra commanded the behemoth and her husband served as the driver/mechanic. The couple fought together in the great battles of 1944–45, in the Baltic states, Poland, Czechoslovakia and in the drive to Berlin.

'We didn't shoot. I cooked porridge for the soldiers … I was given a medal for that … '

A SOVIET WOMAN RECRUIT RECALLS HER WAR

In the Red Army, medical support tasks were wholly integrated with combat, and doctors and nurses served in the front line under heavy fire. All the nurses and some 40 per cent of the doctors in the Soviet military were women. There were many instances of the heroism of Red Army personnel under fire, although some of them were in all likelihood embellished for reasons of propaganda. Vera Krylova enlisted as a student nurse in 1941 and in front-line service dragged hundreds of wounded comrades to safety. In August 1941 at the height of Operation Barbarossa, when German armies were racing across the Soviet Union, the wounded Krylova is said to have taken command of an ambushed company whose officers had been killed and, riding a horse in a two-week running battle, led the survivors back to Soviet lines. A year later, in another improbable tale, she was reported to have singlehandedly charged a German tank formation, hurling grenades as she went and enabling her comrades to evacuate their position.

Whatever the precise truth of these exploits, they nevertheless reflect the courage of Red Army women in the front line. Perhaps a more typical memory of a woman's war is that of one veteran who, recalling her service, reflected: 'We didn't shoot. I cooked porridge for the soldiers … I was given a medal for that … I dragged cauldrons and mess tins about. Heaven knows, they were heavy. I remember our commander saying, "I'll shoot holes through those mess tins … How are you going to give birth after the war?" '

In the highly specialized military discipline of sniping, women of the Red Army enjoyed a very high reputation and rate of success. Sniping was a deadly skill that was highly prized on the Eastern Front, which saw many savage city battles, notably that for Stalingrad (August 1942 – January 1943).

In the summer of 1941 Ludmilla Pavlichenko exchanged her history studies at Kiev University for service in the Red Army's 25th Rifle Division. Pavlichenko was to become one of approximately 1,600 female snipers who fought with the Red Army during the war, of whom some 500 survived the conflict.

In 1941 Pavlichenko fought at Odesssa, on the Black Sea, recording 187 kills. In the summer of 1942 she was at Sevastopol in the Crimea, which fell to the Germans after a long and bitter siege. In June 1942 she was wounded by mortar fire and shortly afterwards was pulled out of front-line combat. By then her score had risen to 309, including 36 enemy snipers.

Now a national heroine, Pavlichenko was despatched on a morale-boosting tour of North America, visiting President Roosevelt in the White House and travelling across the United States in the company of Eleanor Roosevelt. The Americans dubbed her 'Sniper Number One' and presented her with a Colt revolver. Folk singer Woody Guthrie even wrote a song about her. On her return to the Soviet Union, Pavlichenko spent the rest of the war training snipers before resuming her career as an historian. She died in 1974.

Sniper Tatiana Baramzina, who was tortured and killed by the Germans.

Nina Lobkovskaya attended a Red Army sniper school in the winter of 1942 and then served with the Third Shock Army on the Kalinin Front. She recalled: 'When we arrived, we spent the days in constant observation of the enemy's front line. When we came back for a night and went to bed, our memory held the picture of the terrain in every detail, with every leaf, every blade of grass standing out. And, as we arrived back to our observation positions the following day, we noticed the slightest of changes. This observation technique we had acquired at the sniper school proved very useful.'

Lobkovskaya marched all the way to Berlin with her unit. During its westward drive the women snipers' formation in which she served was redesignated a Guards Company. She was badly wounded in 1944 in heavy fighting in the Baltic, and finished the war with a tally of 89 kills. She was just 20 years old, with a round Russian face, teasing smile and turned-up nose.

Tatiana Baramzina served as a sniper in a rifle regiment with Third Belorussian Front from April 1944, and in three months accounted for 16 of the enemy. On 5 July 1944 she was captured by the Germans and brutally tortured. Her eyes were gouged out and she was then shot at point-blank range with an anti-tank rifle. In March 1945 she was posthumously awarded the Gold Star and created a Hero of the Soviet Union. By the end of the war, the markswomen trained at the Soviet Union's Central School for Snipers had accounted for some 12,000 German troops.

Over 100,000 of the Red Army women were decorated during the war, including 86 women who received the Hero of the Soviet Union medal, the USSR's highest award for valour. Three women – sniper Petrova, machine-gunner Stanilizhene and air gunner Zhurkina – were awarded all three classes (bronze, silver and gold) of the Order of Glory, the most highly respected soldiers' decoration.

In Britain during the Second World War, women of the Auxiliary Territorial Service (ATS) played a vital role in the nation's Anti-Aircraft (AA) Command. The idea was first mooted in 1938 by its commander General Sir Frederick Pile, with advice from Caroline Haslett, a distinguished engineer, on the suitability of women for this role in home defence. Training for mixed AA batteries began in the spring of 1940, to meet an estimated shortfall in AA Command of some 1,100 officers and 18,000 men, and the first mixed battery was deployed on 21 August 1941 in Richmond Park, on the outskirts of London. The first German aircraft to be shot down by a mixed battery crashed near Newcastle on 8 December 1941.

Britain's Mixed Anti-Aircraft Batteries 1939–45

ATS women operating a sound locator at a mixed AA battery in January 1943. The officer commanding the first mixed battery to bring down a German bomber commented: 'As an old soldier, if I were offered the choice of commanding a mixed battery or a male battery, I say without hestitation I would take the mixed battery. The girls cannot be beaten in action, and in my opinion they are definitely better than the men on the instruments they are manning ... '

At full strength a mixed battery contained 189 men and 229 women, including officers. At the outset, each battery had 11 male and three female officers, the latter performing administrative and welfare duties. However, in 1943 the first female Technical Control Officers began to assume operational responsibilities on gun sites in Home Command.

On the site, women operated all the equipment except the guns, handling the radar, predictors and radio communications. Pile, an unlikely feminist, saw no logical reason why women should not fire the guns, but he was overruled. The wartime history of AA Command patronizingly observed of the women in mixed batteries: 'They have the right delicacy of touch, the keenness and the application which is necessary to the somewhat tiresome job of knob twiddling, which are the lot of the instrument numbers. In principle, also, women will take on all the duties of mixed searchlight detachments.'

The searchlight batteries had been the first operational ATS units within AA command, a pioneer 'experimental' battery having been established in April 1941 and manned by an all-ATS crew wearing male battledress. An ATS version of battledress was subsequently introduced in specifically female sizes and in a finer 'Saxony serge'. But however finely dressed, the women on searchlight duty were still not allowed to return fire if machine-gunned by enemy aircraft.

Work on the searchlight batteries was demanding, and included the shifting of tons of earth, filling and laying sandbags, renovating derelict sites, logging all aircraft and transmitting messages between command posts and gun operations rooms. The British wartime leader and prime minister Winston Churchill's daughter, Mary, was one of the first women to volunteer for duties with a mixed battery.

The idea of men and young women working together, sometimes in remote and physically arduous conditions, was approached with caution by the army. Initially, it was decided to combine ATS volunteers with men who had just joined up, on the basis that the latter's lack of military experience would not prejudice them against working alongside women. Great care was also taken in the appointment of male officers, often relatively old, fatherly or schoolmaster types, in an attempt to minimize friction in the batteries.

The mixed batteries played a vital role in the summer and autumn of 1944, when a significant proportion of AA Command's resources was

---

HIT AND MISS

In 1942 Dorothy Calvert was serving as a radar operator on an AA gun emplacement near Cheltenham, Gloucestershire: 'We had been gazing at the tubes for hours, and we were all feeling rather boss-eyed, trying to keep our concentration fixed on our job … On my elevation tube I saw, or thought I saw, one "blip" slowly moving across, and it had been drilled into our heads that one "blip" without a small "blip" behind was the enemy. I nudged the girl next to me who checked her tube and mine. It was there alright.'

Calvert's sergeant, also a woman, rang the command post, which checked their range bearing and elevation and opened fire. Calvert takes up the story: 'The poor old radar cabin was shaking with the bangs, and we girls were shivering with the excitement of it all. After a few shots the target was lost, which could mean only one thing. We had scored a hit … Oh boy! Our first hit – we'd show them!'

The next day, in the battery's mess hall, Calvert and her comrades were introduced to an RAF aircrew, all of whom were wearing their flying gear. The pilot told them: 'Yes, you got us in about six shots.' Calvert was devastated: 'I felt as if I had been shot down. I had been on cloud nine and now I was down to earth with a bang. I looked at the others, and I could tell that they were feeling just as deflated as me … Then

the pilot said (which I thought was super of him): "Don't take it to heart, it wasn't your fault as our Identification Friend or Foe signal had broken down – it could have happened to anyone." Well he had put things right for us, we had not done anything wrong on the sets, but somehow it did not make me feel any better. The thing that stopped me from howling was that the aircrew were safe.'

A British radar operator tracking the movement of enemy aircraft during the Second World War.

deployed to southern England to deal with the threat posed by German V-1 flying bombs. Many batteries were transferred to the south coast, where the men and women who serviced them had an uninterrupted view of the V-1s as they approached Britain. They were in the front line.

The crews lived under canvas surrounded by seas of mud and in improvised accommodation. One gunner, Lynne Griffiths, remembered: 'The huts we lived in were holiday chalets with walls as thin as cardboard. I remember we always seemed to have wet feet and wet blankets.' Moreover, the women were living and working with guns massed all around them. The noise of the barrage was deafening, the sky pockmarked with thousands of exploding shells. Tin hats were the order of the day, and at night the women snatched sleep with their helmets balanced over their faces. A newspaper reported that the favourite story of the men on one site was that when they shot down their first V-1, they ran into the shelter as it plummeted earthward: 'but the ATS just stood around and cheered, although the bomb crashed down only a few hundred yards from where they stood! Later the girls learned to dash into their slit trenches for safety as quickly as any man.'

> ### 'In three days our battery shot down over a hundred [V-1s]. We were very proud.'
>
> Lynne Griffiths on her AA unit's success

Ruth Negus vividly recalled the pressure of primitive conditions and non-stop action: 'We lived in denims during the day and changed into battledress after work. The flying-bomb battle made life very intense. We slept completely dressed and in plimsolls. It was difficult for us to get a proper wash or any sleep as everyone was fully stretched. Even the cooks and orderlies were pressed into service. All leave was cancelled and mail censored. I was in personal agony as I had a whitlow on my finger and the only treatment was soaking it in water. When I went to the medical officer, he just lanced it with a scalpel before it was ready and even before asking me to sit down. That was followed by an abcess in my ear for which the ear was syringed with cold water, and after that a series of sties. No antibiotics then!'

By the autumn of 1944, the V-1 menace had been overcome by the combination of massed AA batteries firing shells armed with proximity fuses, and fast fighter aircraft. The V-1 had proved to be an inaccurate weapon, but the area of Greater London was a very big target. By early September, some 21,000 Londoners had been killed or wounded by approximately 1,000 'doodlebugs', as they were dubbed. About 15,000 houses had been destroyed. This second Blitz prompted a new wave of evacuation, and every evening thousands sheltered in the London Underground system. At the height of the battle, Lynne Griffiths was stationed at Folkestone, in Kent, which was dubbed 'Hellfire Corner.' She remembered that: 'in three days our battery shot down over a hundred [V-1s]. We were very proud.'

The Warsaw Ghetto uprising was one of the rare engagements of the Second World War in which women fought alongside men, showing beyond doubt what women could do when given weapons and allowed to take part in combat. The heroism of the Jewish women involved in the Warsaw Ghetto Uprising was such that it received the grudging admiration of the German commander of the forces against which they made their courageous but doomed last stand.

Women of the Warsaw Ghetto Uprising
1943

At the outbreak of the Second World War, there were some three million Jews in Poland, of whom about 300,000 lived in the capital, Warsaw, where they formed about one-third of the city's population. The Warsaw ghetto was established by Poland's German occupiers in the autumn of 1940. Within a matter of days, an 11-mile (18-km) wall, 3–6 metres (10–20 ft) high and topped with broken glass and barbed wire had been erected in order to isolate an area of 2.5 square miles (6.5 square km) east of the River Vistula. The original population of the area had been moved out and replaced by some 138,000 Jews. No Jews were allowed to leave the area, with the exception of a handful employed in war-related industries. Thousands more Jews were transported to Warsaw from cities and towns across Poland, and eventually approximately 433,000 Jews were incarcerated in the ghetto. Thousands of its inhabitants died every month from starvation and disease.

For those trapped in the ghetto, communication with the outside world was both illegal and fraught with danger.

July 1942 saw the first shipments from the Warsaw ghetto to the gas chambers of Treblinka, a death camp only 40 miles (64 km) away. The Jewish Council, a body established by the Germans, was ordered to supply 6,000 people a day for 'resettlement'. Few had any inkling that this was a death sentence. A German poster offered three kilos (nearly 7 lb) of bread and a kilo (some 2 lb) of jam to all those who reported for resettlement on 29–31 July.

However, the truth about Treblinka was discovered by a member of the *Bund*, the underground Jewish socialist party in Poland. The news was

Nazi troops round up Jewish fighters during the Warsaw Ghetto Uprising of 1943. Photograph from SS commander Jürgen Stroop's report on the action in May to Heinrich Himmler.

published in the *Bund* newspaper, but made little or no impact on the situation. By September 1942 the population of the ghetto had fallen to 60,000. The decision to resist the liquidation of the ghetto was led by *Zydowska Organizacja Bojowa* (ZOB), 'Jewish Combat Organisation', a group of some 500 young male and female Zionists opposed to the *Bund*, who up to that point had remained isolated and powerless. From December 1942 onwards the ZOB began to acquire small quantities of arms with the help of a clandestine body, the Polish Home Army, formed in September 1939 by Karas Tokarzewski, who within a few months had been arrested. By the spring of 1943 the Polish Home Army was commanded by General Tadeusz Bór Komorowski.

On 18 January 1943 the Germans embarked upon a renewed round-up in the ghetto. This time it met armed resistance, and the operation was abandoned after four days of fighting. The mood of fatalism that had previously pervaded the ghetto was lifted. Taxes were imposed on wealthy inhabitants of the ghetto to obtain fuel and arms from outside its walls, and the ZOB received some additional weapons from the Polish Home Army. Training and weapons drill was stepped up. Bunkers were prepared with supplies of food and water.

On 19 April 1943 a contingent of 3,000 SS troops supported by tanks and flamethrowers, and commanded by SS General Jürgen Stroop, was sent into the ghetto with orders to clear out the remaining inhabitants and destroy the buildings. They were met with small arms fire and grenade attacks. Small detachments of armed Jews totalling some 750 male and female fighters armed with grenades, Molotov cocktails, 17 rifles and a handful of pistols engaged the SS in a running battle. The Jews were meant to go like lambs to the slaughter, but they fought like tigers, using hidden bunkers and secret escape routes. Stroop himself, who had previous experience fighting partisans, reported on the battle in the ghetto: 'Jews and Jewesses shot from two pistols at the same time ... Jewesses carried loaded [weapons] in their clothing ... At the last moment they would pull out hand grenades ... and throw them at the soldiers.'

The battle lasted for 27 days. On 8 May the headquarters bunker of the ZOB at 18 Mila Street was overrun and its leader Mordecai Anielewicz was

'Jews and Jewesses shoot from two pistols at the same time ... Jewesses carried loaded [weapons] in their clothing ... At the last moment they would pull out hand grenades ... and throw them at the soldiers.'

SS GENERAL JÜRGEN STROOP ON THE TENACITY OF THE WARSAW GHETTO FIGHTERS

The Polish Catholic Irena Sendlerowa, a welfare officer in Warsaw's health administration, was a member of *Zegota*, a secret organization established in the Second World War by the Polish government-in-exile in London to rescue Polish Jews. She was permitted to enter the Warsaw Ghetto, which had been established by the Germans in the autumn of 1940, and by 1942 contained some 433,000 Jews. Wearing a Star of David, which the Germans forced the Jews to wear as a mark of identification, she handed out money, clothes and medicines, and smuggled children to safety through the sewers or hidden in workmen's bags before placing them with friendly families, convents or orphanages.

She noted the children's names on cigarette papers, which she sealed in glass bottles and buried in a colleague's garden. In the autumn of 1943, following the liquidation of the ghetto, she was arrested and tortured by the Germans. She managed to bribe her way out of execution, but was left permanently crippled.

It was not until 2007, when one of the children she had saved revealed Sendlerowa's courage to journalists, that her story became widely known. In that year she was honoured by the Polish government for 'rescuing the most defenceless victims of Nazi ideology' – the Jewish children – and nominated for the Nobel Peace Prize. Sendlerowa, crippled but serene, was insistent that she had done nothing extraordinary, observing: 'I was brought up to believe that a person must be rescued when drowning, regardless of race or nationality.'

Irena Sendlerowa in old age. In 1965 she was given the title of 'Righteous Among the Nations' by the Yad Vashem Holocaust memorial organization in Israel.

killed. Stroop proceeded methodically, using fire rather the sword. Water, gas and electricity were cut off and buildings set ablaze block by block. Cellars were cleared with 'smoke candles'; as their occupants emerged, they were mown down. Even so, several dozen fighters escaped through the sewers. Eight days later Stroop called a halt to the operation. He said his forces had captured 56,065 Jews and announced that he was going to blow up the Great Synagogue on Tlomack Street as a sign of victory.

At the final count, over 7,000 inhabitants of the ghetto were killed and another 7,000 transported to Treblinka. Around 300 Germans had died in the fighting. The Polish Jews had provided their fellow Poles with a heroic example of resistance. Their cause had been hopeless, but their courage was superb. In the process they had demonstrated the effectiveness of urban guerrilla warfare waged with unflinching determination against a better armed and numerically superior enemy.

In 1943 the effective head of the Special Operations Executive's F (French) Section was not its director, Colonel Maurice Buckmaster, but his assistant Vera Atkins. This placed the Romanian-born Atkins in an uncomfortable position because until 1944, when she became a naturalized Briton, she was an enemy alien at the heart of British intelligence operations in Occupied France (Romania had joined the war as an ally of Germany in June 1941). This anomaly explains Atkins's many successes as a spymistress and also her principal failures in the shadowy world of the Special Operations Executive.

Vera Atkins
1908–2000

Vera was born in 1908 in Galatz (now Galati), Romania, the daughter of a prosperous Jewish timber merchant, Max Rosenberg, and an English mother. The young Vera was intelligent and multilingual, and attended a finishing school in Switzerland.

In the 1930s Romania was a seething hotbed of spies. Both Vera and her father shared informal links with British intelligence (MI6). In 1934 she gained employment as a 'foreign correspondent' with the Pallas Oil Company working as an intermediary with foreign clients. The job gave Vera access to useful information about Romania's strategically important oil industry and offered her opportunities to travel widely. In addition, her friendship with the German ambassador in Bucharest, Count Friedrich von der Schulenburg, who was hostile to the Nazi régime, placed her in an excellent position to supply her British contacts with useful diplomatic and economic information about central Europe.

In 1932 Vera's father died bankrupt, and in 1937, as anti-Semitism grew in Romania, she moved with her mother to London, adopting the latter's maiden name of Atkins. In June 1940, while serving with the Chelsea Air Raid Precautions (ARP) group, Atkins was approached to join the Special Operations Executive (SOE) by an old friend from her days in Bucharest, and in March 1941 she joined F Section as a secretary.

At SOE's headquarters on London's Baker Street, Atkins rose rapidly from her post of secretary to become a key member of F Section. From early 1942 her 'confidential work' included the selection of female agents, of which there was a growing number; their preparation and briefing before despatch to Occupied France; maintaining contact while they were in the field; debriefing on their return; and liaising on a very guarded basis with her agents' next of kin. The last duty required a cold-blooded

'France has lost a battle, but France will win the war'—these words by Charles de Gaulle were often associated with this lithograph that envisaged the outcome of the war, including the aid of the French Resistance. Vera Atkins played a key role in forging contacts between the British clandestine sabotage agency, the SOE, and the networks of freedom fighters within Occupied France.

professionalism as Atkins's agents trusted her not to tell their families the truth about their activities and, if they fell into German hands, their fate.

Of the 470 agents despatched by F Section, 118 failed to return after German intelligence successfully penetrated a number of the section's networks. The most serious setback suffered by F Section during the war was the disabling of the large 'Prosper' network, based in Paris, as a result of the treachery of its field air-movements officer, Henri Déricourt, a former stunt pilot who was responsible for the reception and return to England of agents in the field.

By the autumn of 1943 there was mounting evidence that 'Prosper' had been fatally compromised. This Buckmaster chose to ignore. Atkins and Buckmaster enjoyed an extremely close working relationship, and the former harboured the gravest doubts about Déricourt's integrity – in the 1990s she told her biographer Sarah Helm that she 'knew he was rotten from the very start'. Nevertheless, Atkins was unable to challenge Buckmaster or limit the damage to 'Prosper'. Several factors tied her hands.

WOMEN IN SOE

The Special Operations Executive (SOE) was the brainchild of Britain's wartime prime minister Winston Churchill, and was formed at his behest in July 1940. Its purpose was to gather intelligence, undertake sabotage, and support Resistance movements in the countries of Europe and the Far East occupied by Germany and its allies. By the summer of 1944 SOE employed some 10,000 personnel overall, of whom about 3,200 were women. Roughly half of the personnel were agents in the field or awaiting despatch.

Although the majority of agents in the field were men, women played a significant role in SOE, particularly in the French (F) Section, which was responsible for operations in Occupied France, the most significant theatre of SOE operations. In the course of the war, F Section sent 470 agents into the field, of whom 39 were women. In all 118 failed to return, among them 13 women.

Until 1943, the man principally responsible for recruiting men and women for field work in SOE was Selwyn Jepson, who in peacetime had been a crime writer. Jepson accorded women complete equality with men in training for field operations, although he initially encountered stiff opposition within SOE. He later defended his decision: 'In my view women were very much better than men for the work. Women, as you know, have a far greater capacity for cool and lonely courage than men. Men don't work alone; their lives tend to be always in company with other men. There was opposition from most quarters until it went to Churchill, whom I had met before the war. He growled at me, "What are you doing?" I told him and he said, "I see you are using women to do this" and I said, "Yes, don't you think it's a very sensible thing to do?" and he said, "Yes, good luck to you". That was my authority.'

In the field an SOE network, or circuit, depended on three figures – a courier, a wireless operator and an organizer. Most of SOE's female field agents in France worked as couriers, travelling around as messengers and liaison officers. Because they were constantly on the move, couriers ran the highest risk of arrest. It was thought that in this situation women would find it easier to invent plausible cover stories, and would attract less attention than men, who from early 1942 were liable to be picked up by the Germans from the streets of France and sent to Germany as forced labour. Women were also less likely to be body-searched and thus could more easily secrete messages.

There was a strong, albeit unacknowledged streak of casual anti-Semitism within SOE, of which Atkins was well aware. Moreover, her status in 1943 as an enemy alien at the heart of the British intelligence establishment obliged her to temper her true feelings with extreme caution. Urgency was added by an episode that had occurred before Atkins joined SOE. In 1940 she had travelled to Nazi-occupied Belgium on a private mission to negotiate with German intelligence, the *Abwehr*, a safe passage to Istanbul for a Jewish cousin, Fritz Rosenberg. If F Section had known that she had passed a substantial sum of money to the *Abwehr* to secure his safety, her position within SOE would have been fatally undermined. It was perhaps inevitable that to survive in the wartime secret world, and in the ensuing peace, Atkins became an implacable guardian of her own secrets.

Vera Atkins (second from right) photographed in the company of other SOE operatives at a reunion in 1984. On the far left is her former boss, Colonel Maurice Buckmaster.

On 24 March 1944 Atkins became a British citizen and two weeks later was made F Section's intelligence officer. At the end of the war SOE was dissolved and many of its embarrassing secrets buried. But the war was not over for Vera Atkins. In January 1946 she travelled to liberated Europe with the rank of squadron officer to assist Allied war crimes investigators. She took with her a list of missing agents, of whom 13 were women.

Atkins was a relentless and implacable interrogator, rarely displaying emotion. However, even on this mission she was careful to cover her tracks. The traces left by one SOE agent in particular, Noor Inayat Khan ('Madeleine'), a victim of the 'Prosper' débâcle and Déricourt's treachery, proved immensely difficult to pin down, prompting Atkins to conclude that she had died at Natzweiler-Struthof, a concentration camp in the Vosges. When she found out that 'Madeleine' had in fact died at Dachau, she falsified the records to mask her initial error.

After the war, Atkins became the unofficial keeper of the F Section flame, adviser to film productions celebrating the heroism of agents she had handled, such as Violette Szabo ('Louise'), and guardian of the agency's most awkward secrets. Temperamentally unable to admit any error, she became skilled at deterring or deflecting probing questions raised by some of the postwar chroniclers of SOE, regularly weeding the large collection of wartime files she kept in her home. Her impregnable reserve prompted many fanciful theories about her motives, including the contradictory allegations that she was a German double agent or tool of the Kremlin.

Inayat Khan's brother took a more guarded view, recalling that Vera Atkins was 'not charming, but remarkable in her own way.'

In August 1943, the month Pearl Witherington completed her SOE training, an official report concluded: 'She is loyal and reliable but has not the personality to act as a leader. She is so cautious that she seems to lack any initiative and drive.' This harsh verdict ranks high among the many spectacular misjudgements the SOE top brass made about its own personnel. Within a year Witherington had assumed command of a *maquis* army some 3,000 strong, operating in the Valence-Issoudin-Châteauroux triangle. The Germans were so concerned by the activities of Witherington's network, code-named 'Wrestler', that they placed a bounty of one million francs on her head.

Pearl Witherington
1914–2008

Cecilie Pearl Witherington was born in Paris, the eldest of her British parents' four daughters, on 24 June 1914. Later she grimly recalled that 'I had no childhood'. She did not attend school until she was 13 and her father, an alcoholic, died young. Pearl became the family breadwinner, working as a secretary. When Nazi Germany invaded France in May 1940, Witherington was employed as a shorthand typist in the British embassy and had become engaged to a Frenchman, Henri Cornioley. She decided to evacuate her family through Spain to Gibraltar, where they embarked on a ship sailing to Liverpool, arriving in July 1941.

Witherington found another secretarial job at the Air Ministry before presenting herself at the Baker Street HQ of the Special Operations Executive (SOE). She later recalled that, far from submitting tamely to an interview, she subjected the head of SOE's F (French) Section, Colonel Maurice Buckmaster, to a spirited grilling about her future role in his organization.

Codenamed 'Marie', but later known to her French comrades as 'Pauline', Witherington was parachuted into Occupied France on 22 September 1943. There was no one to meet her and she spent the night on top of 20 tons of ammunition disguised as a haystack. She then joined the 'Stationer' network in central France run by Maurice Southgate, code-named 'Hector' and a veteran of the Dunkirk evacuation of 1940. Working as a courier, Witherington covered many miles, posing as the representative of a cosmetics company. Crucial to her survival in such a hostile environment was what she referred to as her 'sensitivity to atmosphere' and, as a last resort, a gun. An SOE training report of July 1943 observed that Witherington was 'probably the best shot (male or female) we have yet had'.

Pearl Witherington (Cornioley) wearing her parachutist's wings, finally awarded to her over 60 years after she was dropped into German-occupied France. The Resistance network Witherington co-ordinated played havoc among German forces in the run-up to the D-Day landings.

Life as a courier was gruelling as well as dangerous. Witherington later remembered long winter nights on freezing trains, which resulted in crippling rheumatism. On another occasion she had to wade waist-deep through an icy river, a bicycle slung across her back, to avoid a German patrol guarding a bridge. These hardships sharpened her impatience with her French colleagues and SOE. She reported to SOE headquarters that: 'Something must be done at all costs to co-ordinate the work of these men and have them trained properly, otherwise there will be an unholy mess when the time comes.'

The time to which Witherington was referring was the Allied invasion of Normandy on 6 June 1944. During the spring of that year, in anticipation of Operation Overlord, the SOE networks and the French Resistance were waging a fierce war against communications and war industries in France. In April 1944, 'Stationer' brought the Dunlop tyre factory at Montluçon to a halt with two pounds of well-placed explosive. However, on 1 May Southgate fell into a Gestapo trap and was subsequently sent to the Buchenwald concentration camp near Weimar. He survived this ordeal, but was never the same man again.

'Stationer' was now split into two circuits, 'Wrestler' and 'Shipwright', which were run respectively by Witherington and Southgate's principal wireless operator, René Maingard (codenamed Dédé). As the head of 'Wrestler' and now known as 'Pauline', Witherington controlled a private army of 3,000 *maquis* fighters. With the help of Henri Cornioley, she reorganized the network into a formidable fighting force. One of 'Wrestler's' outstanding achievements was to cut the principal railway line from Paris to Bordeaux, which in the run-up to D-Day remained almost permanently out of action. The German signals regiment stationed near Orléans also suffered unrelenting disruption from 'Wrestler' – so much so that by the time it was evacuated to Germany it had failed to restore any of its major telephone circuits.

> ' ... *probably the best shot (male or female) we have yet had.'*
>
> REPORT ON WITHERINGTON'S CRACKSHOT SKILLS

So effective had 'Wrestler' been that the Germans placed a bounty of one million francs on Witherington's head. They came within an ace of capturing her. On 11 June 1944 German troops fought a pitched battle, lasting some 14 hours, with an element of Witherington's army. In the firefight, fought under a blazing sun, the Germans lost 86 men while the *maquis's* losses were 24 dead, including civilians and badly wounded fighters who were finished off on the spot to prevent them falling into German hands. During the battle Witherington was separated from Cornioley and hid in a cornfield: 'moving only when the wind blew the corn, hiding behind my very large handbag.' When night fell, she was able to slip away.

By the late summer of 1944, 'Wrestler' had taken some 18,000 German troops prisoner. In a report written in April 1945, General Sir Colin Gubbins, the executive head of SOE, strongly recommended that Witherington should be awarded the Military Cross or, failing that, an OBE. She received neither and her reward, if such it can be called, was a civilian MBE. On 20 October 1945 Witherington returned the MBE with a letter containing a stinging rebuke, pointing out that she had spent a year in the field and, had she been caught, she would have been shot. The British authorities were thus shamed into awarding Witherington a military MBE.

Witherington married Henri Cornioley in October 1944 and after the war the couple settled in Paris, where she worked as a secretary in the World Bank. By the time the new century dawned, Pearl Cornioley had

The daughter of a French mother and an English father, Szabo grew up in south London. As a teenager she haunted shooting galleries, becoming a crack shot. Early in the Second World War she married a young Free French officer, Étienne Szabo, and had a baby girl.

After service in the Auxiliary Territorial Service (ATS) and First Aid Nursing Yeomanry (FANY), and now a widow, she joined the Special Operations Executive (SOE). In April 1944, during the build-up to D-Day, she was flown to France in a Westland Lysander light aircraft. Her mission was to establish if one of SOE's networks had been penetrated by German intelligence.

Having found that the network's operational usefulness was at an end, she returned to France on 6 June, parachuting in with the task of reviving the 'Salesman' network around the city of Limoges. On 8 June, while with a *Maquis* colleague, she was captured near Oradour-sur-Glane by an advance unit of SS Panzer Division *Das Reich*. Szabo covered the escape of her colleague with a Sten gun, holding off the SS troops before her ammunition ran out and a suspect ankle – injured in parachute training – gave way. Two days later, in a reprisal action, Oradour was destroyed by a *panzergrenadier* battalion and some 640 of its inhabitants slaughtered.

Szabo was initially held in Fresnes prison near Paris, then imprisoned in Ravensbrück concentration camp, where she was executed along with two other female SOE agents on 26 January 1945.

Violette Szabo and her husband in 1940. She was given the codename 'Corinne' for her covert operations in Occupied France.

become one of SOE's most distinguished survivors. In 2004 at the British embassy in Paris she was presented with the CBE by Queen Elizabeth II, who told her: 'we should have done this a long time ago.' Two years later, and six decades after she had parachuted from a Halifax bomber into Occupied France, she was awarded her parachute wings. She declared that she was: 'tickled pink, because I was somewhat miffed when no one thought to give me them all those years ago. But I don't consider myself a heroine. Not at all. I am just an ordinary person who did her job during the war.'

In the annals of the Special Operations Executive, there are few more remarkable examples of iron nerve and lonely courage than those displayed by the Polish-born Countess Krystyna Skarbeck, who operated under the nom de guerre of Christine Granville.

Christine Granville
1908–52

Granville was born into a noble but impoverished Polish family in May 1908, the daughter of Count Jerzy Skarbeck and Stephanie Goldfeder, an assimilated Jew and member of a then-prosperous banking dynasty. As a child during the First World War, Skarbeck endured the German occupation of Poland, which left her with little love for her country's powerful neighbour. Nevertheless, at the age of 18 she married Charles Getlich, a wealthy young Pole of German stock. The marriage was swiftly dissolved, and in November 1938 she married the adventurer Jerzy Gizycki. The couple then departed for the capital of Ethiopia, Addis Ababa, where Gizycki had been appointed Polish consul.

The couple were in British East Africa when on 1 September 1939, Nazi Germany invaded Poland. They made their way to London, where Skarbeck volunteered to work as a spy. She had already drawn up a plan of action. She proposed to the initially sceptical British authorities that she should travel to Hungary, then a neutral state but strongly supportive of Nazi Germany, with the aim of waging a one-woman propaganda war in Budapest, the Hungarian capital. She also proposed intelligence-gathering missions into occupied Poland by skiing over the Tatra Mountains.

Skarbeck left for Budapest in December 1939. There she met Andrejz Kowerski, a pre-war acquaintance and an officer in Poland's only motorized division, known as the 'Black Brigade' from their dark leather uniforms. After Poland's defeat, the one-legged Kowerski (he lost the limb in a shooting accident in 1938) had escaped from internment in Hungary and was now working undercover as a used-car dealer. Skarbeck joined forces with him and began her work in Poland, crossing Hungary's mountainous northern border to establish links with the Polish Resistance and extract Polish and Allied personnel. Yet she was unable to persuade her mother to leave Warsaw, where she was teaching in a school run by the Polish underground; she would later die in a concentration camp.

It was not long before Skarbeck's activities in Poland attracted the attention of German intelligence, and in early 1941 she and Kowerski (who by now was her lover) were pulled in and interrogated by the Gestapo.

Displaying characteristic presence of mind, Skarbeck bit so hard on her tongue during questioning that she drew quantities of blood, convincing a Hungarian doctor that she was suffering from tuberculosis, the disease that had killed her father in 1930. The ruse secured her release on parole, and that of her lover, and they promptly escaped to Yugoslavia in the boot of a car driven by the British ambassador in Budapest, Sir Owen O'Malley, a personal friend. (Kowerski drove to the border in his own car, claiming he was delivering it to a Yugoslavian customer.) O'Malley's parting gift to the Poles was two British passports. Skarbeck became Christine Granville and Kowerski became Andrew Kennedy. As neither spoke any English, elaborate cover stories were concocted to explain their new identities.

Granville and Kennedy reached Egypt via the Balkans and Turkey. In Cairo, however, they found themselves under a cloud of suspicion raised by fellow Poles-in-exile. The latter refused to believe that they had made good their escape without the connivance of the enemy. In particular they queried the couple's passage through Syria, then controlled by Vichy France and used as a refuelling stop for German military aircraft en route to Iraq, run by a military junta whose leader was in the pay of the Third Reich. But Granville's accusers reckoned without her extraordinary charm and resourcefulness, which she had used to extract visas from a pro-Vichy consul.

After a hiatus, Granville joined the French (F) section of the SOE station based 17 miles (27 km) west of Algiers and codenamed 'Massingham'. The air route to southern France from Algeria was shorter than that from England, enabling operations in this vital sector in advance of D-Day (6 June 1944) to be more easily mounted and supported.

At 'Massingham', Granville honed her wireless skills, underwent weapons training and received the papers and clothing that would enable her to pass in Occupied France. Her hair was coiffed in the latest French style and her

Christine Granville during her wartime service with SOE. After the war, her lovers included the writer Ian Fleming, who reputedly based the character Vesper Lynd in *Casino Royale* on her.

dentistry underwent minute examination to enable any anomalies to be incorporated into her cover story. She was ordered to ready herself for imminent departure when SOE received a request from the Anglo-Belgian Francis Cammaerts ('Roger'), running the 'Jockey' network, to replace his female courier, Cecily Lefort, who had fallen into German hands. On 6 July 1944 Granville parachuted into France, under the codename 'Pauline' – the name also used by Pearl Witherington (see pages 244–247).

Cammaerts's network stretched from the Alpes Maritimes to the Ardèche, a huge area of southeast France. At its heart was the Vercors, an immense, rocky bastion and haven for the *Maquis*, which controlled vital lines of communication and launched raids along the Rhône valley. It was both a citadel and fertile recruiting ground for the Resistance.

Granville thrived in the testing environment of Occupied France, a completely independent woman answering to no one. She soon acquired a reputation for ice-cool resourcefulness. One night, hiding from a German patrol in a ditch, she was found by the patrol's tracker dog, a large German Shepherd. Granville quietly placed her arm around the dog's neck, inviting it to settle down beside her and lick her hand. She could hear the handler blowing his whistle, but the dog did not bark or budge. It later became Granville's devoted pet and stayed with its new mistress until the liberation.

> ' ... *her short, carelessly-combed dark hair and the complete absence of make-up on her delicately featured face gave her the appearance of an athletic art student ... '*
>
> A FELLOW SOE AGENT ON CHRISTINE GRANVILLE

On a mission with partisans near the Italian border, Granville was stopped by another German patrol and ordered to raise her hands. She did so, revealing two live grenades; she told the Germans that they had a choice – they could let her and her companions go or be blown to pieces. Discretion proved the better part of valour and the Germans moved on.

Granville's slight figure belied her immense stamina. She was a tireless walker in the High Alps, and on one mission in the Col de la Madeleine persuaded the garrison there – Poles forced into service by the Germans – to abandon their posts and leave the route free for the Americans advancing north after the 'Anvil' landings in southern France.

Granville's most audacious exploit was her rescue of Cammaerts, the SOE operative Xan Fielding and a French colleague, who on 11 August 1944 had been captured at a roadblock by the Gestapo. Her reaction to the news was swift and decisive. She reconnoitred the jail in Digne, where the SOE men were being held, whistling 'Frankie and Johnny', a call sign that Cammaerts quickly answered. She then persuaded his two principal jailers that she was not only the wife of one of the SOE prisoners but also the niece of Field-Marshal Montgomery, commander of the British 21st Army

Mary Lindell, the comtesse de Milleville, was a British-born stalwart of the French Resistance in the Second World War. Codenamed 'Marie-Claire', she was in charge of a Resistance network in Lyons running an escape route out of Occupied France for Allied airmen, soldiers and refugees.

Although married to a French aristocrat, Lindell remained resolutely British. In 1980 she told an interviewer that in 1940 after the fall of France: 'we were sick to death of the French and knew that someone would have to stay behind and stand up to the Jerries and see things through.'

In 1942 she smuggled to safety the only two survivors of a daring British commando raid on German blockade-running ships at Bordeaux, the so-called 'cockleshell heroes'. Major 'Blondy' Hasler and Marine Bill Sparks, were successfully escorted through southern France and over the Pyrenees into Spain by one of Lindell's sons.

In the 1980s Lindell revealed that she had paid Klaus Barbie, the head of the Lyons SD (the security element of the SS) 40,000 francs for the release of her son Maurice from the prison at Fort Montluc. Striking a deal with one of Barbie's subordinates, she produced a wad of notes, tore it in half and told him he could have the rest when her son was delivered safely to friends in Lyons. Barbie kept his word, though Lindell noted that Maurice arrived so badly beaten up that he looked like 'strawberry jam'. Her younger son Octavius died at Mauthausen concentration camp.

In 1944 she was shot through the head by the Gestapo and imprisoned in Ravensbrück where she recalled, with studied understatement, 'conditions were pretty dim for the general public'. After the war Lindell was awarded the *Croix de Guerre* for the second time (having won her first working as a nurse on the Western Front in the First World War) and was appointed OBE.

In the postwar years, the tiny but indomitable figure of the comtesse de Milleville was often to be seen at meetings of the RAF Association in Paris, where she lived with her dachshund Tommy.

Group. Granville explained that the Allies were on their way and the war would soon be over (the Allies landed in the south of France four days later). The price for the release of the SOE men was two million francs and safe passage for the jailers. Granville arranged for the money to be dropped by an aircraft flying from Algiers on the night of 16 August. Four days after their arrest, the SOE men were driven out of the prison and freed by their captors. That night one of the messages broadcast by the BBC was: *Roger est libre. Félicitations à Pauline* ('Roger is free. Congratulations to Pauline').

After the war, the British paid off Granville with a George Medal, an OBE and £100. She divorced Gizycki in 1946. She had influential friends and from 1947 a British passport, but could find no outlet for her restless energy. After working as a telephonist and a saleswoman, she became a stewardess on an ocean liner, wearing her many decorations on her uniform, prompting puzzlement among passengers and resentment among her colleagues. On 15 June 1952 she was stabbed to death in the lobby of a seedy London hotel by George Muldowney, a besotted fellow steward.

The politician and journalist Aidan Crawley, who as a young diplomat got to know Granville in Hungary in 1940, said of her: 'When I discussed bravery with her, she laughed and said that when she was in the field and a crisis occurred, she was generally too busy to be frightened. She was an eminently practical soldier.'

In Nazi-occupied Europe the largest and most successful escape line transporting downed Allied airman, escaped POWs and Resistance workers to safety was the 'Comet' Line running from Belgium into Spain. Its mastermind was a petite nurse turned commercial artist in her mid-20s. Her name was Andrée de Jongh, but she was known as Dédée or 'Little Cyclone' by all who knew and admired her.

Andrée de Jongh
1916–2007

The line made its début in August 1941 when the demure de Jongh, wearing a simple blouse, skirt and bobby socks, turned up at the British consulate in Bilbao on the northern coast of neutral Spain. She informed the consul that she had brought three fugitives with her from Brussels – two Belgian officers and a British private named Colin Cupar, who had been stranded after the Dunkirk evacuation in May 1940. She made only a modest request for financial assistance and promised that she would return with more British servicemen.

MI9, the secret British agency established to encourage escape and evasion in Occupied Europe and often at loggerheads with the Secret Service (MI6), provided financial assistance, but in all other respects de Jongh went her own way. With the help of her father, Frédéric, she established a trail of safe houses along which she could move her charges, from Brussels through Paris and on to the western Pyrenees, where she received sterling support from loyal Basques.

She declined London's offer of radio operators, fearing that their transmissions would compromise security. She also insisted that the escape line would be an all-Belgian operation. Furthermore, in contrast to the other escape line running from northern France and Belgium – the 'Pat Line' led by Albert Guérisse, whose *nom de guerre* was 'Pat O'Leary' – de Jongh was determined to avoid Vichy France and take a more dangerous route to Spain through German-occupied France. The last house in the Basque region on the Franco-Spanish border was invariably in the village of Urrugne. Here the evaders were sheltered before meeting Basque guides organized and led by a huge man, Florentino Goicoechea. It was Florentino's task to lead the party across a gruelling terrain of rivers and mountains, with Dédée urging them on from behind.

In one respect, de Jongh heeded advice from British intelligence. She specialized in bringing back downed Allied airmen, in whom much time and training had been invested. Initially MI9 codenamed de Jongh's escape

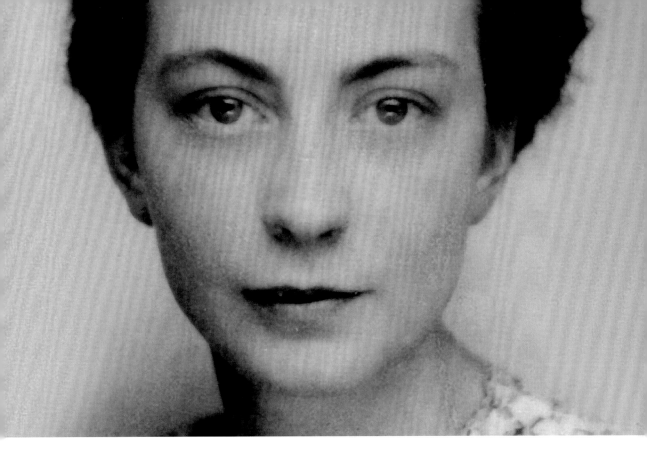

line 'Postman', because she referred to her charges as 'packages'. In 1942, however, the name was changed to 'Comet' after she delivered the crew of a British bomber, downed over Belgium, in less than a week. Eventually the line ran from Brussels through German-occupied France, over the Pyrenees to the British consulate in Madrid and then to Gibraltar. Security was paramount: the Comet Line's 'safe houses' always had two exits and were usually staffed by elderly, childless couples who lived scrupulously quiet lives. The line itself consisted of a series of self-contained boxes. The personnel in each box remained unaware of the identity of their counterparts in the adjacent boxes. As the 'packages' passed from box to box, they were left at pick-up points to await the arrival of a new courier. The couriers communicated in code from public telephone boxes or by pre-arranged signals – for example, a pot plant placed in a window to indicate the presence of a German patrol.

From the outset the Gestapo were hard on the heels of 'Comet'. Dédée's sister was arrested in Brussels in February 1942, obliging her and her father to flee to Paris, where they stayed in a succession of apartments funded by MI9. Nevertheless, from July to October 1942 the line brought out 54 'packages', most of them aircrew.

By Christmas 1942, Paris was becoming increasingly dangerous. On her next trip to Spain, Dédée took her father with her. At Anglet, near Bayonne, they stayed with Madame Elvire de Greef ('Tante Go'), who ran an advanced

Andrée de Jongh crossed the Pyrenees many times with Allied escapees before her arrest by the Germans. A historian writing on her rescue network, the Comet Line, has described it as: 'the greatest of escape lines in Europe in numbers of rescues as well as the most sophisticated, longest-operating and most successful.'

post on the French side of the border. Severe weather prevented Dédée's father from accompanying her into Spain, and it was on this leg of the journey that Dédée and her party were detained by police on 15 January 1943. One of her charges, a pilot, talked, blowing Dédée's cover. In 16 double journeys across the mountains she had escorted 118 people. On this occasion her party was handed over to the Germans. Worse was to follow. A month later the 'Pat' Line was broken and Guérisse arrested. In June 1943 Frédéric de Jongh, now escorting parties across Paris, was betrayed by a double agent, Jacques Desoubrie, and executed. Dozens of their colleagues suffered a similar fate. However, in spite of the loss of their leaders, and the grievous damage they had suffered, both lines survived.

The remarkable 'Tante Go' was also arrested, but had the presence of mind to talk herself out of trouble. She knew too much about German dealings in the local black market and threatened to spill the beans. On her release, she resumed work for 'Comet' until the arrival of the Allies. It was not until the spring of 1944 that traffic along the Comet Line finally slackened, mainly because of the severity of Allied bombing in the build-up to D-Day. To alleviate the situation, MI9 established a new escape route, the 'Shelburne' Line, to ferry downed airmen directly to the coast of Brittany and thence to England. The last airman to be passed into Spain crossed the frontier on 4 June 1944. In all, 'Comet' had helped some 600 Allied servicemen.

Dédée's captors could not believe that this engaging young woman had organized Comet and, after a spell in Fresnes prison, near Paris, she was sent to the concentration camps at Mauthausen and Ravensbrück. For two years she survived on a diet of dirty potato and turnip soup, worked as a nurse and kept her head down. By the time she was freed by advancing Allied troops in April 1945, she was severely ill. Guérisse also survived the war.

In 1946, after recovering her health, Dédée went to Buckingham Palace to receive the George Medal, the highest British civilian award for bravery available to a foreigner. She was also awarded the American Medal of Freedom and appointed a Chevalier of the *Légion d'honneur*. In 1985 she was created a Belgian countess. In the postwar years she worked with lepers in the Belgian Congo and Ethiopia. When her health began to fail she returned to Brussels. In 2000 she recalled: 'When war was declared I knew what needed to be done. There was no hesitation. We could not stop what we had to do although we knew the cost. Even if it was at the expense of our lives, we had to fight until the last breath.'

> *'When war was declared I knew what needed to be done. We could not stop what we had to do although we knew the cost. Even if it was at the expense of our lives, we had to fight until the last breath.'*
>
> 'DÉDÉE' ON HER WARTIME SERVICE

In the summer of 1940, when France fell to Nazi Germany, Peel (then Andrée Marthe Virot) was running her own beauty parlour in the port of Brest, the naval base and industrial harbour in western Brittany. She soon became involved in the local Resistance as 'Agent Rose', supplying the Allies with information about German naval installations and troop movements and the results of British bombing raids. In three years with the Resistance, Peel helped to save the lives of over 100 Allied aircrew. Her team used torches to guide Allied aircraft to improvized landing strips, or gunboats to remote coastal locations, from which the airmen were then smuggled to safety.

In 1943 Peel was forced to flee to Paris when a comrade betrayed her to the Germans after his family was tortured by the Gestapo. In Paris she was betrayed for a second time shortly after D-Day, arrested and taken to Gestapo headquarters, where she was stripped naked, underwent a form of 'waterboarding' and was savagely beaten around the throat, maltreatment that left her with permanent injuries. She was subsequently transferred to Ravensbrück, the concentration camp in Mecklenburg, where she narrowly escaped death on several occasions and survived an attack of meningitis.

Eventually Peel was transferred to Buchenwald, the holding camp in Weimar, where she was able to send messages to friends and family in Brest via French POWs working in the fields around the camp. At the end of April 1945, as Allied troops closed in on Buchenwald, Peel and a number of fellow prisoners were lined up before a firing squad, only to be saved a by last-minute intervention by the commander of approaching US troops, who telephoned the camp commandant and ordered him, if he wanted to live, to halt the killings.

Peel was awarded the *Croix de Guerre* (with palm and silver star), the Cross of the Voluntary Fighter, the Medal of the Resistance, the Liberation Cross, the American Medal of Freedom and the British Commendation for Brave Conduct, the last a massive understatement for this most gallant of Frenchwomen. She later married an Englishman many years her junior and in 1999 published her autobiography, *Miracles Do Happen*. Five years later she was awarded the *Légion d'honneur*, which was presented to her by her brother, General Maurice Virot.

Ravensbrück on the day it was liberated (16 April 1945). The sign on the hut reads: 'German political prisoners welcome their American friends.'

Virginia Hall was a woman of unique distinction. In the Second World War she served in the field with both the British Special Operations Executive (SOE) and its American equivalent, the Office of Strategic Services (OSS); she was the only American female civilian to be decorated with the Distinguished Service Cross, second only to the US Medal of Honor; and in the postwar years she was in at the birth of the Central Intelligence Agency (CIA). However, not the least of her achievements was that Hall was operating, often in conditions of great danger, with a prosthetic lower leg. The Gestapo, who were under no illusions about her courage and skills in tradecraft, considered that the 'lady with the limp' was one of the most dangerous Allied agents in France, insisting 'we must find and destroy her'.

Virginia Hall
1906–82

Hall was born to a life of privilege in a wealthy Baltimore family, and was an energetic sportswoman and linguist in her youth, later becoming fluent in French, Italian and German. At the family summer home in Maryland, she learned how to milk cows, a skill that would subsequently serve her in good stead in Occupied France.

In July 1931 she joined the staff of the US embassy in Warsaw. She later served in Tallinn (Estonia), Vienna and the Turkish city of Izmir. It was during this posting that Hall suffered a disabling shooting accident while hunting snipe. Gangrene set in and her leg was amputated below the knee. Her mobility was restored when she was fitted with an artificial limb, which gave her a pronounced limp and which she christened 'Cuthbert'.

After the accident in Turkey, Hall was obliged to resign, as the US State Department would not employ anyone with an amputation 'of any portion of a limb'. When war broke out in September 1939, she was in Paris and promptly joined the French Ambulance Service. After the fall of France in June 1940, she made her way through Spain to England, where she obtained employment as a code clerk in the US embassy. By the end of the year she had joined the Special Operations Executive (SOE).

Hall's first SOE assignment began when she arrived in Vichy France in August 1941, three months before the United States entered the war. She was able to operate under her own name as an accredited journalist. On 11 December 1941, four days after the Japanese attack on Pearl Harbor, Hitler declared war on the United States, and Hall became an enemy alien.

This picture by the artist Jeffrey W. Bass, showing Virginia Hall radioing London from Occupied France, was painted in 2006 to commemorate her achievements as an OSS/SOE operative. It is entitled *Les Marguerites Fleuriront ce Soir* ('The Daisies will Bloom Tonight'), a reference to the cryptic messages signalling air-drops of supplies.

By then, she had shifted her centre of operations to the city of Lyons, some 75 miles (120 km) southeast of Vichy. Here her work for SOE began in earnest. She made contact with the French underground, recruited French citizens, set up safe houses for incoming agents and established an escape line back to England for Allied POWs on the run.

The Allied invasion of North Africa in November 1942 brought about the end of Vichy France's fragile autonomy as German troops marched in. Hall was ordered to leave France. She set off in the depths of winter across the Pyrenees, accompanied by two Frenchmen and a Belgian army officer, following a Spanish guide. It was an arduous journey and she signalled SOE headquarters that she fervently hoped 'Cuthbert' would not hold her back. Forgetting who 'Cuthbert' was, Baker Street replied: 'If Cuthbert troublesome, eliminate him.'

Hall and her companions were arrested on the Spanish frontier and taken to Figueras prison, where she persuaded her cellmate, a prostitute, to smuggle a letter to the US consul in Barcelona. Hall was freed within six weeks and made her way to Madrid, where she was assigned to SOE's escape and evasion department working under cover as a *Chicago Times* journalist. For her work in France, she was awarded the MBE. Although Madrid was seething with Allied and Axis spies, Hall did not find the Spanish capital congenial. She signalled SOE's F Section that she was wasting her time: ' ... after all my neck is my own. If I am willing to get a crick in it, I think that's my prerogative.' Hall returned to England in November 1943 to receive training in wireless telegraphy and to transfer to the Office of Strategic Services (OSS) with the rank of second lieutenant.

Hall returned to France in a motor torpedo boat in March 1944, landing near Brest in Brittany. Now codenamed 'Diane', her mission was to work as a wireless operator for the OSS network 'Heckler'. She was accompanied by another OSS agent, Peter Harratt, codenamed 'Aramis'. Their task was to establish 'Heckler' in the Haute-Loire region of central France. Hall had been provided with the identity of 'Marcelle Montaigne', a spinster and social worker. However, she was now a marked woman, well known to

The American-born Brousse, code-named 'Cynthia', played a vital role in a daring operation launched by the American Office of Strategic Services (OSS) to steal, photograph and return naval codes held in the Vichy French embassy in Washington during the run-up to the November 1942 Allied landings in North Africa.

Before 1939 she led a globe-trotting life as the wife of a British diplomat. In that year she left her husband and assumed her maiden name of Thorpe. After the outbreak of war she became an agent for the British Security Co-ordination (BSC), an intelligence-gathering network based in New York. An attractive woman, she was tasked with charming information from Italian diplomats before moving on to the Vichy French, with whom the US still enjoyed diplomatic relations, in a joint operation with American intelligence.

In May 1941 Thorpe became the mistress of Charles Emmanuel Brousse, a former French naval pilot who was an aide to the Vichy ambassador. With his help she supplied BSC with a stream of diplomatic

AMY ELIZABETH BROUSSE
1910–63

cable traffic between the Vichy government and its Washington embassy. In June 1942 she persuaded Brousse to entertain her in the Vichy embassy where, at the third attempt, the couple removed the French naval codes from a safe in the naval attaché's office. An inquisitive embassy guard was forced to beat a hasty retreat when he stumbled on the couple naked in the office. The documents were photographed and safely returned. They proved particularly helpful during the Operation Torch landings in North Africa.

'Cynthia' later served with the British Special Operations Executive (SOE), but never went operational again. However, the break-in had a bonus, as it later provided indirect cover for the maintenance of the Ultra Secret, the British cracking of the German Enigma code. Information about the Washington break-in was leaked to the Germans to allay suspicions that Enigma was being read. 'Cynthia' later married Brousse, who had been interned in the United States, and settled down with him in a hilltop château near his native Perpignan.

German intelligence. As she and 'Aramis' were constantly on the move across the countryside, exchanging one safe house for another to evade German radio direction finders, Hall artfully manipulated her physical appearance to make herself next to invisible, transforming herself from a handsome 38-year-old into an old peasant woman herding cows.

During the critical period from mid-July to mid-August 1944, Hall sent 37 messages to London, detailing German troop movements in the days following the Normandy landings. A *Maquis* group of some 30 men provided her with security, helped her to mark drop areas and retrieved material that had landed miles from the drop zone. From August she also had the help of a joint SOE/OSS three-man unit, known as a 'Jedburgh', whose task was to arm and train three battalions of local militias known as *Forces Françaises d'Intérieure* (FFI) for guerrilla and sabotage operations against the retreating Germans. In this fluid campaign, Hall and her Resistance colleagues provided daily intelligence on local conditions, harassed the enemy, and disrupted their communication lines, blowing up bridges and derailing trains.

In Paris in September 1944, another OSS agent, Julian Defourneaux, noted the impact of war and disguise on Hall's appearance: 'I was completely surprised … She looked like an old lady with dark gray hair, dressed completely in black, with a black pearl choker which relieved to a degree the severity of her appearance. However, she still looked like a queen … She exuded authority … and there was an alertness about her, as if she were still watching for an ambush. I had the feeling that she was so iron-willed that the Germans didn't really want to tangle with her.'

On 27 September 1945 General 'Wild Bill' Donovan, commander of the OSS, presented Hall with the Distinguished Service Cross. In 1948 she joined the National Committee for Free Europe, a front organization for the newly formed Central Intelligence Agency (CIA) and an arm of Radio Free Europe. Three years later Hall joined the CIA in Washington as an analyst on French politics. In 1952 she became one of the first women operations officers in the Office of the Deputy Director of Plans. She prepared political action projects, interviewed exiles from behind the Iron Curtain, and planned stay-behind resistance and sabotage networks to be activated in the event of an invasion by the Soviet Union.

In 1966 Hall retired at the mandatory age of 60 to live on a Maryland farm. In December 2006, 24 years after her death, her niece, Lorna Catling, was presented with a certificate signed by King George VI, which should have accompanied the award of Hall's MBE in 1943. Her Majesty's Government had mislaid it for 63 years.

> *'She sometimes carried her detachable brass foot in a pack or leg pack. I have always had the greatest respect for that lady. Her courage knew no bounds.'*
>
> AN OSS COLLEAGUE ON HALL'S BRAVERY

Gulovich was born in the Slovak village of Jakubany, the eldest of five daughters of a Greek Orthodox priest. She trained as a teacher, and was given her first teaching job in a village near her family home. These respectable, even pedestrian beginnings gave no indication of the dash, courage and endurance she would shortly bring to wartime action of the most dangerous sort.

Maria Gulovich
1921–2009

By the spring of 1939, Czechoslovakia had been entirely swallowed up by Nazi Germany. The urge to seize the Czech armaments industry and its tank fleet hastened Germany's rush to war in the late summer of 1939. When Hitler moved against Poland, the occupation of Czechoslovakia enabled the German armies to outflank the Polish forces.

In 1943 the Soviet Union began to infiltrate military missions into Slovakia to organize partisan warfare. In contrast, British and American intelligence (SOE and OSS) had experienced great difficulty in mounting operations in Nazi-occupied Czechoslovakia. It was not until 1944 that an OSS mission arrived in the country to establish contact with the Czech Resistance. In August 1944 the Slovak Independent Army (SIA), encouraged by Red Army advances in Hungary and Ruthenia, rose up against the Germans, seized the small mountain town of Banska Bystrica and radioed appeals for help. Gulovich, who had moved away from her hometown during the war years, joined the Slovak Independent Army.

Fluent in Russian, Hungarian, German and Slovak, Gulovich initially worked for a Red Army colonel attached to the SIA, translating frontline intelligence from Slovak or German into Russian. By the end of October 1944, however, their stronghold was in danger of being cut off by German forces, and the SIA had to conduct a fighting withdrawal through the Tatra Mountains towards the Hungarian border and the Red Army's front line.

Police hold back angry crowds as the first German troops enter Prague on 5 March 1939. Maria Gulovich played a vital part in infiltrating Allied agents into Nazi-occupied Czechoslovakia.

On 30 October Gulovich was recruited as a guide and translator by a 20-strong OSS mission, codenamed 'Dawes', sent to Czechoslovakia to support the insurgents and evacuate downed Allied airmen. Now they were caught in the SIA's retreat, battling through rugged terrain in foul winter weather. German patrols were everywhere, and on 7 November seven members of the Dawes mission were captured while foraging. As the weather deteriorated, Gulovich developed gangrene in her right leg, and her life was saved only after an improvised operation performed by the Associated Press war correspondent Joseph Morton.

Maria Gulovich (second from right) with OSS colleagues in Prague in 1945. She is talking to Allen Dulles, who became head of the CIA in 1953.

In mid-November the Dawes group took shelter in a mining camp, where partisan medical teams treated the victims of frostbite. The mission then pushed on towards the Hungarian border. Two more of its members were betrayed to the Germans as they attempted to requisition horses. After another exceptionally gruelling march, Gulovich and her OSS comrades made a rendezvous with a British SOE unit at Velky Bok, a remote mountain resort.

However, on 26 December the Germans arrived to round up the Dawes mission. Gulovich evaded the sweep, having already set off that day with two members of the mission to join other members of the Allied special forces higher up the mountainside. They watched from a distance as their companions went into the bag; all of them were later shot at Mauthausen concentration camp. Three weeks later, in the company of the two survivors of the Dawes mission and two SOE men, the exhausted, lice-ridden Gulovich reached the seeming safety of the Soviet lines, fully aware of the short Russian way with dissidents like her.

Soviet intelligence officers subjected Gulovich to hours of interrogation, which she handled with great composure, insisting – at least partially truthfully – that her companions were part of a military mission looking for downed Allied pilots. Gulovich also ingeniously thwarted an attempt by the Russians to separate her from her companions, a setback that she would not have survived. She persuaded the Russians to allow her to marry one of the SOE men, which gave her British citizenship. Gulovich and her companions were then taken to Budapest en route to the port of Odessa on the Black Sea. Gulovich gloomily realized that once they reached Odessa, her fate would be sealed; she would join the ranks of the millions of those who disappeared in war-torn Eastern Europe.

In Budapest, Gulovich desperately stalled for time while she and her companions tried to contact the Allies for help. In a drama that would have done justice to the Alfred Hitchcock thriller *The Lady Vanishes* (1938), Gulovich, her two colleagues and other refugees, slipped to safety under the noses of their Red Army guards. She was flown to Bari in Italy, and assigned to OSS units in Caserta and Salzburg. In OSS uniform she visited her family in Czechoslovakia before travelling as an exchange student to the United States to attend Vassar College. In May 1946 the 24-year-old Gulovich was awarded the Bronze Star for her work with the OSS between October 1944 and May 1945. She then settled down to a quiet life in California, where the climate was kinder to her permanently frost-bitten limbs.

The American equivalent of the British Special Operations Executive (SOE), the Office of Strategic Services (OSS) was established in 1942 to support Resistance movements in Axis-occupied countries.

Friction sometimes arose between OSS and SOE, particularly over dealings with the Vichy authorities in North Africa. This prompted General Eisenhower, the Allied Supreme Commander in Europe, to bring the two agencies under the umbrella of the Special Forces Headquarters, which formed part of the Operations Division of the Supreme Headquarters Allied Expeditionary Force (SHAEF).

The OSS was run by General William 'Wild Bill' Donovan, a decorated First World War hero and postwar New York lawyer. In its early days recruitment for the OSS was mainly from a pool of fashionable and well-connected young men and women on America's East Coast, earning the agency the nickname 'Oh So Social'.

Initially the OSS structure was divided into several main branches: Research and Analysis (R & A), the amassing of background material to aid the planning of operations; Special Operations (SO), clandestine activities including sabotage and guerrilla warfare; and the Counter-intelligence Branch (X-2), which monitored and manipulated enemy intelligence operations and liaised with the British over their penetration of the Enigma code, which the Germans had thought unbreakable.

Few women played an active part in OSS operations in the field. In the somewhat patronizing words of General Donovan: 'The great majority of women who worked for America's first organized and integrated intelligence agency spent their war years behind desks and filing cases in Washington, invisible apron strings of an organization which touched every theatre of war.' Nevertheless, women like Virginia Hall (see pages 256–259) more than proved their courage in the field. Another highly effective field agent was Canadian-born Betty Lussier, who worked for the X-2 counter-intelligence branch and was one of the select few privy to the Ultra secret (the breaking of German codes) and joined one of the top-secret Special Liaison Units (SLUs) tasked with passing Ultra-derived information to Allied commanders in the field in Europe while simultaneously preserving the all-important secret itself.

In August 1944, following the Allied landings in the south of France, Lussier was forbidden to follow her unit to the front line. She nimbly avoided this restriction by hitching a ride with the Army Air Corps, landing at Grenoble and eventually linking up with an SLU attached to the US Seventh Army. The persistent Lussier was formally reassigned to X-2 duties and went on to control a counter-intelligence unit in southwest France, which infiltrated nests of collaborators and stay-behind members of German military intelligence.

A 'Jedburgh' team of the OSS studying plans before being dropped into Occupied Europe.

Hanna Reitsch was a German aviator of exceptional ability and a diehard Nazi who was fanatically loyal to her Führer, Adolf Hitler. She was the first woman to fly a helicopter, a rocket plane and a jet fighter. For her services to aviation, she was the only woman to be decorated with the Iron Cross First Class and Second Class. In April 1945 she had the dubious fortune – for a woman of her convictions – to witness Hitler's last days in the Berlin *Führerbunker*, as the Red Army closed in, and the Third Reich spiralled towards destruction.

Hanna Reitsch
1912–79

Reitsch was raised in an intensely patriotic family in the east German province of Silesia. She was bitten early by the flying bug, and as a small girl yearned to: 'soar like the storks in their quiet and steady flight, the buzzards circling ever higher in the summer air.' In 1931 she joined the gliding school at Grunau. Gliding was an ostensibly civilian sport, but in the 1920s it also served a military purpose as a way of circumventing the ban on powered flight imposed on Germany in 1919 by the Versailles Treaty.

In her final test as a glider pilot, Reitsch set an endurance record for women of five and a half hours. By the time she attended medical school in Berlin, aviation had become the ruling passion in her life. She acquired a 'heavier-than-air' licence and also set an unofficial gliding altitude record of over 1,500 metres (5,000 ft) and extended her endurance record to 11½ hours.

At a fraction over 1.5 metres (5 ft) tall, the diminutive, hard-driving Reitsch was an intensely feminine woman in a man's world. With the German Institute for Glider Research, she travelled to South America where she flew stunts for a film, *Rivals of the Air*, in Argentina and Brazil. Now a German national heroine, she travelled the world, smashing records wherever she went. At the 1936 Berlin Olympics she was a member of an élite German team tasked with giving aerobatic displays. On the insistence of Ernst Udet, the First World War flying ace who had been appointed technical director at the German Air Ministry, Reitsch was appointed *Flugkapitän* (Flight Captain), a rank normally reserved for the most senior pilots of Lufthansa, the German national airline.

In September 1937 Udet invited Reitsch to join a team of test pilots at Rechlin, an air base at which new aircraft designs for the *Luftwaffe* – unveiled by Hitler in 1935 – were flown and evaluated. Here she tested the dive brakes on the Ju87 Stuka dive-bomber and flew an early helicopter, the Fa61, in the presence of the American aviator Charles Lindbergh. She also demonstrated this helicopter, with its rotors over each wing, in the huge roofed *Deutschlandhalle* stadium in Berlin.

In the early war years, Reitsch remained at Rechlin as a test pilot, flying fighter and bomber aircraft and ferrying Nazi leaders and senior officers around Germany and Occupied Europe. She also tested modified He111 and Do17 bombers equipped with a device to cut the cables of barrage balloons. During one test flight, a cable shaved off several of her Do17's propeller blades. Reitsch coolly handled this emergency and landed safely. For this feat she received the Iron Cross, Second Class. At Rechlin she also helped to develop and fly the Me321 Gigant, a massive transport glider capable of carrying 100 fully equipped troops plus a crew of seven or 9,750 kilos (21,500 lb) of cargo. A powered version, the Me323, was later used extensively as a heavy transport machine in North Africa.

Hanna Reitsch in July 1938 in front of a DFS-108 *Habicht* ('Goshawk') glider. Two years earlier, she had piloted one of these gliders into the main stadium at the Berlin Olympics.

In the spring of 1940 Reitsch advised the German high command on the daring raid of 10 May, when nine troop-carrying gliders were landed on top of the supposedly impregnable Belgian fort at Eben-Emael, guarding the vital bridges at the confluence of the Albert Canal and River Maas, and put its guns out of action. Before the operation Reitsch had personally tested the gliders. In 1942 she tested the Me163 Komet, a unique ultra-short-range defensive jet fighter that could climb to over 9,000 metres (30,000 ft) in 90 seconds, but had an alarming tendency to explode like a bomb as it landed on its ski undercarriage.

Reitsch later likened flying the Komet to 'thundering through the skies on a cannonball'. On 30 October 1942 on her fifth flight, her launching undercarriage failed to drop away from the plane's fuselage and she crash landed. Sitting semi-conscious in the cockpit, she felt blood pouring down her face and raised her hand to discover that she had lost most of her nose. This did not stop her reaching for pencil and paper to record her impressions of the crash. Only then did she pass out. Reitsch had suffered multiple fractures to her skull and spent five months in hospital before emerging to test her nerve and restore her sense of balance with a stern régime of tree- and roof-climbing.

Now the holder of an Iron Cross First Class, she turned her attention to developing suicide aircraft under the direction of SS-Obersturmbannführer Otto Skorzeny. The idea had been suggested by Hitler early in 1944. Reitsch and Skorzeny formed the Leonidas Squadron, similar to the

NAZI GERMANY'S FEMALE 'HELPERS'

In Nazi Germany women were defined by the 'three Ks' – *Kinder, Kirche und Küche* ('children, church and kitchen'), which encompassed the National Socialist ideal of womanhood. The war work of good German women was to breed, in large numbers, the children of the future, the Aryan dream.

Nevertheless, the demands imposed by the Second World War called into being a number of uniformed German women's auxiliary formations, the *Helferrinnen* ('helpers') serving the signals corps, the air force and its anti-aircraft batteries, the army, the navy and the Waffen-SS. Their role was principally clerical, although Heinrich Himmler's SS sanctioned a more flexible approach to the running of its concentration and death camp empire.

During the conflict there were some 3,500 female camp guards, though even at Ravensbrück, the camp designated for the training of female SS personnel, they constituted less than 10 per cent of the SS establishment. They did not have to meet the same racial criteria as SS men, nor was their blood type tattooed on their bodies. However, they could rise to a position of command as senior overseers, a post in which they were the equal of their male counterparts. Many, such as Hermine Braunsteiner and Irma Grese, were even more depraved and brutal than their male colleagues.

In the last two years of the war, many *Helferrinnen* were drafted into the Reich Labour Service to deal with bomb damage caused by the increasingly heavy Allied raids. Others served in radar stations, the fighter control network and anti-aircraft and searchlight batteries. By 1945, in contrast to their British opposite numbers (see pages 232–235), they were firing anti-aircraft guns. By the end of the war, some of these women and those guarding communications hubs had been supplied with small arms.

Japanese *kamikaze* units that flew Okha flying bombs against US warships in the Pacific. However, the German high command rejected the concept and the Leonidas Squadron never saw action. Even so, late in the war Reitsch test flew a manned version of the V-1 flying bomb, the *Reichenberg*, which was intended for use against Allied shipping and launched from beneath a He111 bomber.

On the morning of 26 April 1945, as the Third Reich entered its death throes, Hitler summoned *Luftwaffe* general Robert Ritter von Greim, Reitsch's lover, to the *Führerbunker*. Reitsch joined this suicidal trip. Von Greim flew from Rechlin to Gatow, the only Berlin aerodrome still in German hands, in a Fw190 fighter with Reitsch stuffed into the rear fuselage through a small emergency opening. They had a fighter escort of some 40 aircraft, many of which were lost in the flight.

From Gatow, the couple then flew into the besieged city in a Fiesler Storch light aircraft. Reitsch was forced to take over the controls after von Greim was badly wounded in the foot by ground fire. After landing the Storch aircraft near to the Brandenburg Gate, they commandeered a passing car to take them to the Chancellery. In the *Führerbunker*, von Greim was promoted to the rank of field marshal and, in succession to the disgraced Hermann Göring, appointed commander of what remained of the *Luftwaffe*. The Führer then thoughtfully provided Reitsch and von Greim with cyanide pills.

In the small hours of 29 April, von Greim and Reitsch were ordered to fly out of Berlin to arrest Heinrich Himmler. They took off in a small Arado aircraft, shells bursting around them, a sea of flame below, and flew on to Grand Admiral Dönitz's headquarters at Plön, on the Baltic. They failed to arrest Himmler, but after Hitler's suicide, Reitsch angrily confronted the Reichsführer SS and accused him of betraying the Führer. When Himmler protested that Hitler had been insane, Reitsch retorted vehemently if not wholly accurately: 'Hitler died bravely and honourably, while you and Göring and the rest must now live branded as cowards and traitors.'

Reitsch's postwar career was marked by more international gliding triumphs. In 1952, as the only female competitor, she came third in the World Gliding Championship in Spain. In 1959 she was invited to India by prime minister Jawaharlal Nehru to establish a gliding centre. In the 1960s she spent several years in Ghana. There was a *rapprochement* with aviation enthusiasts in the United States – she visited the White House in 1961 – and a protracted battle to clear her name of the taint of Nazism. Privately, she was unrepentant – she maintained that the only bad thing about the Second World War was that the Third Reich lost it. In her life Reitsch had burned like a furious little flame and, perhaps inevitably, she burnt herself out. She continued to set gliding records until her death, from a heart attack, on 24 August 1979.

Hanna Reitsch giving a Hitler salute during a visit to her home town, Hirschberg in Silesia, in April 1941. In 1970, she stated: 'I am not ashamed to say I believed in National Socialism.'

Dubbed 'the most successful female spy in history' and codenamed 'Sonya', Ruth Hamburger Beurton ('Werner' was a *nom de plume* when she wrote her memoirs) always denied that she was a spy. To the end of her long life she insisted that she was no more than 'a member of the Red Army, in the reconnaissance service'.

Ruth Werner
1907–2000

Werner was born Ursula Ruth Kuczynski in Berlin, the daughter of Polish Jews who were supporters of the German Communist Party, and joined the Communist Youth League when she was 17. In 1929 she married her first husband Rolf Hamburger, an architect and Soviet agent, and went with him to Shanghai, where he had taken a job with the British-administered Shanghai municipal council.

In China, Ruth Hamburger was shocked by the extremes of wealth and poverty and was soon moving in revolutionary and communist circles. She met Agnes Smedley, the American journalist and triple-agent, and also her lover and collaborator, the German journalist and Soviet spy Richard Sorge, who ran a network of agents in Japan and was privy to many international secrets. Sorge persuaded Hamburger to work for the GRU (Soviet military intelligence) and gave her the codename 'Sonya'. She later described this as 'one of the most decisive events of my life'.

At Sorge's suggestion, Sonya travelled to Moscow where she underwent training in espionage and radio communications at the GRU's headquarters. She travelled widely as a GRU agent before returning to China, where she worked with revolutionary forces fighting the Japanese on the Manchurian border. In 1937 Sonya returned to Moscow for promotion to the rank of GRU major, advanced training and the award of the Order of the Red Banner, the highest honour then available to a non-Soviet citizen.

In 1938 Sonya settled her children in England, where her father and brother Jürgen, had been living since the mid-1930s, and was then ordered by the GRU to Switzerland. In the late 1930s and wartime years neutral state was a happy hunting ground for espionage networks, among them the Soviet-controlled *Rote Kapelle* ('Red Orchestra') and the so-called 'Lucy' ring, also controlled by Moscow, but which in the war years was used by British intelligence to channel discreetly laundered information about German military intentions to the Soviet Union. These were treated with the greatest scepticism by the Soviet leader Josef Stalin.

In Switzerland Sonya met Allan Foote, a British member of the 'Lucy' ring, who introduced her to her second husband, Len Beurton, an English veteran of the International Brigades of the Spanish Civil War. The GRU had ordered Sonia to divorce Rolf and marry Beurton, in order to secure a British passport. She married Beurton in February 1940 and received her passport in May. But before the couple could travel to England, their children's nanny – furious because she was not allowed to accompany her charges to England – informed the British consular representative in Montreux of the couple's links with Soviet intelligence. For the first but not the last time, the warning was ignored by the British security services.

In England, Sonya and her family moved into a large house in the village of Great Rollright, near Oxford. From 1942 this provided her with an ideal location for working as a courier with the German émigré scientist and atom spy Klaus Fuchs, a naturalized Briton employed at the atomic research establishment at Harwell. Sonya had been put in touch with the scientist by her brother Jürgen, who had known Fuchs during his communist past. Jürgen was to finish the war as an officer with the American Office of Strategic Services (OSS), an intelligence and espionage agency modelled on the British Special Operations Executive (SOE) and the forerunner of the CIA. In the war years, Jürgen's anti-fascist credentials and communist sympathies proved no bar to his working for US intelligence, indeed would have been considered an advantage.

Ruth Werner was a staunch believer in Communism and claimed to have been ignorant of Stalin's crimes. 'I fought against fascism', she proudly proclaimed in later life. 'Whatever else, I can hold my head up high because of that.'

Physicist and spy Klaus Fuchs, pictured while working at Los Alamos, New Mexico, on the Manhattan Project to assemble the Allied atomic bomb. The secrets he passed helped the Soviet Union develop the A-bomb by 1949.

After a series of meetings with Fuchs in Banbury, Sonya passed a stream of information on the British atomic programme either to her Soviet controllers in London, or directly by radio to Moscow. In late 1943 Fuchs joined the Manhattan Project in the United States and thereafter passed into the hands of other controllers. At the end of the war, Sonya's brother, now a lieutenant-colonel in the US army, supplied her with details of the results of the Strategic Bombing Survey, the American assessment of the air campaign against the Third Reich.

In 1946 Moscow mysteriously and abruptly broke off all contact with Sonya. Within a year both her own and her husband's cover had been exposed by Foote, and she was paid a visit by British Special Branch officers. Sonya later recalled: 'They left us calmly and politely but empty-handed.' Sonya and her husband kept their nerve and British intelligence did not return.

In 1950 Sonya and two of her children left Britain for East Germany on the day before Fuchs stood trial for betraying the West's atom secrets to the Soviet Union. In her autobiography (*Sonya's Report*, 1991) she reflected: 'Either it was complete stupidity on the part of MI5 never to have connected me to Klaus, or they may have let me get away with it, since every further discovery would have increased their disgrace.'

Subsequently suspicion fell on Roger Hollis, then head of MI5's F Division and responsible for the surveillance of Soviet agents. In the late 1920s Hollis had worked as a journalist in Shanghai and may have met Sonya at this early stage in their careers. He was later to become director general of MI5. It has never been conclusively demonstrated that Hollis was a Soviet agent.

In 1969 Sonya received her second Order of the Red Banner. She lived long enough to see the Berlin Wall come down, a small white-haired woman with a prominent nose, peering intently through heavy spectacles. In an interview shortly before her death, she fondly remembered England and English friends, but had no regrets about her fight against fascism and few reservations about Stalinism. In her autobiography she observed: 'I had not worked those 20 years with Stalin in mind. We wanted to help the people of the Soviet Union in their efforts to prevent war, and when war broke out against German fascism, to win it.' She dismissed German reunification, referring to it as an 'annexation'. She was one of the last of the generation who had dedicated their lives to communism in the belief that they were striving for a more just and humane society.

It was said of Daphne Park that she looked more like Miss Marple than Mata Hari. Matronly but with a Rolls-Royce mind and an iron reserve, she was dubbed the 'Queen of Spies' after over 40 years spent as an outstanding intelligence agent.

Park spent her childhood in Africa, where she was raised in a mud hut and only turned on an electric light and pulled a lavatory chain for the first time when, at the age of 11, she was shipped back to the United Kingdom via Dar es Salaam. She went up to Oxford in the autumn of 1940, at the beginning of the Blitz, and graduated from Somerville College in 1943. She then volunteered for the First Aid Nursing Yeomanry (FANY), having been tipped off that it was now more than a nursing corps, and spent most of the war in North Africa on coding operations for the Special Operations Executive (SOE).

After the war, Park transferred to MI6 and, under diplomatic cover, worked in a remarkable variety of postings from postwar Austria to Ulan Bator in Outer Mongolia in the 1980s. In all these postings Park displayed exceptionally measured coolness under fire. When in 1956 a mob invaded the British embassy in Moscow in a 'spontaneous' display of outrage against the Suez operation launched by the British, Park seized the opportunity to harangue the demonstrators, in fluent Russian, about the Soviet invasion of Hungary.

Three years later, as Belgian rule in the Congo collapsed, Park refused to take refuge with the colonialists in their fortified cantonment, but took up residence on the road to the airport, where she regularly received African visitors, including the Congo's future (albeit shortlived) prime minister, Patrice Lumumba. For this, she was beaten up by supporters of Lumumba's successor. She talked her way to safety and sought and secured local

DAPHNE PARK
1921–2010

United Nations intervention, which released imprisoned Britons and other foreign nationals. For this she was awarded the OBE.

Although she retained friendly relations with African opponents of white rule in Africa, Park remained an unrepentant Cold Warrior. She blamed the US withdrawal from Vietnam on 'a campaign orchestrated by the Russians' and never wavered from her belief in the 'domino theory', which justified intervention in Southeast Asia. Her hard-line against communism persisted long after the fall of the Berlin Wall because, as she put it: 'leopards do not change their spots overnight.'

Daphne Park on her elevation to the peerage in 1990, as Baroness Park of Monmouth.

Adolf Hitler was implacably opposed to women playing an active role in the waging of war, a paradox in such a highly militarized state as Nazi Germany. With the notable exceptions of Hanna Reitsch and Leni Riefenstahl, the Führer considered that women should be decorative or reproductive rather than active. In this context, a Russian émigré to Germany, Olga Chekhova, achieved fame as Adolf Hitler's favourite screen actress and was an intimate of many in the Führer's close circle, including Josef Goebbels. For many years, however, she was also a 'sleeper' agent for the Soviet intelligence service, the NKVD.

Olga Chekhova
1897–1980

Chekhova was born in the Caucasus, the daughter of German parents, Konstantin and Yelena Knipper. The family had strong theatrical connections – her aunt, Olga Knipper, had been a founder-member of the Moscow Art Theatre, and the wife of Russia's greatest playwright, Anton Chekhov. Olga followed her aunt onto the stage and in 1915 married the actor and theorist Michael Chekhov. Two years after the Russian Revolution she divorced Chekhov, left the Soviet Union and settled in Berlin, where she pursued a successful silent movie career, regularly cast as an elegant and seductive *femme d'affaires*. She became a major star in Europe and acted in more than 40 silent films during the 1920s.

As a Russian émigré with a family still in the Soviet Union, Chekhova became a target for agents of the NKVD, which established contact with her in 1923. In return for allowing her family to join her in Berlin, she agreed to provide her handlers with low-level intelligence. Later, as a movie actor, she survived the transition from silent movies to sound, and in the 1930s her fame grew and with it her apparent closeness to the Nazi élite. She was courted both by the head of the *Luftwaffe*, Hermann Göring, and by the Nazi propaganda minister Josef Goebbels. Goebbels first introduced her to the Führer, who greatly admired her films, in 1933. Photographs and newsreels showing her with an animated Adolf Hitler prompted the NKVD to involve an unwitting Chekhova in a 1943 plot to assassinate him.

Olga Chekhova in her role as the courtesan Feodora in the 1939 German film of Balzac's novel *The Magic Skin*. Meanwhile, in her real life, Chekhova was playing the role of the *femme fatale* Soviet spy.

Although Chekhova's precise role as a Soviet sleeper remains the subject of much conjecture, there is no doubt that her older brother, Lev Knipper, was an NKVD agent. The NKVD planned to despatch Knipper, a former White Russian émigré, composer and fluent German speaker, to Germany to pose as a defector. In Germany he would make contact with

Goebbels was a keen supporter of the German film industry, recognizing its potential as a propaganda tool for Nazism. He referred to Chekhova in his diaries as 'a charming woman', and is seen here in 1936 talking to the movie stars Gustav Fröhlich and Lida Baarová, who became his mistress.

his sister and another 'defector', Igor Miklashevsky, whose uncle – a genuine turncoat – worked as a Russian-language radio announcer for the Nazis. The intention was to use Chekhova's apparent closeness to the Nazi court to bring the assassins and Hitler together.

The plan was doomed to failure. By 1943 Hitler spent the greater part of his time in closely guarded military headquarters in East Prussia or the Ukraine, far from the company of fashionable actresses. Moreover, after the defeat of the German Sixth Army at Stalingrad in January 1943, the threat of a German victory in the east had significantly diminished, as had Stalin's desire to assassinate Hitler.

Chekhova, however, was a remarkable survivor. After the war, she re-established herself in West Germany and, when her screen career faltered, published an entertaining but highly unreliable volume of memoirs entitled, without irony, *I Conceal Nothing* (1955). She later launched a cosmetics company in Munich, which she is alleged to have funded by passing on to the Soviets snippets of information gleaned from NATO officers' wives who patronized her salons.

Like so many of the *femmes fatales* who stalk through the pages of espionage fiction, Vera Eriksen remains a woman wrapped in mystery. The unvarnished truth behind her life and career as a German agent may never be known,

although her life story seems like pure fiction: a mixture of farce, melodrama and tragicomedy.

She was born Vera Starizka in tsarist Russia and was possibly both illegitimate and Jewish. After the revolution, her adoptive family moved to Denmark and settled in Copenhagen. In the 1920s we find her dancing at the *Folies Bergères* in Paris. In 1930, aged 18, she married Count Sergei Ignatiev, the scion of a noble Russian family. Ignatiev, however, cut a less than noble figure and was rumoured to have links with both intelligence and drug-dealing. Through him, Vera was drawn into a world of White Russians and white powder (cocaine), the favourite narcotic of the era.

In 1937, following Ignatiev's death – possibly at the hands of the Soviet secret service – she married a German intelligence officer, Hans Friedrich von Wedel, who introduced her to the *Abwehr* (the counter-intelligence arm of the German high command). In 1938 the couple went to England, where they moved in circles sympathetic to the Nazis. It is possible that during the time the couple spent in England Eriksen had a son, swiftly consigned to an orphanage, who had been fathered not by her husband but by an unknown man. Early in the war, von Wedel died in a car crash, and shortly afterwards Eriksen turned up in Hamburg as the mistress of a Major Dierks, a naval intelligence officer in the *Abwehr*.

On a night towards the end of September 1940, in Operation 'Lena', Eriksen and two other agents, Werner Walti and Karl Drucke, travelled by flying boat from Stavanger, in occupied Norway, to a point near Portgordon in Banffshire, on the west coast of Scotland. They came ashore in a dinghy. Eriksen's mission was to establish contact with a sympathetic Italian countess while posing as her long-lost niece. To this end, she was travelling under the name of Vera Cottani de Chalbur. It has never been established whether the Italian countess existed, or indeed if she too was an agent.

For Drucke and Eriksen, 'Lena' ended at the Portgordon railway station, where they tried to buy tickets to London. Their gutteral accents, salt-caked clothes and utter ignorance of British currency or the price of railway tickets prompted a swift call to the local police. At the police station a search uncovered a box of revolver ammunition, a wireless and accessories, a collection of deeply unconvincing identity cards, a list of place-names that turned out to be airfields and a half-eaten German sausage. Under questioning, their stories became increasingly incredible, and they were arrested. Walti had been somewhat more successful in reaching Aberdeen, boarding a train for Edinburgh. In Edinburgh he was detained by the police while trying to reclaim his suitcase wireless from a left-luggage office.

In June 1941 Drucke and Walti were tried at London's Old Bailey, found guilty and sentenced to death. They were hanged in Wandsworth Prison on 6 August 1941. Eriksen, however, was never brought to trial. Many of the files relating to her case have been lost or remain closed, but it is safe to assume that she was successfully 'turned' by British intelligence, and saved her life by becoming part of the British 'Double Cross' deception in which captured Axis agents continued to send doctored signals to their unsuspecting controllers, as if they were still at large.

Some have speculated that the secret of Eriksen's survival lies in the identity of the child she had in London in the late 1930s, or rather that of the child's father. Nevertheless, all who have studied her case have wondered how German intelligence could have imagined that a cocaine-snorting foreign sophisticate, posing as a member of an aristocratic Italian family, would remain at large for any length of time in wartime western Scotland.

Rumours abound about what became of Vera Eriksen. At the end of the war, she was due to be deported to Germany, but an administrative blunder by MI5 in October 1945 meant that she was 'mislaid' and disappeared without trace, never to be heard from again. Thus ended one of the most hopelessly botched intelligence operations of the Second World War.

Photograph of Vera Eriksen taken in February 1942.

A member of Europe's pre-war gilded youth, Travers became the only woman to have joined the French Foreign Legion in the Second World War and she played an important role in the 1942 breakout from the fortress of Bir Hacheim in North Africa.

Susan Travers
1909–2003

The daughter of a British naval officer who had moved his family to the south of France in 1921, Travers excelled as a tennis player on the Côte d'Azur. Small and striking, she spent the 1930s as a privileged socialite. This carefree life came to an abrupt end with the outbreak of the Second World War. In 1939 Travers joined the French Red Cross. Blood made her queasy, a less than ideal qualification for a nurse, but she qualified as an ambulance driver and in 1940 accompanied the French expeditionary force despatched to help the Finns in their 'Winter War' against the Soviet Union.

In May 1940, after the fall of France, Travers made her way to London to offer her services as a nurse to the Free French. She was attached to a unit of the Foreign Legion (about half of which had refused to fight for pro-German Vichy France) and in September 1940 embarked on the abortive Franco-British expedition to capture the naval base at Dakar in French West Africa, whose garrison had thrown its lot in with the Vichy régime.

After serving as a driver in the Allied campaign in East Africa, where she was dubbed 'La Miss' by the legionnaires, Travers was posted to Beirut as the driver of Colonel Marie Pierre Koenig, who in November 1940 had captured Libreville in French Equatorial Africa. Travers and the dashing Koenig became secret lovers. She told him: 'Wherever you go, I will go too.'

In the spring of 1942 Koenig, now promoted to brigadier-general commanding the 1st Free French Brigade, was sent to hold Bir Hacheim, a fort in Libya at the southern end of the British 8th Army's Gazala Line. Travers went with him, and was in Bir Hacheim on 17 May, when it came under attack by German and Italian units of General Erwin Rommel's Afrika Korps. The Axis forces were certain the fort would swiftly fall. In the event, the defenders held out for over three weeks until the night of 10–11 June when, with water and ammunition exhausted, Koenig ordered a breakout.

Travers had spent much of the siege sheltering in a coffin-shaped fox hole in conditions of sweltering heat. In the breakout she played a more active role. She drove both her commanding officer and another Legion colleague, the White Russian prince Colonel Dmitri Amilakvari (another of her lovers before she met Koenig). Under heavy fire, Travers's car burst through the enemy lines, at one point smashing into several German armoured vehicles. She recalled: 'Shells were falling around us like rain and sudden violent explosions tore the night, showering our car with burning metal … It is a delightful feeling going as fast as you can in the dark. My main concern was that the engine wouldn't stall.' By dawn, some 2,500 of Bir Hacheim's 3,700 defenders, including 650 legionnaires, had reached the safety of the British lines.

After her daring breakout from Bir Hacheim, Travers coolly noted 11 bullet holes in her vehicle, as well as extensive shrapnel damage. She was awarded the *Croix de Guerre* and the *Ordre du Corps d'Armée* for her gallantry.

Her affair with Koenig ended shortly afterwards, but she stayed loyal to the Legion, serving in Italy and France until 1945. In May of that year, she applied to join the Legion officially and was made an officer in its logistics division – the only woman to serve in the Legion in the 1940s.

Travers served in French Indochina, but in 1947 resigned her commission to bring up her children by her husband, Nicholas Schwegelmilk, a sergeant in the Legion. In 1956 she was awarded the *Médaille Militaire*. Poignantly, the medal was pinned on her by Koenig, who by then was France's Minister of Defence. In 1996 she received the *Légion d'honneur*. Four years later, the French government decided as a matter of general policy to allow women to join the Foreign Legion.

MARIE-MADELEINE FOURCADE
1909–89

In Occupied France, one of the foremost Resistance networks run by the British Secret Intelligence Service (SIS, or MI6) was 'Alliance', based in Vichy and led by Georges Lostauna-Lacau, an officer in the French army who had been badly wounded in 1940.

In the summer of 1941, Alliance was betrayed by one of its wireless operators, Bradley Davis. Many key members, including Lostauna-Lacau, were arrested and sent to concentration camps. Lostauna-Lacau was imprisoned in Mauthausen, but survived the war. The network was kept alive by his principal lieutenant, Marie-Madeleine Fourcade, and eventually numbered some 3,000 active supporters throughout France.

They supplied a wide range of intelligence – the location of the *Luftwaffe*'s decoy airfields, reports from inside U-Boat bases and, later in the war, reports on German rocketry. Fourcade gave her agents animal or bird codenames (she was 'Hedgehog'), and in France the network became known as 'Noah's Ark'.

Fourcade was an extremely tough customer. Arrested in November 1942, she escaped and was later exfiltrated by aircraft to London, where she maintained close links with 'Alliance' from a house in Chelsea. She returned to France shortly after D-Day, but fell into enemy hands a second time. She contrived another escape by stripping naked and squeezing through the bars of her cell window. After the war SIS, in paying tribute to Fourcade, stressed that the blunders and betrayals that had threatened to destroy 'Alliance' in 1941 had in no way dimmed her loyalty to the British.

Fourcade recounted her wartime experiences in a book, *Noah's Ark*, published in 1968. She was highly decorated, becoming a Commander of the *Légion d'honneur*. She also founded an organization to help survivors of the Resistance (in the war 'Alliance' had lost some 430 of its personnel). A staunch Gaullist, she became a member of the European Parliament. After her death, friends of Fourcade revealed the name and fate of the traitor Bradley Davis. He had been spotted in Marseilles by another SIS agent, kidnapped, questioned and finally poisoned.

Born an orphan in Florida, Cochran was raised in poverty by foster parents. Nothing in her background indicated the talent that would make her a pioneering aviator and leader in the Second World War. She was eight years old before she was given her first pair of shoes and two years later was working in a cotton mill. She had virtually no formal education, and in later years would take an oral examination for her pilot's licence.

Jacqueline Cochran
1910–80

Cochran worked in a beauty parlour in Montgomery, Alabama, before moving to New York in 1929 as a hairdresser at Saks Fifth Avenue. In 1932, while in Miami, she met the wealthy entrepreneur and aviator Floyd Odlum, whom she later married. Odlum encouraged Cochran to fly, and in the summer of 1932 she obtained a pilot's licence in just three weeks.

In 1934 Cochran set the first of many records when she flew and tested the first supercharger installed on an aircraft engine. In the same year she achieved another first, piloting an unpressurized biplane to 10,363 metres (34,000 ft) while wearing an oxygen mask. Cochran then became the first woman to fly in the 1935 Bendix Transcontinental race, winning the overall title in 1938 in an untried Seversky fighter. In 1938 she was awarded the General William E. Mitchell memorial award for making the greatest contribution to aviation in that year.

War clouds were now gathering in Europe, and the storm broke in early September 1939, when German forces invaded Poland. The day after Warsaw fell to the Nazis, Cochran wrote a letter to Eleanor Roosevelt, the wife of the US president, suggesting the use of female ferry pilots by the US Air Corps. She urged that they could also be used for a wide variety of tasks, indeed almost everything short of flying combat missions. Cochran was in no doubt that the US would become embroiled in the war and that the Air Corps should be prepared.

Cochran was encouraged by General Henry 'Hap' Arnold, head of the Air Corps, to lend her support to the British Air Transport Auxiliary (ATA), which from 1939 had included female flying personnel. In June 1942 Cochran became the first woman to pilot a United States Army Air Force (USAAF) bomber across the Atlantic, part of the Lend-Lease deal between Roosevelt and Churchill that made weapons available to the British. Cochran and a crew of three flew a Lockheed Hudson light bomber and reconnaissance aircraft from Montreal to Prestwick in Scotland. The flight was jokingly referred to as 'a jump across the pond', but such levity conceals the dangers inherent in such an undertaking and the possibility of engine failure over the wastes of the ocean. Cochran had proved her point.

However, in the summer of 1941 it was still by no means clear to the USAAF that there was a place for female ferry pilots to act as effective auxiliaries. But following the surprise Japanese attack on the US Pacific Fleet in Pearl Harbor on 7 December 1941, the rules of the game were radically changed. The United States was

In 1961–62 the 52-year-old Jacqueline Cochran was awarded the Harmon Trophy for establishing eight world records at the controls of her Northrop T-38 Talon jet trainer.

now at war with Japan. Four days later, after Hitler's declaration of war on the United States, it was at war on two fronts.

The drive to recruit ferry pilots – both male and female – began in earnest in the late summer of 1942, when Cochran was in the United Kingdom after the delivery of the Hudson. It saw the formation of Air Transport Command (ATC), commanded by Brigadier-General Harold L. George and responsible for ferrying duties within the United States. George decided as an experiment to establish a squadron of female ferry pilots, the Women's Auxiliary Ferrying Squadron (WAFS) to be commanded by another outstanding airwoman of the period, Nancy Love.

It was inevitable that friction would arise between two such dynamic, ambitious airwomen as Cochran and Love. Cochran was a working girl who by force of will and natural ability had become a national heroine. Love came from a wealthy family, had learned to fly in her teens and had attended Vassar College. The problem was in part smoothed over with some deft organizational juggling. On 15 September 1942 the USAAF announced the formation of a training programme to prepare women pilots to serve with the WAFS. The programme was to be called the Women's Flying Training Detachment (WFTD) and Cochran was appointed its director. Plans were drawn up for the training of 500 women pilots.

Jacqueline Cochran, standing on the wing of a Canadair F-86 Sabre, chats to test pilots Chuck Yeager (left), the first man to break the sound barrier in level flight, and test pilot Bill Longhurst.

In August 1943 the WAFS and WFTD became a single entity, the Women Air Force Service Pilots (WASP). Its Director was Cochran while Love was placed in charge of all the agency's ferrying operations in continental America. More than 25,000 women applied for training with the WASP and eventually 1,074 graduated from its rigorous training programme. They were to fly some 60 million miles (nearly 100 million km) for the USAAF within the United States, suffering 38 fatalities, approximately one for every 16,000 hours flown.

The WASP's 18th and final class graduated at the beginning of December 1944. In his speech General Arnold told the 68 graduates and over 100 returning WASPs: 'Frankly, I didn't know in 1941 whether a slip of a young girl could fight the controls of a B-17 in the heavy weather they would naturally encounter in operational flying. Well, now in 1944 … the entire operation has been a success … It is on the record that women can fly as well as men.'

In the summer of 1939 the Royal Air Force agreed to the formation of a unit, the Air Transport Auxiliary (ATA), to undertake non-combat flying duties. From the outset, the decision was taken to widen the intake to include female personnel.

Initially the ATA's purview included flying mail and performing ambulance duties. Its pilots were qualified aviators ineligible for service in the Royal Air Force. From early 1940, the scope of the ATA's duties widened to include the ferrying of aircraft from manufacturer to air base or between air stations. A women's section was formed under the leadership of Pauline Gower, a pilot with some 2,000 hours of flying experience.

Eventually 166 women served with the ATA, helping to deliver many of the 310,000 aircraft that passed through the Auxiliary's hands during the war. In addition to flying duties, 900 of the 2,000 personnel employed by the ATA as office staff, trainers and maintenance workers were women.

The female pilots were accomplished aviators. Issued only with 'pilots' notes', a simple set of instructions, they had no radio on board and navigated by following the terrain below them, often flying along railway lines. Using these methods, Lettice Curtis, who before joining the ATA had worked as a pilot for a survey company, delivered no fewer than 400 four-engined bombers. She also loved ferrying Spitfires, observing: 'In the air the Spitfire was forgiving and without vice ... The Hurricane was dogged and masculine but the Spit, calling for more sensitive handling, was altogether more feminine, had more glamour and threw its wheels outward in an abandoned, extrovert way. From the ground there was a special beauty about it.'

In the autumn of 1944 the ATA began to deliver aircraft to the advancing Allied armies in northwest Europe. That winter ATA pilots, including many women, braved atrocious weather to deliver their aircraft to forward airfields. Navigation was immensely difficult, as snowfall blotted out all landmarks except forests, thick ice rendered rivers invisible and roads, railways and airfields all but disappeared in the murk. In all, 129 ATA pilots died in service, including the celebrated prewar aviatrix Amy Johnson. Members of the ATA sometimes referred to themselves as 'the Ancient and Tattered Airmen and Women'.

For her services to her country in the Second World War, Cochran received the Distinguished Service Medal. Over 30 years later in 1977, she was among those who successfully lobbied the US Congress for veteran benefits for the WASP. From 1948 to 1970 she served in the Air Force Reserve with the rank of colonel.

With the war over, she returned to record breaking, forming a close alliance with Colonel Fred J. Ascani and Captain Chuck Yeager of the United States Air Force. In May 1953, flying a Canadair F-86 Sabre jet fighter and with Jaeger flying on her wing, Cochran attained a speed of 652.3 mph (1,050 km/h), and became the first woman to break the sound barrier at Edwards Air Force Base in California. Early in 1954 she was awarded the Harmon Trophy as the outstanding female pilot of the year.

In 1961 she set a succession of speed records flying a Northrop T-38 Talon trainer and in the same year, flying the unforgiving Lockheed F-104G Starfighter, recorded a speed of 1,429.3 mph (2,300 km/h), the fastest by a woman. She also claimed a 500 km record with the F-104, recording a speed of 1,127.4 mph (1,814 km/h). A pilot to rate alongside the finest of the heroic age of jet-powered aviation, Cochran subsequently became active in politics and journalism and ran her own cosmetics firm.

During her military service, Keil was awarded the impressive total of 19 medals and ribbons, including four Air Medals, two Presidential Unit Citations, a Second World War Victory Medal, four Second World War battle stars and a Korean Service Medal with seven battle stars.

Lillian Kinkela Keil
1916–2005

Keil was born in Arcata, northern California, and after her father left the family home was brought up by her mother in a convent where she worked as a cleaner. Following high school, she enrolled in a nursing programme at St Mary's Hospital in San Francisco. She later became a flight attendant with United Airlines, which then required its stewardesses to be registered nurses.

At the outbreak of the Second World War, Keil enlisted as a flight nurse with the US Army Air Corps, attending wounded soldiers on casualty evacuation flights from combat zones to hospitals in the rear. Serving with 801st Medical Air Evacuation Transport Squadron, Keil saw service in the Normandy campaign in the summer of 1944 and then during the Battle of the Bulge (December 1944). She later recalled: 'After the Normandy landings, the pace picked up for 801st Air Evacuation crews. Wherever a toehold was established and called a battle zone, that would be our destination. The pilot and co-pilot, my medical technician and I, would scramble aboard a C-47 [Dakota transport plane] crammed full of gas, oil, rations, and medical supplies, and head out over the Channel to the battlefield. Since we carried military supplies, we couldn't hide behind the safety of the Red Cross insignia. Despite that fact, and since sleep was something we never got enough of, I learned to doze with my head resting on my oxygen tank sitting atop an oil drum. We always carried our own

'Wherever we landed, smoke rising in the distance and the dull roar of heavy artillery marked the front line. Everyone pitched in to help unload our supplies. My heart ached for those carefully covered and lying silently in neat rows awaiting another plane for their ride home.'

LILLIAN KEIL ON HER NURSING DUTIES DURING THE ALLIED ADVANCE FROM THE NORMANDY BEACHHEAD

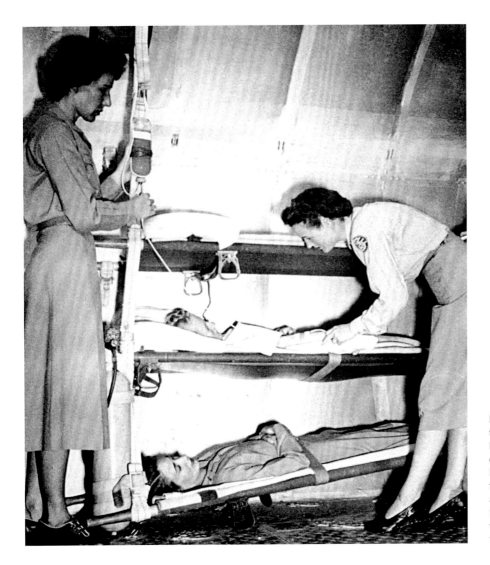

In November 1942 the School of Air Evacuation was opened at Bowman Field in Kentucky, to train flight nurses to act as assistants to flight surgeons. Keil was a leading light in these operations.

C-rations wherever we went, since we never knew when we'd be back or have time to eat.'

In July 1944 Keil's Transport Squadron tracked the progress across France of US Third Army, commanded by General George S. Patton, after it broke out from the Normandy bridgehead. In addition to casualty evacuation, the Squadron's duties included dropping off gasoline, oil drums, ammunition, weapons and supplies. When the Squadron's aircraft were grounded by bad weather, Third Army also found it difficult to move. Fuel supply was vital in this race against time. Keil recalled that General Patton would often send the flight nurses a case of champagne from Rheims to thank them for the delivery of the fuel that was vital to sustain the speed of his army's advance.

Keil followed the front line as it moved across northwest Europe: 'Wherever we landed, smoke rising in the distance and the dull roar of heavy artillery marked the front line. Everyone pitched in to help unload our supplies. Some wounded soldiers were already stabilized by corpsmen in the field. Those on litters came directly from the Mobile Hospital (Mobile Army Surgical Hospital or MASH) with more critical wounds that would require special attention. My heart ached for those carefully covered and lying silently in neat rows awaiting another plane for their ride home.'

Keil had vivid memories of the part she played in the heavy fighting in the Ardennes during the Battle of the Bulge, Hitler's last great offensive in the West: 'I remember the bitter cold … that December. Our planes landed and took off in light snow, or on slippery metal runways. Frostbitten toes and fingers were black and to the bone. Often it was so foggy that we couldn't land. I cried more than once for the wounded anxiously awaiting evacuation whenever our planes could not land. Once we were grounded by a storm, so we stayed aboard our aircraft with the wounded trying to keep everyone warm. During that long and sleepless night, I wondered what the sisters at St Mary's Hospital, who taught me to be a nurse, would think if they could see me now. I also wondered if my job as a stewardess with United Airlines would be waiting for me when I got home, especially that warm tropical Hawaiian route they planned to add.'

> **'I remember the bitter cold … that December. Our planes landed and took off in light snow, or on slippery metal runways. Frostbitten toes and fingers were black and to the bone. Often it was so foggy that we couldn't land. I cried more than once for the wounded anxiously awaiting evacuation whenever our planes could not land.'**
>
> KEIL ON THE HARSH CONDITIONS IN DECEMBER 1944

On these missions, Keil went to great lengths to ensure that she was well made up and that her hair was modishly coiffed. To a wounded soldier she and her colleagues were a powerful reminder of home. Even in the most harrowing situations, she strove to maintain an expression that conveyed to her charges that everything was going to be all right. It was a matter of constant regret that after the delivery of her human cargo, Keil and her crew never learned of their fate.

Keil's service did not end in 1945. In 1950 she also participated in the Inchon landings in Korea. It is estimated that in two major conflicts Keil tended some 10,000 US troops. A 1954 Hollywood movie, *Flight Nurse*, starring Forrest Tucker and Joan Leslie, was in part based on Keil's wartime experiences. Seven years later Keil appeared on the television show *This Is Your Life*, which generated a flood of correspondence from veterans she had tended in Europe and Korea, and could now meet again in happier circumstances.

The first two women to land on the Normandy beachhead on 12 June 1944 were Iris Ogilvy and Mollie Giles, both Sisters in Princess Mary's Royal Air Force Nursing service and members of No.50 Mobile Field Hospital, 83 Group, Royal Air Force. They came ashore on Juno Beach near the town of Courseulles-sur-Mer.

Iris Ogilvy recalled: 'Orders were given to disembark, and we were guided down to the lower deck. I remember standing next to Mollie in the dark, on the left side of the lower deck of the LST (Landing Ship Tank) facing the ramp. I felt as though I was in a monstrous whale, listening to the noises of the vehicles edging their way down the steep ramp to the shore ... We scrambled down the ramp and the next thing I remember was feeling sand under my feet ... "Follow me", said the beachmaster, "I'll take you down here and arrange for a jeep to take you". We had no idea what he meant by "down here", but, after walking a few yards we found ourselves standing by some concrete steps leading to what appeared to be an underground shelter. We quickly descended and suddenly heard the voices of troops. We were given a tremendous welcome. Someone shouted, "Watch out Adolf, you've had it now!" '

'There was torrential rain at times and casualties began to pile up, as it was not possible to evacuate them by air. One night was particularly noisy, due to the gunfire and shelling, and we were all busy dashing about. I stopped by one of the lads, who was very poorly, lapsing into periods of unconsciousness. I made certain that all was well with the various tubing, then hurried off to do other things. After a little while I returned to look at him again. This time he had his eyes wide open and said in a perfectly clear voice, "Where's your tin hat? Who do you think you are, a blinking fairy?" I had forgotten that I was not wearing one. I went to find my hat and hurriedly put it on. I returned to reassure him, to find that he had just died. It was an incident that shook me greatly and that I could never forget.'

American medics administer a plasma transfusion to a survivor from a landing craft that was sunk off the Normandy beaches on 12 June 1944.

Santamaria's career described an extraordinary arc from guerrilla freedom fighter to director of a world-famous literary institution and home for exiled Latin-American artists and intellectuals.

Haydée Santamaria
1922–80

Haydée was born on a sugar plantation in central Cuba to parents who were small landholders. In Havana in 1952, Santamaria and her brother Abel joined the insurgency movement led by the young lawyer Fidel Castro against the Cuban dictator Fulgencio Batista, who had seized power in a military coup. On the morning of 26 July 1953 Santamaria joined Melba Hernandez as the only two women in the 160-strong force assembled by Castro to seize the Moncada barracks in the city of Santiago de Cuba as the first step towards overthrowing the American-backed Batista regime. Among the insurgents were Santamaria's boyfriend and her brother.

The attack on the Moncada was a chaotic failure, and many of those involved were either killed or taken prisoner. Santamaria, her boyfriend, her brother and Hernandez were among those captured. The subsequent trial in the Santiago de Cuba Palace of Justice began before three judges on 21 September and ended on 6 October. At the outset, Castro conducted his own defence and lied under oath to protect his comrades. When he protested against the cold-blooded murder of captured insurgents by the military at the Moncada barracks, he was prevented from returning to the court on the spurious grounds of illness, and then tried separately. Santamaria received a seven-month sentence as the prosecution failed to prove that she had handled any weapons during the attack on the Moncada.

During the trial Santamaria had been subjected to sadistic pressure to make her talk. In her cell she was confronted with a barbaric display in an effort to make her confess her guilt. She was shown an eye, or in some accounts, both eyes and the testicles torn from her brother. Famously, she told her captors: 'If you tore out his eye and he did not speak, neither will I.' Her brother succumbed to torture, as did her boyfriend, but Santamaria did not crack, even when she and Hernandez were terribly burned with cigarettes.

Haydée Santamaria (left) and Melba Hernandez in prison after taking part in the abortive attack on the Moncada barracks in 1953.

While Santamaria was in prison, Castro arranged for a document he had written to be smuggled into her cell page by page. It defiantly justified all his actions and was later published under the title *History Will Absolve Me*. It contained the ringing words: 'I warn you. I am just beginning. If there is in your heart a vestige of love for your country, love for humanity,

love for justice, listen carefully ... I know that the [Batista] regime will try to suppress the truth by all possible means. I know that there will be a conspiracy to bury me in oblivion. But my voice will not be stifled, it will rise from my breast even when I feel most alone, and my heart will give it all the fire that callous cowards deny it ... It does not matter. History will absolve me.' Castro subsequently named the Cuban revolutionary movement after the failed attack on the Moncada barracks of 26 July 1953.

In 1955, following a general amnesty announced by Batista, Santamaria was released from prison and returned to the revolutionary struggle. She worked as a gunrunner, international fundraiser, co-ordinator of the urban underground and combatant in the 26th July movement. Later she fought alongside Castro's lieutenant Che (Ernesto) Guevara in the Sierra Maestra, the mountainous region in southern Cuba. This inhospitable terrain provided a refuge for Castro and a small band of rebels after a second attempt to raise the flag of revolution in December 1956 had been all but destroyed by Batista's army.

It was in the Sierra Maestra that the powerful myths of the Cuban revolution were forged with the help of compliant Western journalists like the American Herbert Matthews, who interviewed its leaders in 1957. The Sierra Maestra became the redoubt for the 26th July movement and then the battleground on which it defeated the numerically superior but inept

Tamara Bunke played a prominent role in the Cuban and other Latin-American revolutionary movements and was the only woman to fight alongside Bolivian communist rebels under Che Guevara.

Bunke was born in Buenos Aires, Argentina, where her German communist parents were living as refugees from the Nazis. In 1952 the family settled in East Germany, but Bunke retained an interest in Latin-American nationalism. After studying political science at Humboldt University, Bunke began working for the East German Ministry of State Security (the *Stasi*), travelling in Western Europe under a variety of assumed names, and sometimes posing as a student of folklore.

In 1960, while working as an interpreter for a Cuban trade delegation, she met Che Guevara. In 1961, a week after the abortive US-backed invasion of Cuba – the co-called 'Bay of Pigs' fiasco – Bunke travelled to Cuba, where she joined labour brigades, worked as a translator and journalist and devoted much time to fostering Cuba's links with Europe and other Latin-

TAMARA BUNKE
1937–67

American countries, often travelling with Guevara.

In November 1964 she went to Bolivia as an undercover agent working for what was to prove Guevara's last guerrilla campaign. Her somewhat unlikely mission was to infiltrate Bolivian high society while posing as a teacher and folk musicologist. In 1966, against Guevara's wishes, she joined a group of Bolivian guerrillas led by Juan Vitalio Acuna. In August 1967, while crossing the Rio Grande at Vado del Yeso, the guerrillas were ambushed by Bolivian troops, who killed Bunke and eight of her comrades. Bunke's body was swept away but was found two weeks later and buried alongside her dead companions. In October 1998 the burial site was identified and her remains were re-interred in Cuba. Bunke's memory is greatly revered in Cuba and 'Tania', her *nom de guerre*, has been adopted by a number of female revolutionaries, including the heiress Patty Hearst during her time with the Symbionese Liberation Army (SLA) in the mid-1970s.

'I warn you. I am just beginning. If there is in your heart a vestige of love for your country, love for humanity, love for justice, listen carefully ... my voice will not be stifled, it will rise from my breast even when I feel most alone, and my heart will give it all the fire that callous cowards deny it ... It does not matter. History will absolve me.'

FIDEL CASTRO ON THE 26TH JULY MOVEMENT

and badly led forces of Batista. The dictator fled Cuba for the Dominican Republic on 1 January 1959, taking with him more than three million dollars amassed through graft and pay-offs. A week later Fidel Castro entered Havana in triumph amid a riot of black and red flags of the 26th July movement fluttering from every rooftop.

After the revolution, Santamaria transformed herself from *guerrillera* to Cuban cultural emissary. Perhaps her greatest achievement was her work as the director of the *Casa de los Americas*, one of the foremost cultural institutions in Latin-America, which over the years hosted and published a pantheon of literary giants, including Gabriel Garcia Márquez, Pablo Neruda, Marta Conti and Alicia Alonso. The *Casa* was responsible for bringing some of the world's greatest dancers, musicians, painters and theatre groups to Cuba, doing much to break down the isolation in which the Castro government found itself from the mid-1960s. Santamaria also fiercely defended young Cuban writers, artists and performers from the dogmatism that muffled free speech in Cuba under Castro.

In the last year of her life Santamaria was badly injured and left in constant pain by a car accident. She was also deeply affected by the death of a close friend, Celia Sanchez, one of Castro's most trusted aides. It was Sanchez who had established the first female combat squad during the revolution in the Sierra Maestra. After Castro came to power, she had been appointed Secretary to the Presidency of the Council of Ministers.

Some have speculated that Santamaria's decline was triggered by the accident and Sanchez's death, combined with her depression about Cuba's increasing material and ideological dependence on the Soviet Union. However, it is more likely that she had reached the end of a long road that began during the horrifying aftermath of the attack on the Moncada barracks. Perhaps Santamaria foresaw her own end in 1967 when she wrote after the death of Che Guevara in Bolivia, where he was leading an unsuccessful peasant uprising: ' ... today I feel tired of living; I think I have lived too much already.' She committed suicide in 1980 on the aniversary of the abortive assault on the Moncada barracks.

The trajectory of Meir's career carried her from Kiev to the Knesset, the Israeli parliament, and to the position of prime minister in the Yom Kippur War of October 1972. In the highly masculine world of Israeli politics, Meir was an 'Iron Lady' long before the term was coined for Margaret Thatcher.

Golda Meir
1898–1978

Golda Meir was born Golda Mabovich in the Jewish quarter of Kiev, in the Ukraine, and later emigrated with her family to join her father in the United States. They settled in Milwaukee, where she trained as a teacher and became a Zionist campaigner. In 1917 she married a sign painter, Morris Myerson, with whom she emigrated in 1921 to Palestine, where they worked for three years on a *kibbutz* (collective farm). The couple later moved to Tel-Aviv, where Golda worked as a clerk and took in washing to support her two children and ailing husband.

By 1928 Meir had become Secretary of the Women's Labour Council and was a rising force in the *Histadrut*, the Jewish labour federation, representing it at international conferences. She was elected as a delegate to the World Zionist Congress, and in the 1930s accompanied missions to the United States and Britain.

After 1946, under the British mandate in Palestine, Meir played a prominent role in the Jewish Agency, the Jewish self-government organization. She succeeded Moshe Sharett as head of its political department, which liaised with the British. As a member of the Jewish Agency's Executive, she played a significant role in raising money in the United States for the nascent state of Israel.

In May 1948, on the eve of the British withdrawal and with armed conflict looming between the Jewish state and its Arab neighbours, Meir was sent by the Jewish leader David Ben-Gurion on a secret mission. Disguised as an Arab woman, and accompanied by Ezra Danin, a conduit between the Jewish Agency and Arab leaders, Meir crossed into Jordan to meet King Abdullah in an attempt to persuade him to join an Anglo-Jordanian pact. King Abdullah, however, was already committed to an invasion of Palestine and Meir returned to Tel Aviv to report the failure of her mission and the imminence of war. On 14 May 1948 she was one of the 25 signatories of the declaration establishing the state of Israel.

In January 1949, after the Israeli War of Independence, Meir was elected to the *Knesset* as a Labour candidate and appointed Minister of

Golda Meir shortly before her death in 1978. Her obituary in the *New York Times* paid fitting tribute to her standing as a stateswoman: 'The miracle of Golda Meir was how one person could embody the spirit of so many.'

Labour and Social Security, the only woman in the Ben-Gurion administration. In 1956 she became Israel's foreign minister and was closely involved in the secret negotiations, this time with the French, which preceded the Israeli campaign in the Sinai peninsula, itself timed to coincide with the Anglo-French occupation of the Suez Canal zone. Subsequently, Meir was instrumental in restoring relations with the United States following the Suez débâcle and providing assistance to emerging nations in Africa. Now a widow, she was asked by David Ben-Gurion to take a Hebrew name and she chose 'Meir', which means 'to burn brightly'. She always stood out from the 'suits', the male politicians all around her, an imposing but warm figure whose heavily lined features were in later years strongly reminiscent of the US president, Lyndon Baines Johnson.

Meir became Israel's prime minister in 1969 after the sudden death of Levi Eshkol. She was the world's third female premier after Sirimavo Bandaranaike of Sri Lanka and Indira Gandhi of India, and governed through a select band of advisers known as her 'kitchen cabinet'. In 1972 she authorized the relentless international pursuit by Mossad, the Israeli secret service, of the terrorists responsible for the deaths of 11 Israeli athletes at the Munich Olympics. But her administration came to be dominated and defined by the Yom Kippur War, which burst upon Israel on 6 October 1972, when the Egyptians crossed the Suez Canal. In the months leading up to the operation, Israeli military intelligence had failed to interpret correctly the many danger signals it had received during the steady Egyptian build-up. Indeed, on 26 September Israel's ambassador in the United States, Yitzhak Rabin, had declared that: 'There never was a period in which Israel's security situation seemed as good as now.'

However, early on the morning of 6 October, when it was clear that an attack on Israel was imminent, Meir overruled a proposal by the chief of staff of the Israeli Defence Force (IDF), General David Elazar, to make a pre-emptive air strike on Egypt's ally, Syria. Meir knew that Israel had to be seen by the world to be the victim of aggression and could not risk the withdrawal of US support, without which Israel might have been forced to launch a nuclear response to the Egyptian and Syrian assault.

Throughout the October War, Meir retained a firm hand on the helm while those about her faltered and panicked as the crisis threatened to grow out of control. In three weeks of bitter fighting, Israel secured victory against Egypt and Syria, but at heavy cost in men and weapons. The spring of 1974 saw the publication of a report by the Agranat Commission, which had been appointed to draw lessons from the débâcle. It was highly critical of all aspects of Israel's political and military leadership. Its two most prominent victims were the defence minister and leading member of the kitchen cabinet, General Moshe Dayan, and Golda Meir herself. When the commission's findings were made public, they both resigned. Her military victory proved fleeting: war still bedevils the Middle East.

The only child of Pandit Jawaharlal and Kamala Nehru, Gandhi was born into India's political aristocracy and became the nation's prime minister in 1967. Four years later, having swept to victory in a second general election, Gandhi led her country into a war with Pakistan in which India secured a decisive victory.

In 1947 Hindu India and the smaller Muslim state of Pakistan had both gained their independence from the British in an orgy of bloodletting. In 1971 the major war that had been threatening to erupt between the two nations ever since the partition of the subcontinent finally erupted. East Pakistan had declared itself the independent state of Bangladesh. West Pakistan attempted to suppress the independence movement, and the ensuing civil strife claimed hundreds of thousands of lives. Up to ten million Bengalis fled to India, where initial support for a guerrilla response gave way to preparations for a full-scale military intervention.

Gandhi prepared the ground with consummate skill. In August she signed a 20-year treaty of friendship with the Soviet Union, which ensured that China, an ally of Pakistan, would stay out of the conflict. in the autumn of 1971 Gandhi launched a diplomatic offensive, touring Europe and ensuring that Britain and France would join the United States, which she visited in early November, in blocking any pro-Pakistani resolutions in the United Nations Security Council.

At the beginning of December 1971, Pakistan attempted to forestall the growing threat of an Indian invasion of Bangladesh by launching a pre-emptive invasion of Kashmir and the Punjab. The Indian air force survived attacks on its airfields, and the next day the Indian invasion of East Pakistan began. Within 13 days the Pakistani commander in Bangladesh had surrendered, while in West Pakistan the Indian army halted the Pakistani advance. By 17 December the war was over and Pakistan had lost Bangladesh.

The 1971 war was unique in that the Indian political leadership exhibited a proper understanding of the use of military power to achieve a clear national aim. Vital to this success, and a tribute to Indira Gandhi's accomplished handling of the crisis, was the use of the Indian navy. As East and West Pakistan were two separate geographical entities separated by over more than 1,600 miles (2,575 km), the only way Pakistani forces in East Pakistan could be sustained was by sea. Indira Gandhi decided that the Indian navy was to be given the strategic task of denying East and West Pakistan access to war supplies by mounting a comprehensive naval blockade, a mission carried out with complete success. Not for nothing was Gandhi sometimes compared to the Indian goddess Durga, who rode on a tiger.

Indira Gandhi in 1956, in the company of her father Jawaharlal Nehru, India's first prime minister.

Holm joined the US military in 1942 and retired three decades later, after becoming the first woman in any branch of the service to rise to the rank of two-star general. In an oral history that Holm recorded for the Library of Congress in 2003, she observed: 'I set about trying to open up as many fields as I could to women, using any gimmick I could.'

Jeanne Holm
1921–2010

Born in Portland, Oregon, Holm trained as a silversmith and enlisted in 1942 after the US Congress established the Women's Army Auxiliary Corps (WAAC). In 1943 she was commissioned as a third officer, the WAAC equivalent of a second lieutenant. By 1945 she was a captain in charge of the 106th WAC Hospital Company at Newton D. Baker General Hospital, West Virginia, but at war's end returned to civilian life to gain a university degree, attending Lewis and Clark College in Portland.

The first female general in the United States Air Force, Holm was the prime mover behind the expansion of women's roles in this service in the 1960s and 1970s.

Holm remained a reservist, and in 1948, during the blockade of West Berlin by Soviet forces, she was recalled to active duty, then in 1949 transferred to the United States Air Force (USAF). One of her early assignments was to the post of War Plans Officer for the 85th Air Depot Wing in Germany during the Berlin Air Lift and in the early stages of the Korean War. She was the first woman to attend the Air Command and Staff School at Maxwell Air Force Base, Alabama, before being posted to USAF headquarters in Washington. From 1957 to 1961 she was based in Naples, responsible for supervising manpower needs at the headquarters of the Allied Air Forces for Southern Europe.

From 1961 to 1965 Holm served in Washington as a congressional staff officer, after which she was promoted to the rank of colonel and appointed the director of the WAF (female personnel in the USAF). In this position Holm was a powerful force for the opening up of career opportunities for women in the USAF and the abolition of discriminatory regulations. Holm later acknowledged that her own rise in the Air Force, and her success in securing greater opportunities for women, owed much to the early impetus

'In the military a racist is not allowed to act like one, but it's sort of winked at to be sexist.'

HOLM ON INSTITUTIONALIZED SEXISM IN THE AMERICAN MILITARY ESTABLISHMENT

Dubbed 'Amazing Grace' and 'the First Lady of Software', Hopper chaired the committee that developed COBOL, the automatic programming language that in the 1940s launched computers as a universal instrument.

A New Yorker, Hopper grew up with a love of geometry and maps, and later confessed that she would have become an engineer on graduating from Vassar College, had that career path been open to women in the 1920s. She graduated from Yale with a degree in mathematics and returned to Vassar to teach.

In December 1943 Hopper joined the US Navy Reserve and was posted to the computer laboratory at Harvard, where she had a life-defining encounter with the first large-scale computer in the United States, the Mark I. In 1947, when Hopper was a lieutenant assigned to the Bureau of Ordnance computation project, a breakdown in one of the circuits of a Mark II Aiken Relay Calculator was found to have been caused by a trapped moth which was removed with tweezers, prompting Hopper to coin the term 'bug'.

She remained in the Reserve after the war and joined the company that was developing Univac I, the first commercial computer. The company subsequently merged with the Sperry Corporation, and it was with Sperry that Hopper worked on the project that led to COBOL. After retiring from active duty in 1966, Hopper was recalled to serve again with the Naval Data Automation Command (NDAC), where she was tasked with imposing a standard on the US Navy's plethora of computer languages.

In 1983 she received a unique presidential promotion to the rank of rear-admiral, becoming head of NDAC and working in the Pentagon for the next two decades. A slight figure radiating energy, Hopper was an old-fashioned patriot, happy to encourage her subordinates to cut through red tape. She wore her medal-bedecked uniform at every opportunity, smoked like a chimney and had no time for feminists. She once observed: 'I'm thoroughly in the dog house with the women's liberation people. They once asked me if I had ever met with prejudice, and I said I've always been too busy to look for it.'

The world's first computer 'bug': the moth that was found to be behind the malfunction of the Mark II calculator at Harvard in September 1947.

of the newly-fledged women's movement of the 1960s. Holm noted that she had become a full colonel and head of the WAF a little more than a year after the publication of Betty Friedan's groundbreaking feminist text *The Feminine Mystique* in 1963.

In 1970 Holm submitted her retirement papers, but was persuaded to remain in the service by its personnel chief, General Robert J. Dixon, who was a staunch supporter of increased opportunities for women. A year later Holm was promoted to the rank of general, gaining another star in 1973. In 1976 the separate status of the WAF was abolished and women were accepted in the military on much the same basis as men. In 1976, the year after Holm retired, women began pilot training in the USAF, but it was not until 1991 that the US Congress lifted its ban on women flying in combat aircraft. Two years later the Department of Defense lifted its prohibition on women flying combat missions.

> *'She came up at a critical time, when there was a big move in the Air Force that wanted to do away with women altogether. She was the one person who was smart enough, shrewd enough, and persuasive enough to handle that job.'*
>
> BRIGADIER-GENERAL JEAN E. KLICK ON HOLM'S IMPACT

Holm spent her last two years before retirement as Director of the Secretariat of Air Force Personnel. After her retirement she remained immensely active, working on the Defense Manpower Commission and serving as a member of the Advisory Committee on Women in the Services. She remained fiercely critical of the lingering effects of male prejudice in the US military, castigating what she stigmatized as the 'boys will be boys' attitude towards sexual harassment. She once said: 'In the military a racist is not allowed to act like one, but it's sort of winked at to be sexist.'

Holm wrote two books about women in the military: *Women in the Military: An Unfinished Revolution* (1982, revised in 1992–94 to incorporate women's combat and military experiences in the invasions of Grenada and Panama and the Gulf War); and *In Defense of a Nation: Servicewomen in World War II* (1998). In 2003 she worked with Linda Witt on *"A Defense Weapon to be of Value": Servicewomen of the Korean War Era* (2005). She died on 15 February 2010 of pneumonia in both lungs. In 1990 the USAF's Brigadier-General Jean E. Klick said of Holm: 'I can say in absolute candour and honesty that we wouldn't have had women in the Air Force without Jeanne Holm. She came up at a critical time, when there was a big move in the Air Force that wanted to do away with women altogether. She was the one person who was smart enough, shrewd enough, and persuasive enough to handle that job.'

Thatcher's reputation as the 'Iron Lady' was earned during the Cold War and strengthened by her steadfast conduct of the Falklands conflict, a rare example in the post-1945 era of a female politician's standing being enhanced by the ready adoption of a military solution to problems in international relations.

Margaret Thatcher
1925–

Born Margaret Roberts, the daughter of a Lincolnshire grocer and local politician, she was not conscripted for military service in the Second World War and later studied chemistry at Oxford University. While at Oxford, she became president of the University's Conservative Association. This set the tone for her later successful battles, since the Conservatives had a strictly segregationist policy at the time. No women were admitted to membership, so she had to fight to get the constitution changed before she could even apply to join. In 1950 and 1951 she stood unsuccessfully as the Conservative candidate for Dartford in Kent. She then turned to the law, qualifying as a barrister in 1953, but it was not until 1959 after many attempts that she obtained a seat in parliament as the successful Conservative candidate for the north London constituency of Finchley.

In 1975, following the Conservative defeat in the second general election of 1974, she ran against and defeated the incumbent Edward Heath for the post of party leader and became the first female party leader in British politics. In May 1979 Thatcher was elected as Britain's first woman prime minister. An enthusiastic monetarist and disciple of the hardline economist Milton Friedman, she launched an all-out attack on inflation, dominating her cabinet and earning the nickname 'Iron Lady' for her robust attitude towards the Soviet Union's invasion of Afghanistan. It was typical of her that she embraced the sobriquet, which was originally intended by the Soviets as an insult.

From the start of her premiership, Thatcher approached the British Foreign Office with a great degree of wariness, if not mistrust. Even so, in 1979 she agreed in principle with a Foreign Office proposal that the sovereignty of the disputed Falkland Islands in the South Atlantic should be handed to Argentina, which also claimed sovereignty, provided that the views of the islanders were taken into account.

However, the ruling Argentine military junta, headed by General Leopoldo Galtieri, was already committed to the occupation of the Falklands, irrespective of the subsequent British negotiating positions. Its resolve had been hardened by Thatcher's backing for the 1981 decision by her defence secretary, John Nott, to withdraw the ice patrol ship HMS *Endurance* from the South Atlantic. Emboldened by what the members interpreted as British weakness, and convinced that Thatcher's NATO ally, US president Ronald Reagan, would not intervene in this regional dispute, the junta went ahead with its plans. In March 1982 an Argentine force occupied the whaling station at South Georgia, a British dependency some 1,000 miles (1,600 km) south of the Falklands. At the beginning of April an Argentine task force landed in Port Stanley, the Falklands' main port, and swiftly secured the lightly garrisoned islands.

On Saturday 3 April, in an emergency session of the House of Commons, Thatcher announced that: 'a large task force will sail as soon as all preparations are complete. HMS *Invincible* will be in the lead and will leave port on Monday.' She was able successfully to negotiate the opening phase of the Falklands crisis for a number of crucial reasons: her own unbending determination to expel the Argentines; support from the Royal Navy's high command, who assured her that an opposed landing in the Falklands, if it came, was feasible although fraught with danger; and the incompetence of the Argentine junta, whose intransigence enabled the British to seize and retain the moral high ground in the United Nations. Later, Britain's ability to sustain the operations to retake South Georgia and the

Margaret Thatcher at the height of her power in 1986 riding on a Challenger tank. A resolute war leader, she remains a deeply divisive figure for her economic and social policies, notably her championing of entrepreneurial individualism over the welfare state. She once notoriously claimed: 'There is no such thing as society.'

In the early 1970s Argentine society was in a state of deep crisis. Strikes and student demonstrations frequently boiled over into riots. Politically motivated bank robbery, kidnappings and the assassination of military and police officers by left-wing guerrillas became part of everyday life. Death squads of troops in civilian clothes, waged a murderous campaign against political opponents.

On 24 March 1976 a military junta took power in a bloodless coup, promising to 'rescue' Argentina from the failures of civilian government. Society rapidly became militarized and any form of dissent rooted out. During the following seven years of military dictatorship, thousands of Argentines – doctors, teachers, journalists, trade unionists – were abducted, tortured and murdered in what became known as Argentina's 'dirty war'. During this lawless period an association, the Mothers of the Plaza de Mayo, was formed by women who had met each other while searching for their missing sons and daughters.

The woman who founded the association, Azucena Villaflor, along with 13 other women, began

Gathering of the Mothers of the Plaza de Mayo in 2006. Their peaceful protests from the 1970s onwards were a brave and principled stand against a murderous junta.

to demonstrate in the Plaza de Mayo, in front of the presidential palace, the Casa Rosada, on 20 April 1977. By then, Villaflor had been searching for her son and daughter-in-law for six months.

In December 1977 Villaflor herself was taken away to a military concentration camp.

The Mothers of the Disappeared met every Thursday to protest silently outside the presidential palace. The military hired hooligans from the slums of Buenos Aires to intimidate them, but the Mothers of the Plaza de Mayo held firm in silent reproach. After the Argentine military handed back its authority to a civilian government in 1983, the Mothers of the Plaza de Mayo pressed successive civilian administrations to provide a clear accounting of the death toll in the 'dirty war'. The military has admitted that at least 9,000 individuals remain unaccounted for, although the true number is probably closer to 30,000. Three of the founders of Mothers of the Plaza de Mayo, Azucena Villaflor, Esther Careaga and Maria Eugenia Bianco, also joined the ranks of the 'disappeared', until their bodies were recovered and identified in 2005. On 8 December 2005 Villaflor's ashes were laid to rest in the Plaza de Mayo.

Falklands was ensured by the considerable active logistical and diplomatic help of the Americans, although she had no time for any hint of appeasement in the American stance.

On 8 April she left the US Secretary of State, General Alexander Haig in no doubt about where she stood. Haig recalled her: 'rapping the table and referring to the position taken by Neville Chamberlain with respect to the invasion of Czechoslovakia, years before [in 1938–39]. In which she referred to Chamberlain saying: "This distant land, these people about whom we know so little and with whom we have so few common interests." And then she referred to the 40 million casualties from World War II.' One of Haig's team, Thomas Enders, the US Under Secretary of State for Latin-American affairs, while not sympathetic to the British position, could not help but be impressed by the prime minister: 'She was brilliant in these meetings. Dominant on her side. Better briefed than anyone else. Forceful in argument.'

In the following ten weeks Thatcher assumed an almost Churchillian mantle, imperiously rounding on querulous journalists after announcing the recapture of South Georgia (26 April) and commanding them: 'Just rejoice at the news ... rejoice!' She displayed immense stamina and a voracious appetite for detail, and did not shrink from sanctioning tough decisions when it came to changing the rules of engagement – notably on 2 May, when the elderly Argentine cruiser *General Belgrano* was torpedoed and sunk by the submarine HMS *Conqueror* outside the maritime exclusion zone established by the British around the Falklands.

> **'She was brilliant in these meetings. Dominant on her side. Better briefed than anyone else. Forceful in argument.'**
>
> US POLITICIAN THOMAS ENDERS ON THATCHER

On 14 June Margaret Thatcher told the House of Commons that 'the Argentine forces are reported to be flying white flags over Stanley.' The prime minister herself and the Conservative Party drew immense benefit from the victory. Margaret Thatcher had risked all, and triumphed. Her role in the run-up to the conflict was less clear. That she and her government had unwittingly played a part in encouraging the Argentine military junta to invade the Falklands was apparent in the circumspect words of the Franks Report on the war, published in January 1983. Yet the report shied away from attaching personal blame to Mrs Thatcher and her cabinet.

In the 1983 general election, in spite of very high unemployment figures of three million, the Conservative Party coasted to victory over a demoralized and disorganized opposition. Thatcher's second term in office was marked by higher public spending and fierce clashes with major trade unions, a battle of her own choosing, which she won. She revelled in her warrior image, captured in one iconic photograph as she rode in the turret of a Challenger tank, resplendent in a white anti-flash suit, a modern Boudicca in a 20th-century chariot.

However, in 1987, after she had secured an unprecedented third term, her chariot wheels fell off. 'Thatcherism' had entered the language, but she fell out with her cabinet and her partners in Europe, and became an electoral liability. Her bolder colleagues came to the reluctant but inevitable conclusion that Margaret Thatcher was now a handicap rather than a heroine, and told her that she had to go. On the night she left 10 Downing Street for the last time as prime minister, the pitiless cameras caught bitter tears in the eyes of the Iron Lady. She was later created Baroness Thatcher.

In the Second World War, the unprecedented demands imposed by 'total war' widened the role of women in the military and paved the way for the postwar integration of women into the US armed services. However, in the conflict of 1941–45 strict limits were placed on the nature of their service: for example, women serving in the Women Air Force Service Pilots (WASP) could ferry combat aircraft but, in contrast to their Soviet counterparts, could not fly them in combat.

Women in the US Military since 1941

In 1948 the Women's Armed Services Integration Act authorized the US military to recruit women on a permanent basis, formally integrating them into the US armed forces for the first time. The number of women in the forces was capped at a fixed percentage of the total strength, two percent for enlisted women and ten percent for officers. It was not until November 1967, in the middle of the war in Vietnam, that the two percent cap was lifted.

In 1972 the military draft was ended and an all-volunteer force was reintroduced. This, and a renewed consideration of widening the range of military specialities open to women, took place alongside the bitter battle for the Equal Rights Amendment, which focused attention on sex discrimination and the status of all women in the United States.

By 1976 one in every 30 recruits in the United States armed services was a woman. In the same year military academies were opened to women recruits. However, the services continued to chew over the seemingly intractable problem of committing female personnel to combat. They eventually came up with the Direct

Combat Probability Coding (DCPC), in which 'direct combat' and 'close combat' were treated as one and the same on a sliding scale of seven probabilities (P1 to P7).

The first occasion in which women in the US Army were placed in harm's way came in 1989 when, in Operation Just Cause, 800 women soldiers joined the 18,400-strong expeditionary force that invaded Panama. In the ensuing years the arguments over the deployment of women in fighting roles have ranged over a number of familiar themes: the problem of sex in an integrated army; the physical differences between men and women in upper body weight and aerobic capacity; and, for better or worse, how they affect integrated training programmes and operations in the field, where morale and unit cohesion are of paramount importance, and high-tech equipment and body armour can weigh up to 57 kg (125 lb).

It was in Operations Desert Shield and Desert Storm, the defence of Saudi Arabia and the subsequent liberation of Kuwait (August 1990– February 1991) that the integration of women into the US Army was put to the test. When the Iraqi dictator Saddam Hussein invaded Kuwait on 2 August 1990, more than 11 percent of those on active duty in the US

A US Air Force servicewoman (left) and her male colleague guarding a C-130 *Hercules* transport plane during military operations in Afghanistan in April 2008.

armed forces were women. For the first time, they would be called upon to demonstrate their effectiveness in positions that hitherto had been the exclusive preserve of men.

The US forces in the Persian Gulf eventually included some 37,000 women; 26,000 in the Army, 3,000 in the Navy, 2,200 in the Marines, 5,300 in the Air Force and 13 members of the Coast Guard. In Operations Desert Shield and Desert Storm women were called upon, among other things, to crew Patriot missile batteries, fly helicopters on reconnaissance missions, serve in the military police and intelligence and to drive convoys over the desert close to enemy positions. They were not assigned to any ground combat with the infantry, armoured, artillery or special operations units.

The continued restriction on women in close combat was applied to support units that were 'collocated', that is, operating 100 percent of the time with direct ground-combat units. This policy, restated in 1994, proved particularly frustrating to highly qualified servicewomen in the theatre like Martha McSally, who piloted a Fairchild Republic A-10A *Thunderbolt II* close-support aircraft: 'After I became a fully-qualified combat-ready A-10 pilot, I discovered there was a policy that still limited me from fulfilling all the responsibilities of my job. Prior to 2005, all A-10 squadrons were responsible for providing battalion air liaison officers (BALOs) to specific army ground combat battalions. BALOs are trained to provide advice and co-ordination on integration of air power for the battalion. They also control air strikes to support ground forces by talking to the pilots on the radio. These pilots train and deploy on the ground with their assigned units when called, and many A-10 pilots served in this capacity on the ground in Desert Storm and Iraqi Freedom (the second Gulf war). In order to qualify as a BALO, a pilot had to attend a three-week training program, pass a physical-fitness test, and go through a local certification program, which includes controlling live air strikes. I earned distinguished graduate

Airman Raynelle Brown fuels up a Seahawk helicopter on the US aircraft carrier *Nimitz* during operations in the Persian Gulf in June 2007. The US Navy's first gender-integrated warship was the aircraft carrier *Eisenhower* with 415 women among the crew of 4,967 who set sail in 1994. By 2010 both the US Navy and Royal Navy were actively considering the introduction of women to the crews of submarines. However, for a number of years the Norwegian, Australian, Canadian and Spanish navies have allowed women to serve on combat submarines.

status at the school, aced the gender-blind physical-fitness test, and became certified as a BALO. However, due to my gender and the collocation policy, I was prohibited from being assigned to an Army unit.'

Between 2002 and 2006 more than 155,000 women deployed to Iraq and Afghanistan. By the spring of 2010, 125 women had lost their lives in the two theatres and many more had been grievously wounded. The nature of both these conflicts posed acute problems for those wrestling with the doctrine of 'collocation', as in these theatres, where an Improvised Explosive Device (IED) or a rocket could strike anywhere, the notion of a 'front line' did not apply.

In an asymmetrical war, insurgents can appear from nowhere when, for example, a convoy takes a wrong turning. As Lieutenant Dawn Halfaker, a military policewoman who lost her right arm in a rocket-propelled grenade (RPG) attack while on a reconnaissance mission in Iraq, observed: 'Women in combat is not really an issue. It is happening. Everyone pretty much acknowledges there are no rear battle areas, no forward line of troops.'

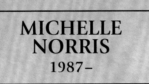

MICHELLE NORRIS
1987–

Michelle Norris was the first woman in the British Army to be awarded the Military Cross for bravery in action in Iraq on 11 June 2006. Private Norris, nicknamed 'Chuck' after the American martial arts movie star, was serving as a medical orderly with C Company, 1st Battalion the Princess of Wales Regiment when her unit was caught up in a fierce night-time firefight with a well-organized force of some 200 insurgents in Al Amarah.

The Warrior armoured vehicle in which the 1.5 metre (5 ft)-tall Norris was travelling came under heavy fire when it attempted to recover another Warrior that had run into a ditch. Norris's commander, Colour Sergeant Ian Page, who was standing with his head above the turret hatch, was hit in the face by enemy fire. The 19-year-old Norris climbed onto the back of the turret to tend Page's injuries, and was spotted by an insurgent sniper who fired three rounds at her, one of which hit the radio mounted on the side of the turret inches from her leg. She was then pulled back into the turret by the driver, and they dragged Page to safety. The Warrior was driven to a helicopter landing point,

while Norris worked hard to prevent her wounded comrade from succumbing to shock. Norris and Page were evacuated by a British Lynx helicopter flown by a US Marine, Captain William Chesarek, who was part of an officer exchange programme.

Commenting on her actions, Norris's commanding officer, Lieutenant-Colonel David Labouchere, said: 'Private Norris acted completely selflessly and, in the face of great danger, concentrated on her job and saved someone else's life. She is part of a larger team, all of whom are acquitting themselves admirably when faced with danger.' Lieutenant-Colonel Labouchere recommended that Norris should be decorated for her bravery, and the award of a Military Cross was gazetted in December 2006. She received the decoration from Queen Elizabeth at Buckingham Palace on 21 March 2007. Chesarek was awarded the British Distinguished Flying Cross for his part in the action. Reflecting on her award, Norris remarked: 'I know some people doubt we [women] can work in the front line. I hope I've proved we can.'

'In 1984 I was attending the US Air Force Academy and told my first flight instructor that I was going to be a fighter pilot. He just laughed, but after Congress repealed the prohibition law in 1991, and I was named as one of the first seven women who would be put through fighter training, he looked me up and said he was amazed I had accomplished my goal.' – Colonel Martha McSally, USAF.

Martha McSally
1966–

In her career with the United States Air Force (USAF), Martha McSally scored two notable firsts. She was the first woman to fly combat operations and subsequently became the first woman in the service to command an air combat unit.

McSally graduated from the US Air Force Academy in 1988 and studied for a master's degree at Harvard University's School of Public Policy. In 1993 she was one of the first seven women to be trained as fighter pilots by the USAF. In 1995–96, during a tour of duty in Kuwait, she became the first woman in the service to fly a combat mission, piloting a Fairchild Republic A-10 Thunderbolt close-support attack aircraft over southern Iraq to enforce the no-fly zone in support of Operation Southern Watch.

In 2001, while based in Saudi Arabia, the feisty 1.6 metres (5ft 3in) McSally was embroiled in a dispute with the US military over a directive requiring female service personnel to wear an *abaya* – an Islamic head-to-toe robe – when not on duty. McSally, a devout Christian, deemed the dress code 'ridiculous and unnecessary', and argued that women serving in the military in Saudi Arabia should be able to wear their uniforms on official business, and dress in long pants [trousers] and long-sleeved shirts when off duty. Backed by a conservative think-tank, the Rutherford Institute, she would not back down, and successfully argued her case in the US Supreme Court before accusing the USAF of discriminating against her for rocking the boat in an admittedly sensitive policy area. On 24 June 2002 the US Senate voted 93–0 in favour of an amendment to prohibit the Department of Defense from requiring or formally urging servicewomen stationed in Saudi Arabia to wear the *abaya*.

In 2004 Lieutenant-Colonel McSally was vindicated when she took command of 354th Fighter Squadron, based at Davis-Monthan Air Force Base, Arizona. Characteristically, McSally said of her new command: 'We are the pointing end of the spear. I understand the marching orders, and we will be prepared to deploy ... with an aggressive attitude that we will win.'

Colonel Martha McSally – the first woman pilot in the US Air Force to fly in combat and to serve as a squadron commander – pictured in front of her A-10 Thunderbolt ground-attack aircraft, which fires milk-bottle sized rounds at rates of 2,100 or 4,200 shots per minute.

McSally served in Afghanistan in Operation Enduring Freedom, where her squadron flew some 2,000 missions, accumulated over 7,000 combat flight hours and expended over 23,000 rounds of 30 mm ammunition. She recalled the first time she deployed her weapons in combat in the rugged terrain of Afghanistan: 'We needed to identify all the many friendly positions working with a controller on the ground. We got eyes on the area, and needed to then ensure we had the right target area, given the friendlies were so close and in multiple directions in a winding, steep canyon. Friendlies were now climbing up the canyon to get away from the enemy and get outside the safe distance of our gun. I shot some rockets to confirm the enemy location, and we honed the target.'

However, the mission rapidly became more complicated: 'On my last rocket pass, my heads-up display failed with all our complicated weapon sights. I had to rely on the very archaic back-up called "standby pipper" which was a hard sight. I needed to quickly get ready to shoot the gun manually, where I had to be at an exact dive angle, airspeed and latitude when opening fire in order to be accurate. We destroyed the enemy on several passes. We train for this type of malfunction, but I never would have imagined shooting the gun in a standby 'pipper' in combat like this.'

McSally became a full colonel in December 2006. She reflected: 'I hope I am a role model to both men and women because we are a fighting force and should not be concerned with the differences between us.' A forthright advocate of gender-neutral policies in the integration of women into the armed forces of the United States, she has written in characteristically robust terms of her own experience: 'As the first woman assigned to my combat A-10 Squadron in 1994, I realized that there were some concerns about a woman's integration into the unit. I knew that I needed to show my competency and capability. I performed very well in my combat-ready checkout program and won a squadron bombing competition despite being the least experienced pilot in the squadron. I earned respect as a fighter pilot, when performance is the ultimate, impersonal gender-neutral standard. Within 60 days of my arrival in the squadron, we deployed to Kuwait for Operation Southern Watch. Pilots were lodged in an area separate from the other troops. I worked with my commander to ensure I stayed in pilot lodgings with my team-mates. I lived in a trailer with four male pilots (in my own small room), and we shared a small bathroom with a shower. We maintained appropriate boundaries, exercised discretion and fostered an atmosphere of respect for personal privacy. During that deployment, my unit became a cohesive team based on our combat mission focus, and my gender was simply not an issue.'

> *'I hope I am a role model to both men and women because we are a fighting force and should not be concerned with the differences between us.'*
>
> MARTHA MCSALLY ON HER DISTINGUISHED SERVICE RECORD

Hester was the first woman since the Second World War to receive the Silver Star, the third-highest US military service award. Her undoubted courage nevertheless highlighted the dilemma facing the US military over the role played by female personnel in ground combat in theatres like those of Iraq and Afghanistan where there is no 'forward area' on the battlefield. In these contexts the battlefield is non-linear and occurs in a 360-degree radius around the troops involved. Perforce, women are involved in ground combat every day and are vulnerable to being injured, killed or captured. They come under fire in ambushes, risk death at the hands of improvised explosive devices (IEDs) and, by the same token, deploy their own weapons against the enemy.

Born in Bowling Green, Kentucky, Hester joined the National Guard in April 2001 and was posted to Iraq as a sergeant in the 617th Military Police Company, 503rd Military Police Battalion (Airborne). On the morning of 20 March 2005, Hester's squad was shadowing an unarmed supply convoy when it was caught in an insurgent ambush south of Baghdad. Under fire from AK-47s, machine-guns and rocket-propelled grenades (RPGs), Hester manoeuvred her ten-man squad into a flanking position to cut off the insurgents' line of retreat, before launching an attack on the irrigation ditches and an orchard from which they were firing.

Working with her squad leader, Sergeant Timothy Nein, Hester attacked the enemy trench line with M203 grenade-launcher rounds and M4 rifle fire, killing three of the insurgents. At the end of a fierce skirmish, 27 insurgents were dead, six were wounded, and one had been taken prisoner. Nein was also awarded the Silver Star for his part in the action.

Leigh Ann Hester, the first woman ever to be cited for valour in close-quarters combat, at the award of her Silver Star.

Like the British Second World War Hurricane pilot Douglas Bader, US pilot Ladda 'Tammy' Duckworth lost both her legs in 2004 when her helicopter was shot down in Iraq. In recovering to launch a political career as a fierce critic of the Iraq War, she displayed a courage comparable to that of the legendary wartime ace of RAF Fighter Command, who had both legs amputated after a crash in 1931.

'Tammy' Duckworth
1968–

'Tammy' Duckworth was born in Thailand, the daughter of a Thai mother and an American father who boasted family roots all the way back to the Revolutionary War. Her family later moved to Hawaii, where she graduated from the University of Hawaii in 1989 with a degree in political science, to which she added a master's degree in international affairs from George Washington University. As a graduate student at George Washington, Duckworth joined the Reserve Officers' Training Corps (ROTC) in 1990 and two years later became a commissioned officer in the Army Reserve, attending flight school where she chose to fly helicopters because it was one of the few combat jobs open to women.

As a member of the Illinois National Guard, Duckworth was subsequently deployed to Iraq, where on 12 November 2004 the UH-60 *Black Hawk* helicopter she was co-piloting was hit by a rocket-propelled grenade (RPG) fired by Iraqi insurgents. In the explosion and crash she suffered massive injuries to her legs and severe damage to her right arm. It took eight days for Duckworth to regain consciousness, and when she came round she asked why her feet hurt, unaware that she had lost both her legs.

On 3 December 2004 Duckworth was awarded the Purple Heart, and three weeks later was promoted to the rank of major at the Walter Reed Medical Center, also receiving the Air Medal and the Army Commendation Medal. She was fitted with artificial legs, which have enabled her to regain mobility and play a leading role in creating the Intrepid Foundation, which is dedicated to the care and rehabilitation of injured veterans.

Duckworth quickly became a vocal critic of the Bush administration's policy on the provision of veteran care, and the US Army's slowness in addressing the problem. She stated that although she had disagreed with Bush's decision to go to war she had nevertheless done her duty, adding that the United States would have been better advised to pursue those

A UH-60 Black Hawk of US 101st Airborne Division, the famous 'Screaming Eagles', whose distinguished history stretches from the Normandy landings to the campaigns in Iraq and Afghanistan. Duckworth flew a Black Hawk in Iraq in 2004.

> **' ... a brave woman wounded in Iraq, who represents all of those with their own battles ahead of them, and their own stories to tell.'**
>
> SENATOR BOB DOLE ON 'TAMMY' DUCKWORTH

behind the attacks on Washington and New York on 11 September 2001, particularly Osama Bin Laden, rather than invade Iraq.

Duckworth was inspired to embark on a political career while recuperating from her injuries at Walter Reed. Here she read the biography of former Republican presidential candidate Robert Dole, *One Soldier's Story*. Dole, who had been severely wounded while fighting in Italy in the Second World War, paid tribute to Duckworth, describing her as: 'a brave woman wounded in Iraq, who represents all of those with their own battles ahead of them, and their own stories to tell.'

In March 2006 Duckworth became the Democratic nominee for the US House of Representatives in the sixth district of Illinois, a Republican stronghold. The following September she was chosen by the Democratic Party to respond to President George W. Bush's weekly radio address. Duckworth went straight on to the attack: 'Instead of a plan or a strategy, we get shallow slogans like "Mission Accomplished" and "Stay the Course" ... Those slogans are calculated to win an election. But they won't help us win our mission in Iraq ... I didn't cut and run, Mr President. Like so many others, I proudly fought and sacrificed, my helicopter was shot down long after you proclaimed "mission accomplished" ... We need a Congress that will ask the tough questions and work together for solutions rather than attacking the patriotism of those who disagree ... It is time to encourage Iraqi leaders to take control of their own country and make the tough choices that will stop the civil war and stabilize the country.'

'Tammy' Duckworth addressing US veterans at Arlington, Virginia, on 2 June 2005. Despite her injuries, she remains a major in the Illinois National Guard.

MARIE T. ROSSI
1959–91

Major Rossi was the first US woman soldier to fly operationally into Iraqi-held territory in the first Gulf War. She was killed in an air accident the day after a ceasefire had been declared in Operation Desert Storm.

A graduate of River Dell Regional High School, New Jersey, she studied psychology at Dickinson where she was an outstanding cadet in the ROTC (Reserve Officer Training Corps). In the first Gulf War, Rossi commanded Company 'B' of the 159th Aviation Battalion, 24th Infantry Division, which played an important role in Desert Storm, ferrying fuel and ammunition to 101st and 82nd Airborne Divisions.

Three days before she lost her life, Major Rossi told a CNN interviewer: 'Sometimes you have to disassociate how you feel personally about going into war and, you know, possibly see the death that's going to be there. But personally, as an aviator and a soldier, this is the moment that everyone trains for – that I've trained for – so I feel ready to meet the challenge. I don't necessarily personally like it; if I had the opportunity and they called a ceasefire tomorrow that would be great.' Major Rossi died on 1 March 1991 when the CH-47 *Chinook* transport helicopter she was piloting flew into an unlit microwave tower at night and in bad weather near her base in Saudi Arabia. Three other crew members died in the crash. Major Rossi is buried in Arlington National Cemetery and her epitaph reads: 'First Female Combat Commander to Fly into Battle.'

In her campaign, Duckworth was also fiercely critical of the wasteful management of the war in Iraq, pointing out that the lavish meals with which she and her colleagues were provided were no substitute for properly equipped and maintained hardware. She singled out the waste of huge sums of money on civilian contractors to perform tasks that could have been undertaken at a fraction of the cost by the US military.

Her Republican opponents launched an expensive mailing campaign against Duckworth, attacking her as 'unhinged' and unpatriotic. The spirited Duckworth hit back with her own mailing campaign in which she accused her opponent, State Senator Peter Roskam, of telling 'ghost stories' that grossly distorted her position on numerous issues, including illegal immigration. The previously admiring Robert Dole endorsed Roskam, as did the Veterans of Foreign Wars.

Duckworth nevertheless received a number of significant newspaper endorsements, and support in a television advertisement from Barack Obama, then a US Senator from Illinois (Duckworth returned the favour with a prime-time speaking slot at the 2008 Democratic National Convention). Roskam, however, replied with insinuations that a victory for Duckworth would also be a victory for the Arabic news network Al Jazeera. Duckworth lost the election by a narrow margin. Her work as Director of the Illinois Department of Veterans' Affairs has prevented Duckworth from re-entering the political fray. This salutary tale tells us that not only is politics a dirty business, but also that 'Tammy' Duckworth is a brave and undaunted woman.

Index

Page numbers in italic refer to illustrations.

Picture Credits

8 Wikimedia Commons/The Louvre; 11 Wikimedia Commons/Archaeological Museum of Herakleon; 13 Photos.com; 14 akg-images/Joseph Martin; 17 akg-images; 18 Wikimedia Commons; 21 akg-images; 23 Wikimedia Commons; 25 Wikimedia Commons/The Louvre; 26 Wikimedia Commons/The Louvre; 29 akg-images/UNITED ARTISTS/Album/AKG; 30 Wikimedia Commons; 31 Wikimedia Commons/ Museum of Art; 33 Wikimedia Commons; 35 Wikimedia Commons; 37 akg-images/Erich Lessing; 38 akg-images/Bildarchiv Steffens; 41 Women's Museum, Hanoi; 43 Wikimedia Commons; 45 © Sotheby's/akg-images; 47 Shutterstock/WitR; 49 akg-images; 51 Wikimedia Commons; 53 akg-images/Erich Lessing; 57 akg-images/Erich Lessing; 58 akg-images/François Guénet; 61 Steve McCurdy/BCS Publishing; 62 Wikimedia Commons; 65 akg-images/Joseph Martin; 66 Wikimedia Commons; 69 akg-images/Erich Lessing; 71 The Print Collector/ HIP/TopFoto; 73 Wikimedia Commons; 76 akg-images/British Library; 79 Wikimedia Commons; 81 McManus Galleries/Dundee City Council; 83 Photos.com; 85 akg-images/François Guénet; 86 Wikimedia Commons; 89 Wikimedia Commons; 90 Society of Antiquaries of London, UK/The Bridgeman Art Library; 91 © Fotomas/TopFoto; 93 Wikimedia Commons; 95 Wikimedia Commons/Rijksmuseum, Amsterdam; 97 Wikimedia Commons; 98 Shutterstock/alehnia; 101 Wikimedia Commons; 103 Wikimedia Commons; 105 © 2006 TopFoto/Wermer Forman; 106 Wikimedia Commons; 109 Michael Cooper/Westport House/11th Marchioness of Sligo; 110 © The British Library/HIP/TopFoto; 111 The Granger Collection/TopFoto; 113 Wikimedia Commons; 114 Photos.com; 117 Private Collection/ The Stapleton Collection/The Bridgeman Art Library; 118 Wikimedia Commons; 121 Album/Oronoz/AKG; 123 akg-images; 125 LADY BANKES OF CORFE CASTLE A miniature painted by Henry; Bone (1755-1834) enamel on copper, Kingston Lacy, The Bankes Collection; (The National Trust) (c)NTPL/Derrick E. Witty; 126 Shutterstock/Joe Gough; 129 © The British Library/HIP/TopFoto; 131 © E&E Images/HIP/ TopFoto; 133 Royal Marines Museum, Portsmouth, UK/ Peter Newark Pictures/ The Bridgeman Art Library; 138 Wikimedia Commons; 137 Photos.com; 140 Wikimedia Commons; 143 akg/North Wind Picture Archives; 145 akg/North Wind Picture Archive; 146 akg/North Wind Picture Archive; 148 Musee de la Ville de Paris, Musee Carnavalet, Paris, France/Archives Charmet/The Bridgeman Art Library; 150 Wikimedia Commons; 153 Â©RIA Novosti/TopFoto; 154 Wikimedia Commons/Library of Congress; 155 Wikimedia Commons/Library of Congress; 156 akg/North Wind Picture Archive; 159 Three Lions/Getty Images; 160 Album/Oronoz/AKG; 163 Wikimedia Commons; 165 © The British Library/TopFoto; 166 Wikimedia Commons; 169 Hulton Archive/Getty Images; 171 Wikimedia Commons; 172 Wikimedia Commons; 173 Wikimedia Commons; 177 Wikimedia Commons; 179 Wikimedia Commons; 181 Getty Images; 183 Wikimedia Commons; 185 Wikimedia Commons; 186 akg-images; 189 The Granger Collection/TopFoto; 193 © 2002 Topham Picturepoint; 194 Wikimedia Commons; 197 Wikimedia Commons; 199 The Granger Collection/ TopFoto; 201 Roger-Violet/ TopFoto; 203 Wikimedia Commons; 205 Wikimedia Commons; 206 Imperial War Museum; 209 Sean Sexton/Getty Images; 210 Popperfoto/Getty Images; 213 General Photographic Ageny/Hulton Archive/ Getty Images; 217 Private Collection/Archives Charmet/The Bridgeman Art Library; 219 Wikimedia Commons; 221 akg-images/ ullstein bild; 223 Wikimedia Commons; 225 Mansell/ Time & Life Pictures/Getty Images; 227 Wikimedia Commons; 229 Wikimedia Commons; 231 Wikimedia Commons; 233 Popperfoto/Getty Images; 234 British Official Photo/Time & Life Pictures/Getty Images; 237 Wikimedia Commons; 239 Wikimedia Commons; 241 © 2002 Topham Picturepoint; 243 © 2004 TopFoto/ UPP; 245 ALAIN JOCARD/AFP/Getty Images; 247 Popperfoto/Getty Images; 249 Apic/Getty Images; 255 Wikimedia Commons; 257 CIA© Jeffery W. Bass; 261 © 2005 TopFoto; 263 Wikimedia Commons; 262 Picasa; 265 Wikimedia Commons; 267 Wikimedia Commons; 270 Manhattan Project/Los Alamos; 271 © 2005 TopFoto/UPPA; 273 Â©ullsteinbild/Topfoto; 274 Â©ullsteinbild/Topfoto; 279 Wikimedia Commons; 280 Wikimedia Commons; 283 U.S. Air Force; 285 Getty Images; 287 Yury Artamonov©Ria Novosti 2010; 290 Keystone/Getty Images; 293 Monty Fresco/Topical Press Agency/Getty Images; 294 Wikimedia Commons/U.S. Air Force; 296 Wikimedia Commons/U.S. Naval Historical Center Library; 299 Time & Life Pictures/Getty Images; 300 Wikimedia Commons; 303 Wikimedia Commons/U.S. Air Force; 304 Wikimedia Commons; 307 U.S. Air Force; 309 Wikimedia Commons/U.S. Air Force; 311 Wikimedia Commons/U.S. Army; 313 Wikimedia Commons

Our thanks are due to the librarians of the Reform Club, the National Army Museum and the Imperial War Museum. To all those who have supported this book, our grateful thanks.

Robin Cross and Rosalind Miles

First published in Great Britain in 2011 by

Quercus Publishing Plc
21 Bloomsbury Square
London
WC1A 2NS

A CIP catalogue record for this book is available from the British Library

UK: ISBN-978-0-85738-077-7
Canada: ISBN-978-1-84866-095-3

Printed and bound in Thailand

10 9 8 7 6 5 4 3 2 1

Designed and edited by BCS Publishing Limited, Oxford.